THINGS
UNSEEN

THINGS UNSEEN

Churches of Christ In (and After) the Modern Age

C. LEONARD ALLEN

LEAFWOOD

PUBLISHERS

THINGS UNSEEN
Churches of Christ In (and After) the Modern Age
published by Leafwood Publishers

Copyright © 2004 by C. Leonard Allen

ISBN 0-9748441-5-2
Printed in the United States of America

Cover design by Rick Gibson

For information:
Leafwood Publishers, Siloam Springs, AR
1-877-634-6004 (toll free)

Visit our website: www.leafwoodpublishers.com

04 05 06 07 08 09   9 8 7 6 5 4 3 2 1

To Leroy Garrett
prophet and priest,
in season and (mostly) out

"…we look not to the things that are seen but to the things that are unseen; for the things that are seen are transient, but the things that are unseen are eternal."

1 Cor. 4:18

Examining our traditions remains for many of us a deep obligation, and for all of us together, a desperate need. But we shall have to acknowledge…that examination of tradition can take place only in the context of unexamined tradition, and that in our examination, our convictions as to the facts are schooled by our traditions. The thinkers of the Enlightenment hoped to bring about a rational consensus in place of fractured tradition. That hope has failed. In my judgment it was bound to fail; it could not succeed.

Nicholas Wolterstorff

Human fallenness almost always leaves its mark. Even theology itself (to borrow a line from Gerard Manley Hopkins) wears man's smudge and shares man's smell.

Michael Bauman

Nothing is simple,
not even simplification.
Thus, throwing away
the mail, I exchange
the complexity of duty
for the simplicity of guilt.

Wendell Berry

CONTENTS

ACKNOWLEDGMENTS

It is a pleasure once again to acknowledge and thank those who have assisted and blessed me in the writing of this book. Thanks first to Kris Miller, Hal Runkel, and Danny Swick, extraordinarily gifted students, for reading portions of the manuscript and making thoughtful comments. It has been a privilege to have taught them and worked with them—and to call them friends.

My deepest thanks to Terry Koonce, Max Lucado, John Allen Chalk, John Wade, Jack and Laura Riehl, Latimer Bowen, the late Don Bowen, J. McDonald Williams, Joseph and Geneva Jones, and the Troy (Mich.) Church of Christ, friends and supporters without whom this book would not have been completed.

Special thanks to Darryl Tippens, Milton scholar and master teacher, and Mike Cope, preacher extraordinaire, whose friendship sustained me during a dark time; to Steve Weathers, an old friend and the best short story writer I know, for whom words weigh pounds yet soar as if lighter than air; to Ian Fair, my former dean, for encouraging me and upholding my work when the season was not politically favorable; to Andre Resner for prompt and helpful reading of several chapters; to Mark Noll of Wheaton College for his serious engagement with my work over the years and for his attention to this book during a busy sabbatical; to the late James McClendon, master craftsman and one of the few theologians I know who prayed for me; and to my daughter Bethany, whose candid but tactful questioning of my original title led to the present, more interesting one.

The dedication to Leroy Garrett recognizes my appreciation for and admiration of him. A lifelong member of Churches of Christ and a Harvard Ph.D. in the history and philosophy of religion, he spent the last forty-five years as a kind of prophet and priest to the fractured and estranged Stone-Campbell traditions and sub-traditions. Unwelcome among mainstream Churches of Christ, indeed viewed as a dangerous and radical figure, he nonetheless continued his prolific ministry of writing and speaking among those who were ready to listen. And he did it with a grace and equanimity that, surely, was possible only by the Spirit of God. The "radical" ideas and practices which he propounded for so many years—nonsectarian faith, fellowship that transcends doctrinal differences, the grace of the gospel—no longer seem radical for many members of Churches of Christ. In that, I'm sure, Leroy finds joy and for that gives thanks.

Chapter 2 originally was presented at a conference on "Primitivism and Modernization," Pepperdine University, Malibu, CA, June 6-9, 1991. An earlier version of Chapter 5 appeared in *Cane Ridge in Context: Perspectives on Barton W. Stone and the Revival*, ed. Anthony Dunnavant (Nashville: Disciples of Christ Historical Society, 1992). A portion of chapter 6 is reprinted from "Silena M. Holman (1850-1915), Voice of the 'New Woman' among Churches of Christ," *Discipliana* 56 (Spring 1996). Thanks to the Disciples of Christ Historical Society for permission to reprint these last two pieces.

Thanks finally to David and Rachel Dillman, Reg Cox, Joe Hatcher, David Parkerson, Kent Smith, Harold and Jeanette Lipford, Carla McDonald, Carol Hutson, Cindy Roper, and Melanie Savage, friends who lovingly sustained my wife and me during the hardest year of our lives.

C. Leonard Allen

CHAPTER ONE

INTRODUCTION:

MARTIN LUTHER, PAT BOONE, AND THE CHURCHES OF CHRIST'S GRAND IDEAL

For over twenty years I was immersed in the task of understanding the theological tradition and heritage of Churches of Christ, and then through writing and teaching helping insiders come to terms with it and outsiders better understand it. It was a preoccupation and perhaps at times an obsession. Often I thrilled at the challenge of it; sometimes I was wrenched by the difficulty of it, since the discoveries I made not only brought me a new freedom and wideness of vision but disorientation and sharp personal struggle as well.

The Churches of Christ in the United States, according to 2003 statistics, number approximately 1,276,500 members in 13,198 congregations.[1] The largest congregations are in Nashville, Tennessee, and Ft. Worth, Texas, and the geographical strength of the body lies in a broad belt connecting these two regions. Churches of Christ originated in the restoration movements begun by Barton W. Stone and Alexander Campbell in the early nineteenth century. Their two movements united in 1832 and were variously called Disciples of Christ and Churches of Christ. By the late nineteenth century a major division was in place: the more conservative, rural, and southern Churches of Christ, and the more progressive, urban, and northern Disciples of Christ. One of the most visible points of division concerned instrumental music in worship: Churches of Christ believed that worship acceptable to God must be a cappella; the Disciples did not. Through the mid-twentieth century Churches of Christ experienced steady growth but since the 1960s have entered a period of ferment, change and, it now appears, decline.

One of the basic challenges I have faced is this: Fundamental to this tradition has been the deep conviction that it does not constitute a human tradition. The phrase "human tradition" was an epithet of sharp opprobrium; Churches of Christ stood in utter contrast to all such "denominational" and apostate things. Indeed, the very use of the phrase "the tradition of Churches of Christ" in this book remains offensive or unsettling to many members. The phrase is troublesome not only due to the implications of the word "tradition" but also because of the capitalization of "Churches." Many members insist that they belong only to the "churches of Christ" and not to the "Churches of Christ," the first phrase speaking of Christ's one true church, the second implying only one denomination of Christ's church. It is not uncommon to see ungrammatical usage employed to preserve this distinction—as in "the Broad Street church of Christ." As a venerable leader recently put it, restating one of the most fundamental convictions of the tradition, true Christians are "opposed to all denominations, for not one nor all of them together make up the New Testament church."[2] So the effort to place Churches of Christ squarely in the stream of real human history, to engage the tradition in a critical way, and to place it alongside other traditions, which has been a key thrust of my work over the last two decades, was a new and jolting perspective for most members of Churches of Christ in the 1980s.[3]

In the mid to late 1980s as co-author Richard Hughes and I were writing our first books, we did not know how these new and critical perspectives would be received.[4] We even faced the possibility that we could lose our jobs at the Church of Christ-related university where we taught. But to our surprise, when the first books appeared in 1988, a door seemed to be open. There was plenty of controversy and sharp attack, to be sure, but there was an amazing explosion of interest. People throughout Churches of Christ, both older and younger members, seemed hungry for these things. In the years since, many hundreds of church leaders— preachers, elders, teachers, and others—have told us how refreshed, stimulated, and broadened they were by these books. And I still hear it, almost every week. Many readers spoke of finding, for the first time, words for the vague and gnawing difficulties they had long experienced with the tradition. "So much of what you wrote," said a typical letter, "gave justification to the feelings I have wrestled with for years. I have struggled since my childhood with both the spiritual wealth and poverty of my heritage, but in this struggle I lacked understanding of why. Your efforts in this book helped answer a great deal of the why."

This critical perspective on Churches of Christ has also helped Christians of other traditions see Churches of Christ in a new and helpful light. It has enabled a spirit of dialogue and understanding to emerge and new bridges to be built. Several years ago I received a letter from a Lutheran pastor in a small Texas town. He had been struck and puzzled by the separateness of the Church of Christ in town and by its attitude toward him. Trying to understand why they had, as he put it, "consigned me to hell," he had recently read two of my books and was writing to say thanks for helping him grasp the logic of their perspective and the history that had produced it.

Many of the issues dealt with in this book are not unique to Churches of Christ. Change the names and some of the lingo, and take into account regional dialects, and many of the challenges and tensions discussed here apply to other American Christian traditions that are seeking direction and renewal in these times.

The era we are now experiencing, which many are calling "postmodern," has brought the blurring of old categories. The clear lines between things we thought we had neatly categorized easily run together. Some aspects of this confusion I enjoy, others make life more difficult. I well remember, for example, the confusion that emerged as readers among Churches of Christ attempted to label my work over the years. Numerous readers labeled me "liberal"—with some even adding the words "modernist" and "agnostic"; numerous others labeled me "conservative"—and it was clear that most of them were not especially happy about that. The two groups of readers, I would judge, were about equal in size. Being able to provoke, and regularly offend, that wide a range of people must say something about the tradition or the times or my contrariness—and maybe about all three.

These are changing, unnerving times. In our culture and our churches, whatever the denomination, anchors are pulling away, things are coming loose. Chaos threatens us. Such times require roots, connections, the weight of healthy tradition. Not an idealized tradition, not a spotless pedigree. But a solid sense of real human forbears with whom we are connected and to whom we are indebted. This sense of a past gives us both strength and humility: the strength of connectedness, the humility of knowing our humanness (and theirs).

But the critical perspective I have helped set out over the years continues to be risky. In this book I risk the impertinence of the person who, finding an elephant in the middle of the living room in the home he is visiting, asks the rather obvious question, "Why is there an elephant in your living room?" The elephant is big and embarrassing, and the family simply does not talk about it. Guests try to be polite but can hardly avoid showing their surprise and curiosity. Some have the impertinence to press the issue—and to speak of it out loud. Such impertinence, perhaps, can be found in this book. At least members of the family may think so.

One sign of the ethos now encroaching upon Churches of Christ is the new and apparently growing sense among its constituency that they simply have not pulled it off: the ideal by which Churches of Christ have long identified and postured themselves—the One True Church, freed of human tradition and fully restored according to the apostolic pattern after more than a millennium of desperate corruption—is not reasonably in touch with the reality. And though a good number of people deep down have probably suspected that over the years, most were not able or willing to acknowledge it, at least in public—and did not know what to do if they did acknowledge it.

Now more and more members, for whatever reason, are not only acknowledging the gulf between the ideal and the actual but also finding the ideal itself flawed. For some Generation Xers and a few intellectuals, it may be a kind of postmodern cynicism that finds any lofty ideal reflexively offensive. For other members, it is a considered theological judgment based upon their reading of Scripture and tradition. For still others, less concerned with the theological issues, it appears to be mostly a desire for personal spiritual fulfillment.

In general, a sense of irony seems to be emerging in the tradition, though almost no one would call it that. It is the sense that, despite long and arduous effort, things did not turn out the way they were supposed to. It is a sense of seeing through pretensions and unmentionables, a sense that beneath the dead seriousness of it all—and it has been a very serious tradition—there is both a pathos and a humor. Seeing that, some tend to cry and some tend to laugh—and some of those who laugh are crying too on the inside. Martin Luther, the great reformer, had a keen sense of such human realities, and he would have understood. But Churches of Christ, having few Lutheran sensibilities, have had a hard time seeing themselves as a mixed bag. Right or wrong, sound or unsound, in the Truth or apostate, the True Church or the false—those have been their stark alternatives.

What to do when the unmentionables are mentioned? What happens when the Grand Ideal is pulled down for revision and realignment? What does it mean when, late in the game, Martin Luther finally trumps Alexander Campbell? When it's time to talk about the elephant in the living room, what does one say?

These weighty questions, forced upon the tradition by the times, are not all bad. It's good to have to talk about the elephant. It's good to face the hidden, unmentionable things. Confession, though unsettling and humbling, can bring one into deeper levels of grace and divine life. A change of eras, which we are presently experiencing, certainly reveals new (or at least redesigned) pitfalls, but it also tends to wake the sleeping, unsettle the settled, prod the smug, anger or alarm the doctrinaire, and do numerous other good things for bored or complacent Christians.

These are not safe and settled times, but they are—or should be—adventurous and exciting times. And as Stanley Hauerwas has reminded us, "God has not promised us safety, but participation in an adventure called the Kingdom. That seems to me to be great news in a world that is literally dying of boredom."[5]

I have found it quite adventuresome, as well as psychologically perilous, to be a theologian in Churches of Christ in these times. Being a theologian is probably always perilous, if not adventuresome, so these challenges do not put me into any special class. But there is a distinctive configuration of theological challenges before Churches of Christ that are particularly difficult given the tradition's history and the present cultural shifts and upheavals. Specifically: How can an anti-tradition tradition face its own very human tradition in a way acceptable to the (anti)tradition? How can it recover a functional Trinitarianism when the Holy Spirit has been virtually equated with the Bible, and when the very word "Trinity" has been deleted from their hymns? How can it engage in more explicit and orderly theological reflection when the tradition has basically assumed that it did not deal in theology but only in Bible facts? How can it engage historic, orthodox Christianity with its ancient creedal tradition in any positive way when the tradition has assumed that creeds are unnecessary, indeed wrong, and that church history is mostly the story of darkness and apostasy? And how can Christian practices and convictions be maintained in a seductively secular and neo-pagan culture when it is assumed that one's resources are simply "the Bible and me"—with nothing in between except something vague called "the way we've always done it"?

The essays in this book do not address, much less answer, all of these questions. But they are a further step toward helping Churches of Christ—and others—gain historical and theological consciousness at a critical time of rapid change and considerable disarray. Four of these essays were prepared, in earlier forms, as lectures for conferences and seminars; and four were written specifically for this volume. A basic theme running through the collection is that the theology of Churches of Christ, despite the pervasive restorationist claims, has been profoundly early modern in its thought structure, so that now, with the receding of modernity and the emerging of a "postmodern" culture, they find some of their basic claims undermined and are thus faced with profound new challenges.

The first three essays focus on the theological method and philosophical framework with which the movement was launched in the first half of the nineteenth century. They show how an early Enlightenment philosophy became invisibly entrenched in the movement and what some of the theological consequences were. The fourth and fifth essays treat lost and hidden strands of the tradition, the recovery of which offer important resources for dealing with the pressures and challenges Churches of Christ face at this time.

The sixth essay examines the central claim of Churches of Christ to be "neither Protestant, Catholic, nor Jew" in light of the Believers' Church tradition, a tradition which in the last fifty years has come to be seen as a distinct "third way" of being Christian in the period since the Reformation.

The seventh essay focuses on the centrality of eschatology for steady and faithful discipleship, particularly in a liberal culture where tolerance and individualism have become the standards. With the passing of Christendom and the emergence of Christians' new cultural status as outsiders, the recovery of a New Testament apocalyptic eschatology becomes a new possibility.

Finally, in the last essay I point to the central dilemma facing Churches of Christ as modernity recedes: with their theology and thought structure rooted firmly in the early modern world, they are finding their message and theology less immediately convincing and more obviously deficient after modernity. But this revelation provides the opportunity to reclaim Christian truth that was compromised or even lost under the pressures and temptations of modernity.

The four epigraphs that begin this book each point to themes that wend their way through these essays. Sometimes they are developed explicitly in the text but more often than not they remain implicit, there between the lines for the reader to draw out with whatever tools, experiences, and yearnings he or she may bring.

My good friend Stephen Weathers, a writer of prize-winning short stories and professor of English, wrote a story some years ago entitled "The Summer of Pat Boone."[6] The story is about a family living on the Gulf coast of the Florida panhandle who are devout members of the Church of Christ. The father runs a fish market, and they all live simple, hardworking lives. In the summer of 1968 they hear a piece of stunning news: Pat Boone, recording star and the most famous member of Churches of Christ, has spoken in tongues, embraced instrumental music in worship, and left the True Church.[7]

That same summer Buddy, the older son in the family, has acquired an electric guitar and dreams of playing rock and roll. Buddy's mother, whose brother played in nightclubs and got killed in a fight, worries about him. And Pat Boone's apostasy hangs in the air like a cloud. When Buddy says that at least Pat was still going to church, the father says, "I'd a lot rather Pat have become a skid row drunk than to have abandoned the New Testament pattern of worship." Buddy has long and sometimes heated discussions with his mother over these issues. Later, at a climactic moment in the story, he stands for a long while at the bay near his house, his guitar in hand, and then in a moment of decision flings the instrument out to sea.

The story captures well the traditional ethos of the thousands of small Churches of Christ scattered across small-town America; and it provides an accurate and touching glimpse into their distinctive, deeply held convictions and how they played out in the lives of ordinary people. That traditional world still remains fairly intact in many of these congregations, though the summer of Pat Boone—1968—can well mark the beginning of a time when it would increasingly be called into question.

I was raised in such a church, and I remember that summer—and the larger things it stood for. I hope that this book, like the previous ones, will help all those who remember, and those both within and without the tradition who do not, better understand Churches of Christ as they move further into the new millennium.

Notes

1. *Churches of Christ in the United States, 2003*, compiled by Mac Lynn (Nashville, TN: 21st Century Christian, 2003), 15, 18.

2. Hugo McCord, "Promise Keepers: The Rest of the Story," *Gospel Advocate* 140 (July 1998), 27.

3. Several Ph.D. dissertations and M.A. theses developed critical perspectives on aspects of the history of Churches of Christ before this time, and several scholarly articles were published in the 1960s-1980s in *Restoration Quarterly*. But the books of Richard T. Hughes and Leonard Allen were the first at the popular or semi-popular level to put Churches of Christ in critical historical perspective. And Hughes' history, *Reviving the Ancient Faith: The Story of Churches of Christ in America* (Grand Rapids, MI: Eerdmans, 1996), is the first comprehensive critical history of this branch of the Stone-Campbell tradition.

4. These writings include *The Worldly Church: A Call to Biblical Renewal* (Abilene Christian University, 1988), with Michael Weed; *Discovering Our Roots: The Ancestry of Churches of Christ* (ACU, 1988); and *Illusions of Innocence: Protestant Primitivism in America, 1630-1875* (University of Chicago, 1988). For an orientation to and assessment of these books, see Mark Noll, "Rethinking Restorationism—A Review Article," *Reformed Journal* (November 1989), 15-21. Noll concluded that this body of work "reinforces the conviction that it is a perilous, but also potentially fruitful, task for believers to pursue, as a Christian calling, the cultural study of their own traditions" (21).

5. Stanley Hauerwas, "Preaching as Though We Had Enemies," *First Things* (May 1995), 48.

6. Stephen Weathers, "The Summer of Pat Boone," *CCTE Studies* 59 (1994), 35-40; a slightly condensed version was published in *Wineskins* 2 (March-April 1996), 12-

15. In correspondence with Dr. Weathers dated March 16, 1994, Pat Boone expressed his appreciation for the story, calling it one of the most sensitive he had ever read.

7. Pat Boone told his story of spiritual awakening and renewal in *A New Song* (Carol Stream, IL: Creation House, 1970). For a polemical response by a Church of Christ author, see James D. Bales, *Pat Boone and the Gift of Tongues* (Searcy, AR: By the author, 1970).

CHAPTER TWO

THINGS SEEN:

STRENGTHS AND WEAKNESSES OF

RESTORATION IN CHURCHES OF CHRIST

THE GREAT RECOVERY

In July of 1835 Alexander Campbell was explaining to William Jones, one of his British followers, something of the history and unique features of what he often called the "current reformation." It was at that time twenty-five years old and facing a crisis of sorts. Campbell reflected back on early influences and on how he became a reformer. He said that as a young man he had studied theological controversies from "Luther, Calvin, Knox, Owen, Glass, Sandeman, Bellamy, etc., down to 1810." From them he acknowledged gaining an immense fund of ideas, but concluded that all this reading "greatly disqualified" him from understanding the Bible. The reason was simple: "there is not to be found in all these reformers a hint upon the true and rational reading of the Book of God." And so it was, he informed his British correspondent, that in 1810 he "began to distrust everything, and take the Bible alone."[1]

This decision at age twenty-two marked a dramatic turning point in Alexander Campbell's life. It thrust Campbell on a ten-year course of intense theological ferment. Upon arriving in America in 1809 he had read his father's *Declaration and Address*, with its eloquent declaration of Christian freedom and call for restoration of simple apostolic faith. Already disillusioned by the discord and traditionalism he had experienced in Irish and Scottish Presbyterianism, the younger Campbell eagerly embraced his father's agenda: to "reduce to practice that simple original form of Christianity, expressly exhibited upon the sacred page."[2]

Upon his father's advice, Alexander plunged into an extended period of intensive study. Between March 1811 and August 1812, for example, he recorded 8,000 pages of reading from 200 different volumes. But his central focus was the Bible itself. In the years that followed he said that he struggled to read the Bible as if he had never read it before, and to make a complete break with all theological tradition. The effort was "arduous beyond expression," he admitted, because he had to unlearn most of what he had been taught of the Protestant theological systems. Thus the Westminster Confession—large portions of which he had memorized as a child—he now came to view as "trash" which the Westminster divines had "interlarded" with scripture. So successful were these efforts to break with the past, he claimed, that after 1812 his mind was "for a time, set loose from all its former moorings." In this state, he concluded, "I was placed on a new eminence—a new peak of the mountain of God, from which the whole landscape of Christianity presented itself to my mind in a new attitude and position."[3]

But by the early to mid 1820s he was sure he had discovered and restored the long lost key—the "true and rational" way of reading the Bible. Though acknowledging his debt to English, Scotch, and Irish influences, he thus claimed for his movement something "wholly new" among all reformation movements; it was, he said, unlike "any ever pled in Europe or America since the great Apostacy."[4] Campbell was aware that many items of his reform agenda were not unique, that he shared them with his predecessors. He knew quite well that he did not stand alone in calling for a restoration of pure, primitive Christianity. With earlier primitivists he shared the basic conviction that scripture presented a pure, fixed, and unalterable norm, and that all "human invention" was illicit and abhorrent. With others he set apostolic and primitive simplicity in sharp contrast to the convolutions and complications of later times. He shared a dire assessment of Christianity's fate in post-apostolic times. "The leprosy of Apostacy," he wrote in a characteristic statement, "has spread over all Christendom, Catholic and Protestant"; as a result, "the christian religion has been for ages interred in the rubbish of human invention and tradition."[5]

Campbell also did not claim uniqueness for the vigorous protests against creeds, the clergy, and the tyranny of Calvinistic orthodoxy that occupied such a prominent place in his work. Throughout his journalistic career, but especially in his early journal, *The Christian Baptist* (1823-30), he blasted the clergy for their greed, pretensions, and manipulation of common folk. He lampooned their "gay equipage, their gewgaws, and all their extravagances in dress," calling them "the most incurable drivellers in the world." He satirized their preaching ("scrap doctors") and their learning ("unteachable metaphysicians"). He fired broadsides at the creeds and confessions of faith through which the clergy kept secure the "manacles, fetters, and chains of antiquated orthodoxy." In all of this, Campbell joined the powerful assault—already mounted by populist religious leaders like Elias Smith, John Leland, Theophilus Gates, and John Taylor—against the mission societies, tract societies, and benevolent agencies of the powerful Calvinist churches in the east. Campbell and the others viewed these societies as part of a grand conspiracy to wrest away peoples' hard-won liberties and to extend ecclesiastical power and control into the west.[6]

Though Campbell was one of the more colorful and skilled satirists of clerical pretensions, he viewed his protests simply as part of the necessary demolition work against the "kingdom of the clergy," a work which others had pioneered. And so, Campbell wrote in 1831 that just because fellow reformer Barton Stone had led the way in protesting against "creeds, councils, and human dogma" and urging union upon the Bible alone, people must not assume that Stone's reform movement was equal to Campbell's. Stone's work, he insisted, was only that of "clearing the forests, girdling the trees, and burning the brush"; he had stopped short of restoring the true faith.[7]

In Campbell's view the spirit of liberty—furthered by reformers like Stone and himself—was fast subverting the forces of tyranny. The long-entrenched creedal orthodoxy was in its "dotage" and the sectarian divisions it had produced were "tottering under the weight of years and the imbecilities of human devices." In this momentous situation many new voices were arising, crying "Lo, here!" and "Lo, there!" But, Campbell insisted, "there is not one voice heard in all the world outside the boundaries of the present reformation, calling upon people to return to the original gospel and order of things."[8]

Here precisely was what Campbell believed to be "wholly new" in his restoration movement. By the mid to late 1820s he believed that he had rediscovered nothing less than "the ancient gospel" and its essential corollary, "the ancient order of things."

The rediscovery of both rested fundamentally upon a particular approach to the Bible—what he termed its "true and rational" reading. In formulating this approach, Campbell wrestled with what for him was a fundamental question: Why are so many good and sincere believers so deeply divided over what the Bible teaches? His answer was that people read the Bible wearing different eyeglasses. One "reads the Bible with John Calvin on his nose, another with John Wesley on his nose, a third with John Gill on his nose...or the good old lights of Scotland." They see only through the grid of creeds manufactured in Geneva, Westminster, Rome, or Philadelphia. As long as people wear these glasses they will see everything with a particular tint yet be utterly convinced of their perfect and unobstructed vision. On this basis they will dogmatize, anathematize, and build their religious fortresses. There is only one way, Campbell concluded, to be honest with the Bible and rise above sectarian strife, and that is by approaching it "without a single inclination to any opinion, theory, or system whatever." Though admittedly a difficult task, one must strive to pick up "the Bible as if it had dropped from heaven into his hands alone."[9]

To help readers make such an unobstructed approach to the Bible, Campbell laid down a basic rule, and this rule lay at the heart of his restorationist hermeneutic. People must confine themselves to "the plain declarations recorded in the Bible," eschewing all the elaborate vocabulary of traditional theology. "We choose to speak of Bible things by Bible words," Campbell said in a frequent refrain, "because we are always suspicious that if the word is not in the Bible, the idea which it represents is not there" either. In this way he swiftly dismissed as useless a host of terms in the historic Christian vocabulary—terms like Holy Trinity, original sin, total depravity, reprobation, imputed righteousness, covenant of grace, sacraments, and eucharist. All the disputes that had swirled around these words for centuries could be safely pronounced irrelevant. No refutation of such doctrines was even necessary—they could be dismissed out of hand as "unauthorized, unscriptural, and schismatical." Indeed one could also jettison as unnecessary the whole library of creeds, confessions, homilies, and commentaries spanning fifteen centuries, for it contained nothing that was not more plainly and precisely taught in scripture.[10]

Besides "purity of speech" as a restrictive principle, the "true and rational" way of reading the Bible demanded another corollary principle: one must read the Bible as a book of facts. The Bible was not a book of "opinions, theories, abstract generalities, nor of verbal definitions" but rather "a book of awful fact, grand and sublime beyond description." "Facts are the Alpha and the Omega of the Bible," Campbell insisted; thus, the "meaning of the Bible facts is the true biblical doctrine." By fact he simply meant, following Francis Bacon, "something said" or "something done." By clearing one's head of all theological speculation and one's speech of all extra-biblical terms and focusing on the bare biblical facts, the Bible would become an open and understandable book. It could be rescued from the "fogs of Calvinism" and the disorienting uncertainties stirred by the array of competing sects. In just the same way that Baconian science, by confining itself to facts, had brought clarity and harmony to nature, so the "divine science of religion," following the same method, would bring clarity and harmony to a badly divided Christian religion.[11]

On this basis Campbell set forth the elements of "the ancient gospel": "gospel facts [death, burial, resurrection, and ascension of Christ], faith, repentance, reformation, baptism, remission of sins, [reception of] the Holy Spirit, sanctification, the resurrection, eternal life." The "ancient gospel," Campbell argued, was simply a series of "facts" which the New Testament placed in a particular order. New Testament preaching began with the biblical testimony to these gospel facts; this testimony, without any other supernatural agency, produced faith; and faith led a person to "obey the gospel," that is, to repent of sins and be baptized for remission of sins. Reception of the Spirit then followed.[12]

Reliance upon the "true and rational" reading of scripture also enabled Campbell to set forth "the ancient order of things." By this he meant the original pattern of church ordinances and order visible in the first apostolic communities and set down primarily in Acts and the Epistles. This portion of the New Testament was the "statute-book of Heaven," providing a precise and uniform code of laws for the church. It clearly legislated congregational autonomy, baptism for remission of sins, weekly observance of the Lord's supper, a plurality of elders and deacons in each congregation, and a simple pattern for worship. This ancient order was specific and complete; any practice or organization lacking an apostolic command or example was simply an illicit novelty.[13]

Together "the ancient gospel" and "the ancient order of things" presented an astounding and glorious prospect: the collapse of the many warring sects and the union of believers in one great body. The movement's founding charter, Thomas Campbell's *Declaration and Address* of 1809, had proclaimed that unity was possible if believers would "reduce to practice that simple original form of Christianity, expressly exhibited upon the sacred page." Alexander believed that he had fulfilled his father's charge; thus the prospect for unity was bright, indeed unity was virtually assured. For who or what could resist the simple logic of his argument? (1) The "ancient gospel and order of things" consisted only of New Testament facts; (2) all the sects already recognized the same basic facts; and (3) the order of these facts was so clear that no one who believed the Bible could mistake it. Therefore, if believers would "purify their speech" and "abandon every word and sentence not found in the Bible," nothing would be left but the gospel facts and division simply could not exist.[14]

But there was more. Faced with such prospects Campbell envisioned nothing less than the dawning of a millennial age of peace, harmony, and Christian triumph over the world. "Just in so far as the ancient order of things, or the religion of the New Testament, is restored," he wrote, "just so far has the Millennium commenced." The "ancient gospel" would be "the instrument of converting the whole human race, and of uniting all christians upon one and the same foundation." One had only to introduce the gospel in "its plainness, simplicity, and force" and it would "pass from heart to heart, from house to house, from city to city, until it bless the whole earth." By the early 1830s, flushed with the rapid growth of the movement, Campbell had little doubt that this millennial march was underway. "Our progress is onward, upward, and resistless," he exulted. "The opposition of the sectarian world [is] as the spider's threads in the path of the elephant."[15]

THE GREAT IRONY

This vision with which Campbell launched his reform movement was grand and hopeful, enthralling by its very simplicity. Campbell caught on early to what the new democratic spirit at work in the young republic might mean for the Christian religion, and in his aggressive accommodation to this spirit we find perhaps his greatest virtue as a reformer. With a native brilliance and prodigious energy, he built up a movement seeking to make Christian faith of, by, and for the common people. He stressed that people possessed the right, indeed the duty, to read the Bible for themselves without the superintendence of mediating elites.[16] Further, in the midst of an "experimental" piety that often ignited the spirit but left one ignorant of the Bible, Campbell insisted that people must not simply revere the book but must open it, read it, and interpret it properly. Finally, he caught up the optimistic, even utopian, hopes of the age in his assurance that Christian unity was actually achievable. The success of the movement resulted, in large part, because Campbell gave people a clear, rational program by which they could do that.

Reciting these virtues—indeed, the genius—of Campbell as a reformer and of the movement he led for nearly fifty years does not mitigate the fact that his original vision resoundingly failed. As we have seen, he envisioned, and for a time truly believed in, the actual downfall of all denominational walls and the grand reuniting of all the "Christians in the sects." But that dream soon was "cruelly refuted by history" (Reinhold Niebuhr). Religious pluralism diminished not one bit; indeed, it continued to proliferate ever more rapidly. The invective against elites and the individualistic, egalitarian appeals of reformers like Campbell and Stone, far from curbing pluralism, actually stimulated pluralism in the young republic. Such an ethos turned out to be a petri dish for the prolific cultivation of new sects and divisions, a proliferation that has continued down to the present time.[17] Among the Disciples of Christ themselves the eventual result was division into three major and many more minor groups, most all of them by this late date long estranged from one another.

Behind all of these developments lies a fundamental, over-arching irony. Put simply, Alexander Campbell's primitivism was, from the very beginning, deeply shaped by the early modern worldview. Campbell viewed his accomplishment as a simple restoration of primitive Christianity, but his restoration was neither simple nor thoroughly primitive. It was actually a complex mix of old and new elements—old elements of biblical tradition and new elements of European and American culture. The movement's basic thought structure was distinctly and profoundly early modern (as opposed to late modern). Its roots lay in what Henry May has labeled the Didactic Enlightenment that grew out of late eighteenth-century Scottish Common Sense thought.[18]

Two central features of Campbell's thought serve to illustrate the point: (1) his way of viewing the Bible, and (2) his assumptions about scientific and moral progress. In approaching scripture, as we have seen, Campbell claimed to have restored its "true and rational" reading. But far from jettisoning all philosophical systems and predilections, as he often claimed, Campbell actually employed a method combining a rigid Lockean epistemology with the Baconianism of the Scottish Common Sense philosophers.[19] The Enlightenment's new scientific view of nature with its order and "system" deeply impressed him. Along with other Protestant theologians of his time, he applied the same thinking to the Bible. "Order is heaven's first law, the Bible's first law, and the Christian preacher's first concern," Campbell insisted time and again. "If nature be a system, religion is no less so. God is 'a God of order,' and that is the same as to say he is a God of system."[20]

Thus Campbell and his followers naturalized the Bible, construing it as a scientific book of "facts." They unwittingly modernized the Bible so that it fit with the Newtonian world of natural laws. The new scientific method had systematized, demystified, and brought nature under control; it did the same thing when applied to the Bible. In good Baconian fashion the Bible became more precise, less mysterious, and more subject to human control.

A second basic feature of Campbell's thought revealing its early modern character is his view of scientific and moral progress. With the stunning possibilities of scientific empiricism just coming into view, the early Enlightenment was marked by enormous confidence in human reason and technique. Utopian visions of human progress emerged. Campbell partook deeply of this spirit. His heroes were "Bacon, Newton, Locke, and all the great masters of science." "What have these mighty minds achieved for science, physical, mental, and moral—for the world!" he exclaimed. Under their ministrations science has "advanced society ten generations in a single century"; its triumphs are "inscribed upon ten thousand pillars." In view of this, he insisted, educational institutions must turn from the ancient classics, which offer no "practical blessings" whatsoever, and focus on the "moderns"—the great men of science and literature since the fifteenth century who had made such grand and practical contributions to human progress.[21]

Campbell placed his own reform movement on the crest of this wave of progress. Could he but establish the five key propositions that had launched his own movement, he claimed, then a great revolution would "regenerate and bless the world in ten thousand ways." The human tongue and pen—"the great moral levers of the world"—provided the key instruments. False religion and moral degeneracy gradually would waste away and the earth would be "enlightened with knowledge, scientific, political, religious."[22] Here was a bright millennial vision incorporating the secular optimism of the Enlightenment squarely into the divine scheme of things.

The irony, then, is that Campbell's primitivism was profoundly modern. It was modern in its reverence for order and system, its view of divine agency in the world, its adulation of scientific empiricism, and its deep confidence in scientific and moral progress. But the primitivist impulse, with its exhilarating sense of complete recovery of originals, veiled this modernity. It served as an enormous screen, masking the cultural particularities and intellectual traditions that remained always at work in the movement.

I take this central irony as an interpretive key to the movement. The story of the later nineteenth-century division of the movement is in part the story of the gradual disentanglement of Campbell's modernism from his primitivism. Thus, the separation of Churches of Christ and Disciples of Christ was, in a word, a separation of primitivists and modernists. To put it this simply, of course, considerably oversimplifies the developments. The aggressive primitivism of Churches of Christ was never simply "primitive" but also partook of the modern in significant and mostly unrecognized ways. Even those Churches of Christ that have been the most separate, the most conservative and suspicious of the modern and innovative, nonetheless unconsciously embraced an earlier "modernism"—an approach to the Bible not then currently modern but formerly modern. In this regard Martin Marty has noted that the various conservatisms of the late nineteenth century "were, in large part, very modern inventions of these counter-modernists."[23] Furthermore, the "modernism" of Disciples of Christ in the late nineteenth century was hardly ever a simple celebration of the "modern" but usually remained cloaked in forms of primitivist language.

But each group assumed a different stance toward the modern world. Churches of Christ maintained (and even heightened) a sectarian stance toward the world, while Disciples moved by fits and starts toward a softer denominational stance. The one was constantly suspicious of culture and alliances with it, the other usually hopeful and optimistic about its promise—it was, after all, American culture and institutions they were

dealing with. The one was marked frequently by apocalyptic (and sometimes explicitly premillennial) eschatology, the other by a postmillennial
outlook attached closely to the progress of science and American culture.
For the one, new developments in culture required above all a redoubling
of efforts to preserve the old, primitively fixed way; for the other, such
developments called for studied adjustments and adaptations. The primitivist Churches of Christ inevitably made certain adjustments (if in nothing
else, at least in resisting modernism), though they did not intend to and
certainly would not have admitted it.

For the Disciples of Christ who embraced the modern, progressive
elements of Campbell's thought, the primitivist elements gradually and
inevitably receded. The steady march toward the Protestant mainstream
correlates rather neatly with this recession. By the early twentieth century
Disciples could be counted among members of the Protestant establishment. They joined, and even led, establishment enterprises such as ecumenical organizations and social agencies.[24] With others of the establishment, they eagerly (but not easily) adjusted to the spirit of the new age.
They struggled to adapt their simple congregationalism to society's new
professional, bureaucratic models, and opened up to the new intellectual
developments of modernity. They built impressive buildings and partook
of the gentility and refinement that was reshaping religion in the new
urban centers. Though turn-of-the-century leaders like Herbert L. Willett
and Charles C. Morrison were too liberal for many Disciples, their progressive spirit and celebration of the *Zeitgeist* would characterize the ethos
of twentieth-century Disciples. Faced with the demands and challenges of
a new age, the old primitivism increasingly appeared quaint, backward,
and outmoded.

The Churches of Christ, in contrast, clung to the primitivist elements
of Campbell's thought, particularly his "ancient gospel and order of things"
and his early opposition to all human "innovations." What Churches of
Christ as a whole did not embrace was Campbell's confidence in scientific and moral progress; indeed, they maintained a powerful anti-modern
stance. To understand this stance we must consider a new element—the
influence of Barton W. Stone.

FROM KINGDOM COMMUNITY TO TRUE CHURCH

R. L. Roberts argued that Churches of Christ owe their first debt to Barton Stone and his "Christian" movement, not to Campbell.[25] To be sure, Campbell's influence, beginning in the 1820s, quickly eclipsed Stone's and became by far the dominant force in the movement. Campbell's precise "ancient gospel and order of things" provided theological structure and rational certainty for those distressed by experimental Calvinism and perplexed by pluralism. It thereby brought polemical success. Furthermore, as we have seen, Campbell brilliantly accommodated and capitalized on the optimistic spirit of the period. Stone's outlook on culture, in contrast, was profoundly pessimistic, and this pessimism was rooted in an apocalyptic worldview largely foreign to Campbell.

This apocalyptic outlook, Richard Hughes argues, was characterized by three closely related features: (1) a call to radical discipleship and separation from the fashions, preferments, and allures of the world; (2) a premillennial eschatology envisioning a coming kingdom, established solely at divine initiative, that would fill the earth; and (3) a disdain for all human government (including America's) and a stance of non-involvement in it.[26] For the early Stonites the kingdom of God was a transcendent reality that alone should claim the Christian's allegiance; as a citizen of that kingdom one placed little hope in all the glowing testimonies to human progress.

This apocalypticism was soon overlaid with and modified by Campbell's biblical patternism; nonetheless, Hughes argues that it remained an important and distinguishing feature of a significant segment of Churches of Christ throughout the nineteenth century (though not necessarily in premillennial form). David Lipscomb of Nashville, Tennessee, became its most important advocate in the second half of the century (see Chapter 5). In the early twentieth century, however, Churches of Christ largely cast off the apocalyptic worldview with its calls for radical discipleship. Lipscomb's apocalypticism was denounced as heresy by some and simply ignored or forgotten by most others.[27] What remained in most cases was a rigid and garrulous form of Campbell's biblical patternism and an exclusivism easily identifying Churches of Christ as the one true, restored kingdom of God. What also remained was a constituency ever more at home with American culture and content with conventional moral standards.[28] The sense of separateness from the world remained a significant factor past mid-century, but it was like a cut flower; severed from its apocalyptic roots and buffeted by the winds of respectability, its days were numbered.

If an apocalypticism indebted to Barton Stone and David Lipscomb marked a segment of Churches of Christ in the nineteenth and early twentieth century, another sizable segment played down the apocalyptic perspective and simply clung to Campbell's early biblical patternism and sectarian view of the church. Indeed, there was a steady tendency among Churches of Christ throughout the nineteenth century to identify the kingdom of God with the restored church as defined by Campbell. This straightforward equation of church and kingdom furthered a separation between eschatology and ethics, and this separation—with its many ramifications—remains one of the greatest theological problems in the tradition.

To understand this divorce and its consequences we must look back to Campbell again, noting particularly two central features of his theology: (1) his dispensational division of scripture, and (2) his view of the kingdom of God.

Central to Campbell's primitivist agenda was a dispensational schema dividing the Bible into three blocks: Genesis 1 through Exodus 19 (the patriarchal age); Exodus 20 through Acts 1 (the Mosaic age); and Acts 2 through Revelation 22 (the Christian age). He argued that only texts from Acts 2 through Revelation could authorize Christian faith and practice. In this view the Gospels fell into the Mosaic dispensation and thus served only a preparatory role. They could not provide the "laws" for Christ's kingdom, for the laws of the kingdom could be set forth only after the kingdom had been established—and that did not occur until the first Pentecost after Christ's ascension (Acts 2).[29] Thus Campbell and many of his heirs thought, for example, that Christians should not pray the Lord's prayer, especially the phrase "thy kingdom come," for the kingdom already had come with the establishment of the church on Pentecost.

Church and *kingdom* thus became virtually synonymous terms. Campbell himself did not flatly equate them and some tension appears in his thought, but among many of his conservative heirs the church/kingdom equation became (and remains to this day) unassailable. For my purposes the key point is this: the kingdom was de-eschatologized; it became an institution fully present in the church, not an expansive, eschatological reality partially manifested in the church. In this way the sense of conversion as inauguration into an eschatological community diminished. The call to a radically transformed, eschatological lifestyle easily became an admonition to "be good" as defined by conventional Protestant morality. Juridical or legal models of the Christian life became dominant, crowding out more personal, covenantal models. Doctrinal precision (knowing the truth) superceded ethics (embodying the truth) as tests of Christian identity. The movement's focus fell heavily upon "restoration of the ordinances of the new institution to their place and power,"[30] not upon the nature and demands of discipleship. Without an apocalyptic framework for the kingdom community, discipleship was easily defined by the moral norms of a "Christian" culture or, more narrowly, of an agrarian Bible Belt subculture.

The doctrine of believer's baptism, prominent in the movement from near its beginning, provides a striking case in point. T. W. Brents, in his standard work of 1874, *The Gospel Plan of Salvation*, set out what became the representative view among Churches of Christ (306 pages of 662 dealt with baptism). Brents noted, for example, that Cornelius the Roman centurion (Acts 10), though already a man of good morals, still needed to be baptized. But he added that since "his conduct was as good before [the new] birth as after it, it follows that the birth did not consist in a reformation of life in this case."[31] Here baptism became, in essence, little more than a formal ordinance required for salvation. Focus fell heavily upon its proper mode (immersion of adults) and basic purpose (remission of past sins), rather than on its place as a vital link between gospel (eschatological message) and ethics (eschatological lifestyle). With baptism thus de-eschatologized Churches of Christ could place enormous stress upon believer's baptism as a formal requirement for salvation and church membership while at the same time adopting many aspects of conventional morality (whether more urban, affluent conventions or more rural, simple ones).

This view has played out in the (unspoken) assumption that as long as people are baptized correctly it is not as important whether they actually follow Jesus in costly discipleship. They can sit in a pew once or twice a week year after year, live private and separate lives, exercise little or no spiritual giftedness, and yet be considered normal or faithful Christians. It is assumed, of course, that conversion should be followed by the "Christian life" and growth in grace, but this life is easily defined in very minimal and culturally accommodated terms.

Something is wrong here. For early Christians both baptism and the Lord's Supper had a concrete ethical and social meaning, not simply a symbolic or "religious" meaning distanced from the actual, vibrant communal life itself. These ordinances were "performative signs" of the new and transformed life that Jesus gave through the Spirit.[32] Among Churches of Christ baptism has tended to become more of a formal ordinance marking entry into an acceptably minimal kind of discipleship than a performative sign moving people into an expectedly full kind of discipleship. Baptism thus becomes formalized and diminished in its significance.[33]

An obscure episode late in Campbell's life serves to epitomize this tendency in the movement toward accommodating the Christian life or ethic to cultural standards. A bright young graduate of Campbell's Bethany College named Walter Scott Russell (whose provocations will be traced more fully in Chapter 4) had begun raising eyebrows in 1857 with articles directly challenging Campbell's strict empiricist theology. In 1859 Campbell mounted a stinging attack. Among many objections, he pointed to Russell's assertion that as followers of Christ we are "to take up our crosses and bear them after him." "How is it that he so reads the Scripture?" Campbell thundered in response.

> Are we among the contemporaries of the Lord when the Cross was in fashion? There is no such phrase nor precept nor oracle in the Acts of the Apostles, none in the preachings of the Apostles from the setting up of Christ's kingdom upon the day of Pentecost to the end of the Apocalypse! The word Cross is not once found in the Acts of the Apostles.
>
> There is now no cross under our government. In other words there is no persecution in our country, or anywhere in Protestant Christendom against Christ or Christianity. Hence no man in these United States has to carry a cross for Christ's sake.[34]

Here, in the heat of controversy or perhaps in the declining powers of old age, Campbell may have written somewhat rashly. But still this passage reflects basic features of his theology, particularly his dispensational schema and his view of the kingdom of God. It also reveals an ethic of cultural accommodation quite removed from the apocalypticism of a Barton Stone or a David Lipscomb. It was this ethic, with its formalism, that was to triumph in the movement in the twentieth century.

THE POWER OF PRIMITIVISM

Now in conclusion I return again to the theme of irony. Restoration-ism, particularly in the American ethos, tends to beget a certain kind of forgetting. It tends to render the intellectual, cultural traditions that shaped it essentially invisible, lopping off the immediate past and thus closing its eyes to the contingencies that past always imposes. For the Christian restorationist wants only the Truth—pure, timeless, and culture-free. But in claiming to enshrine only the primitive and original, a restorationist movement tends to draw into its wake a host of traditional, "modern" assumptions all the more entrenched for remaining invisible. F. J. A. Hort put it well: "The air is thick with bastard traditions which carry us captive unawares while we seem to ourselves to be exercising our freedom and instinct for truth."[35]

Hort's observation points to one of the chief ironies of restorationist traditions, and particularly that begun by Stone and Campbell: the ten-dency to develop powerful traditions propelled by the illusion of existing without tradition. The degree to which this has happened in the Stone-Campbell movement dissolves irony at times into high comedy. We are kept from comedy most often, however, by considering the seriousness and integrity of most of the people who promoted and defended the movement's ideals.

I have focused on the movement's ironic outcomes because the sense of the ironic seems largely absent. But I hasten to add that the establish-ment of irony is not itself a worthy enough goal. For preoccupation with irony tempts one with condescension, resignation, and ultimately cyni-cism. It does so because the disturbing force of irony is not that it mere-ly exposes folly or shortsightedness (a relatively easy task), but rather that it underscores the ultimate inability of even people of great intellect and daring, of great faith and virtue, to pull off what they so ardently—and perhaps brilliantly—envision.[36] When put to Christian use, however, irony can illumine the subtler reaches of the Christian doctrine of sin. It can function like a sharpened chisel, creating an opening wedge for grace to enter the sealed regions of the human heart.

Finally, in highlighting the ironies and illusions to which restorationism in the Stone-Campbell movement has been given, I must say emphatically that I do not thereby dismiss the restorationist vision as altogether illusory.

Illusions beset all human undertakings, and there is no reason to think that Christian restorationists escape them. Modernisms generate more than their share of illusions; indeed, they seem prone to even greater forgetfulness and scorn of the past than most restorationisms. I believe the restorationist impulse to be a powerful means of saying no, of resisting the innumerable forms of compromise, erosion, and domestication that beset Christian faith in new guise in every generation. It maintains a steely cynicism about the benefits of alliances with the new and the modern. It does not condemn everything modern though, as we have seen, it inevitably partakes of the modern against its wishes.

It is becoming common now days for American Protestants, long situated in the mainstream, to call their churches to resist the culture and to become counter-cultural enclaves.[37] Not surprisingly, such calls seem to have become fashionable only as the mainstream has lost its mainstream status. The restorationist vision of which I speak issues such calls when they are not in fashion and when they are easily dismissed by the establishment as self-righteous, uncivil, or merely obscurantist. And indeed all of these attitudes tempt the restorationist: one does not have to look far to find self-righteousness, incivility, and obscurantism in this movement. But in its best impulses and clearest insights, the Stone/Campbell movement proclaimed forcefully that America is not the kingdom of God or even its harbinger, that historic creeds easily become golden calves, that wealth and worldly fashion generally pervert the religion of Jesus, that Christians do not fight Caesar's wars, that denominational compromise and division are scandalous, and that popularity and pragmatism provide no valid tests of Christian truth.

The restorationist vision is fundamentally a means of critique and dissent. For this reason it will never fit comfortably with mainline or establishment forms of Christianity. Its sins tend to be those of severity rather than laxity, blind obstinacy rather than easy compromise, too-quick exclusion rather than too-ready inclusion, irrelevance rather than trendiness. Restorationists are constantly putting burrs under the seats of the sleepy and comfortable. They work from the conviction that accommodation and compromise are far easier and subtler than most suppose and that the call of Christ is higher, more serious, and more demanding than most care to entertain. That restorationists often fail to embody their own ideals should not obscure to our eyes the truth and power of the ideals themselves.

Notes

1. Alexander Campbell, "Letter to William Jones. No. V," *Millennial Harbinger* 6 (July 1835), 305.

2. Thomas Campbell, *The Declaration and Address of the Christian Association of Washington* (Washington, PA, 1809).

3. Manuscript F, Disciples of Christ Historical Society; Alexander Campbell, "Reply," *Christian Baptist* (February 3, 1826), 182; Campbell, "Education—No. II," *Millennial Harbinger* 1 (June 7, 1830), 252; Campbell, "Anecdotes, Incidents and Facts, Connected with the Origin and Progress of the Current Reformation," ibid. 3rd series 5 (June 1848), 344-5.

4. Ibid., pp. 306-7. See also Campbell, "Reply on Union, Communion, and the Name Christian," *Millennial Harbinger* 2 (September 5, 1831), 390, and "The Christian Repository," ibid. 4th series, 7 (November 1857), 627.

5. Alexander Campbell, "Christendom in its Dotage," *Millennial Harbinger* 5 (August 1834), 372-3; ibid. 3 (January 2, 1832), 6.

6. Alexander Campbell, "Third Epistle of Peter," *Christian Baptist* 2 (July 4, 1825); "The Millennium—No. III," *Millennial Harbinger* 1 (July 5, 1830), 313; "Present State of the Presbyterian Denomination," ibid. 5 (July 1834), 360. See Byron Cecil Lambert, *The Rise of the Anti-Mission Baptists: Sources and Leaders, 1800-1840* (New York: Arno Press, 1980), and Nathan Hatch, Democratization, pp. 170-79.

7. Alexander Campbell, "Kingdom of the Clergy," *Christian Baptist* 1 (September 1, 1823); Barton Stone, "Union," *Christian Messenger* 5 (August 1831), 180; Alexander Campbell, "Reply on Union, Communion, and the Name Christian," p. 390.

8. Campbell, "Christendom in its Dotage," p. 374. See also Campbell, "Reply to Mr. Waterman," *Millennial Harbinger* 5 (June 1834), 251.

9. Alexander Campbell, *Debate with Walker*, 2nd ed., p. 207; Campbell, *Millennial Harbinger Extra* 3 (August 6, 1832), 343.

10. Alexander Campbell, *The Christian System* (Bethany, W.V., 1839), p. 102-6; "Letter to William Jones. No. VI," *Millennial Harbinger* 6 (August 1835), 352-3; "Letter to England—No. V," ibid. new series 1 (November 1837), 498.

11. Campbell, *The Christian System*, pp. 2, 6, 107; "Mr. Lynd on the Influence of the Holy Spirit," *Millennial Harbinger* new series 1 (November 1837), 531. On "fact," see also Campbell, "Education," *Popular Lectures and Addresses* (1863; reprint, Nashville: Harbinger Book Club, 1954), p. 243f.

12. Campbell, "Letter to William Jones, No. VI," *Millennial Harbinger* 6 (August 1835), 353; *Christian System*, pp. ; "The Confirmation of the Testimony," *Millennial Harbinger* 1 (January 1830), 8-14.

13. See Campbell's long series, "A Restoration of the Ancient Order of Things,"

beginning in the *Christian Baptist* 2 (February 1825), and especially No. VII (September 5, 1825).

14. Thomas Campbell, *The Declaration and Address of the Christian Association of Washington* (Washington, PA, 1809); Alexander Campbell, "The Millennium—No. I," *Millennial Harbinger* 1 (February 1830), 57-8; Campbell, "A Restoration of the Ancient Order of Things. No. XVII. Purity of Speech," *Christian Baptist* 4 (March 3, 1826), 154.

15. Campbell, "A Restoration of the Ancient Order of Things. No. I," *Christian Baptist* 2 (February 7, 1825), 136; Campbell, "The Millennium—No. I," p. 58; Campbell, "An Oration in Honor of the Fourth of July," *Millennial Harbinger* 1 (July 5, 1830), 309.

16. See Nathan Hatch, *The Democratization of American Christianity* (New Haven: Yale University, 1989), pp. 1-16, 71-77.

17. Ibid., pp. 14, 213.

18. Henry F. May, *The Enlightenment in America* (New York: Oxford University, 1976). May argues that the European Enlightenment ideas that influenced American thought can be grouped into four categories: the Moderate Enlightenment (Locke and Newton), the Skeptical Enlightenment (Voltaire and Hume), the Revolutionary Enlightenment (Rousseau), and the Didactic Enlightenment (Scottish philosophers).

19. For Campbell's own statement of his Lockean/Common Sense premises, see "Education—No. 4," *Millennial Harbinger* 6 (April 1835), 152-4, and "Reason Examined by Interrogatories—No. 1," ibid. 2 (November 7, 1831), 485-7. See also James Ellerbrook, "The Influence of Thomas Reid on the Thought-Life of Alexander Campbell" (B.D. thesis, Christian Theological Seminary, 1947). On his Baconianism see C. Leonard Allen, "Baconianism and the Bible among Disciples of Christ," *Church History* 55 (March 1986), 65-80, and Michael W. Casey, "The Origins of the Hermeneutics of the Churches of Christ: Part Two, The Philosophical Background," *Restoration Quarterly* 31 (1989).

20. Alexander Campbell, "On Prayer and Special Influence," *Millennial Harbinger* 4 (May 1833), 233; Campbell, *Christian System*, pp. 2, 6.

21. Alexander Campbell, "Evidence of the Gospel—No. 3," *Millennial Harbinger* 6 (October 1835), 472; Campbell, "A Word to Neutrals and Partial Reformers," ibid. 3 (January 2, 1832), 40; Campbell, "The Millennium—No. 3," ibid. 5 (November 1834), 549; Campbell, "Education—New Series, No. I," ibid. 3 (August 6, 1832), 408-11. On the Enlightenment background of this progressive spirit, see David Spadafora, *The Idea of Progress in Eighteenth-Century Britain* (New Haven: Yale University, 1990).

22. Campbell, "Millennium—No. 3," p. 549; Campbell, "The Cooperation of Churches—No. I," *Millennial Harbinger* 2 (May 4, 1831), 236; Campbell, "The Millennium—No. 8," ibid. 6 (April 1835), 148. For the persistence of this view in the movement, see W. K. Pendleton, "An Address Delivered Before the American Bible Union," ibid., 4th series, 7 (December 1857), 671-75. On the background to Campbell's millennialism, see Nathan Hatch, "Millennialism and Popular Religion in

the Early Republic," in *The Evangelical Tradition in America*, ed. Leonard Sweet (Macon, GA: Mercer University, 1984), pp. 111-30.

23. Martin E. Marty, *Modern American Religion, Volume 1: The Irony of It All, 1893-1919* (Chicago: University of Chicago, 1986), p. 194.

24. See William R. Hutchinson, "Protestantism as Establishment," in *Between the Times: The Travail of the Protestant Establishment in America, 1900-1960* (New York: Cambridge University, 1989), pp. 13-16. Cf. also C. Howard Hopkins, *The Rise of the Social Gospel in American Protestantism, 1865-1915* (New Haven: Yale University, 1940), pp. 280-98.

25. R. L. Roberts, "The Influence of B. W. Stone vs. A. Campbell in the History of Churches of Christ in America" (unpublished paper); R. L. Roberts and J. W. Roberts, "Like Fire in Dry Stubble—The Stone Movement, 1804-1832 (Part I)," *Restoration Quarterly* 7 (1963), 148-58, "Like Fire in Dry Stubble—The Stone Movement (Part II)," ibid. 9 (1965), 26-40.

26. Hughes, *Reviving the Ancient Faith* (Grand Rapids, MI: Eerdmans, 1996), pp. 92-134.

27. Ibid.

28. For analysis of a telling episode in the 1920s, see Don Haymes, "The Road More Traveled: How the Churches of Christ Became a Denomination," *Mission Journal* (March 1987), 4-8. See also Michael Casey, "From Pacifism to Patriotism: The Emergence of Civil Religion in the Churches of Christ During World War I," *Mennonite Quarterly Review*, 66 (July 1992), 376-90.

29. Alexander Campbell, *Familiar Lectures on the Pentateuch*, ed. W. T. Moore (St. Louis, MO: Christian Publishing, 1867), pp. 266-304; Campbell, *Christian System*, p. 133.

30. Alexander Campbell, "The Ordinances," *Millennial Harbinger*, New Series, 7 (January 1843), 9.

31. T. W. Brents, *The Gospel Plan of Salvation*, 16th ed. (Nashville, TN: Gospel Advocate, 1973), p. 196.

32. James McClendon, "Baptism as a Performative Sign," *Theology Today* 23 (October 1966), 403-16.

33. For a study recognizing this diminution of baptism and calling for its enrichment and renewal, see John Mark Hicks and Greg Taylor, *Down in the River to Pray: Revisioning Baptism as God's Transforming Power* (Siloam Springs, AR: Leafwood, 2004).

34. Alexander Campbell, "Opinionisms—No. 1," *Millennial Harbinger*, 5th series, 2 (August 1859), 436-37.

35. F. J. A. Hort, *The Way, the Truth, and the Life* (New York: Macmillan, 1893), 91.

36. Richard Reinitz describes the sense in which I am using the concept of irony: "We perceive human action as ironic…when we see the consequences of that action as contrary to the original intent of the actor and can locate a significant part of the reason for the discrepancy in the actor himself or in his intention." In this under-

standing, when we are involved in irony the "contradictory outcome is at least in part a result of an unconscious weakness in ourselves," so that "we are seen as bearing some responsibility for a discrepancy." *Irony and Consciousness: American Historiography and Reinhold Niebuhr* (Lewisburg, PA: Bucknell University, 1980), p. 19.

37. See for example Leonard I. Sweet, "From Catacomb to Basilica: The Dilemma of Oldline Protestantism," *Christian Century* (November 2, 1988), 981; Stanley Hauerwas and William Willimon, *Resident Aliens: Life in the Christian Colony* (Nashville: Abingdon, 1990); and Ronald E. Osborn, "The Irony of the Twentieth-Century Christian Church (Disciples of Christ): Making it to the Mainline Just at the Time of its Disestablishment," *Mid-Stream* (1989), 293-312.

CHAPTER THREE

The Odd Embrace of the Modern: Alexander Campbell's New Hermeneutic

THE ANCIENT GOSPEL

In propounding the "true and rational" approach to the Bible and in arguing for the "ancient gospel," Alexander Campbell was shaped deeply by his disgust with the "experimental" piety of Protestant revivalism in the early nineteenth-century. Jonathan Edwards and John Wesley had given this piety its classic shape in the eighteenth-century evangelical awakenings. Both men, though differing on key points, had insisted that God converted people by the immediate work of the Holy Spirit, that is, by a sovereign divine act not contingent upon any human "means" or efforts (though God might well use such means). Further, both taught that conversion followed a basic pattern: (1) an initial awakening to one's dangerous spiritual condition; (2) a period of distress and deepening conviction of one's utter helplessness before God; and (3) an experience of deliverance in which the Holy Spirit filled one's heart with love for God and granted assurance of forgiveness.[1] Theologians like Samuel Hopkins and Andrew Fuller mediated this pattern of conversion to Presbyterians, Congregationalists, and Baptists; wide use of Wesley's sermons spread it among Methodists. Though strict Calvinism faded quickly after 1800 and the preaching of the Second Great Awakening generally proclaimed salvation as free for all, this experimental piety remained prominent in Alexander Campbell's time.

Examples of such conversions abound in the autobiographies of the time. One preacher told how, at age seventeen, he awoke to the fact that he was a "hell-deserving sinner" and how he struggled mightily for the "evidence of pardon." He prayed with great sobs and groans; he attended church services for several weeks, even accompanying his sister to the anxious seat; he went forward to be prayed over, and when that failed, "went forward at every meeting when mourners were called for." Still not receiving deliverance, he resolved never to cease the struggle until he received some token of acceptance with God. Upon finally reaching conversion after several weeks, his mother marveled that he had gotten through so quickly.[2] For others the agonized quest for peace with God often lasted months or even years.

Against this view of conversion Campbell directed a large and disproportionate amount of his voluminous writings over a span of forty years. His longest running journal, *The Millennial Harbinger*, contains over 1600 pages on the Holy Spirit, much of it opposing "spiritual influences" in conversion. He explained in 1837 what had compelled him to write so much on this theme:

> If I had not met with a thousand marvellous tales of miraculous conversions by new or special illuminations, appearances, visions, dreams, that left the soul as dark as midnight...; if I had not met with many preachers...almost as ignorant of the Bible as they were of the Koran, telling incredible tales of what the Lord had done for them, when they could scarcely tell where the Messiah was born, or why it behooved him to die and rise again: I say, if I had not met with multitudes thus deceived and deceiving others about spiritual operations, I should never have had any controversy on this subject.

Campbell believed fervently that such excesses resulted directly from the dominant model of conversion with its "mystic impulses." He thus could call it "the greatest delusion of this our age, and one of the most prolific causes of the infidelity, immorality, and irreligion of our contemporaries."[3]

Campbell therefore sought to counter this dominant pattern of conversion with what he saw as its dangerous and paralyzing subjectivity.

Indeed, he meant to oppose any doctrine of conversion based on "speculation" and contrary to clear biblical fact. To do this he proposed a new *ordo salutis* (sequence of steps to salvation), a pattern he believed was nothing less than the old or original order. He called it "the ancient gospel" and listed its simple elements: "gospel facts [death, burial, resurrection, and ascension of Christ], faith, repentance, reformation [of life], baptism, remission of sins, [reception of] the Holy Spirit, sanctification, the resurrection, eternal life." The problem, he judged, was not that the Christian sects rejected any of these basic biblical facts--they all already believed each of them. The problem was that each sect ordered these facts differently depending on its particular theory of conversion. Some, for example, placed reception of the Holy Spirit before faith and remission of sins before baptism (Regular Baptists); others placed both baptism and remission of sins before faith (pedobaptists).

The "ancient gospel," Campbell argued, was simply the New Testament ordering of these facts. If one took preaching in the New Testament as a model, one found that it began with the testimony to the gospel facts; this testimony, in turn, without any other supernatural agency, produced faith; and faith then led a person to "obey the gospel," that is, to repent of sins and be baptized for remission of sins. Reception of the Spirit then followed gospel obedience. There was no agonized waiting for the Spirit to work, no designated "anxious seat," no lingering doubts about the veracity of one's experience.[4]

Campbell's "ancient gospel" was a simple schema and readily adapted to itinerant preaching. That proved to be its genius in the competitive religious marketplace of Jacksonian America. But Campbell grounded this "ancient gospel" in a deeper, theoretical base indebted to the thinkers of the Scottish Enlightenment, particularly the rhetorician and theologian George Campbell of Aberdeen (d. 1796). Guided by George Campbell's theory of "natural rhetoric" with its focus on the role of testimony, Alexander set out the "natural" (and thus "original") plan of salvation.[5] The New Testament contained a "divine chain of moral and spiritual instrumentality" containing five links: facts, testimony, faith, feeling, and action. These five elements formed a solid chain of cause and effect. The gospel facts first gave rise to inspired apostolic witnesses who reported those facts. These first witnesses then worked miracles to confirm their testimony, since supernatural facts require supernatural confirmation. The Christian preacher likewise testifies to the facts, but the preacher now confirms those facts not with new miracles but only through "argument and evidence"--in the divine economy miraculous confirmation was no longer necessary for that too had entered the factual record and remained available for rational assessment.[6]

This factual testimony, rationally presented and argued, produced faith. Faith arose not from some mysterious spiritual effusion or any "insensible operation" of the Holy Spirit but simply from "the belief of testimony"; indeed, the standard Calvinist and Arminian insistence on such an experience flatly denied the adequacy of God's revelation in the Bible. Campbell adamantly insisted time and again that "all the converting power which the Father, the Son, or the Holy Spirit now exercises upon the human mind, is in the word" and its factual testimony to the Messiah. Thus it followed naturally that "where testimony begins, faith begins; and where testimony ends, faith ends." The work of the preacher, therefore, was clear and focused: it was not to recount spiritual experiences or to enflame the emotions but to "exhibit the evidence" and persuade people to "obey the gospel."[7]

Once instilled by testimony, faith then stirred feelings and prompted moral actions appropriate to the nobility and glory of the Christian religion. "The feelings corresponding with the nature of the fact," Campbell wrote, "are excited or called into existence the moment the fact is known or believed...facts alone can move the affections, and command the passions of man." For this reason Campbell considered the traditional revivalistic pattern of conversion unbiblical and even ludicrous. "To call anything christian experience which transpires or is felt before a person obeys the gospel...appears to me as absurd as to talk of the conjugal experience of an unmarried person." Thus the "ancient gospel" demanded a sharp distinction between true religious affections, which are always called forth by facts, and the unstable and illusory experiences promoted by the Protestant "mystics."[8]

Facts, testimony, faith, feelings, then moral action--this was the strict and inviolable order of the "ancient gospel." To the workings of this order, Campbell adamantly insisted, there could be "no exception, [any] more than against the universality of the laws of gravity."[9]

This focus on the orderliness and inviolability of the conversion process provides a major clue to the appeal of the "ancient gospel" and the rapid growth of Campbell's movement. To those distressed by the terrors of "experimental religion" and put off by the apparent capriciousness of its God, the "ancient gospel" allowed people to take matters firmly into their own hands. The gospel, Campbell proclaimed, "makes no provision for despondency"; neither does it require a person to "become a desponding, trembling infidel before he can become a believer."[10] Rather, people can use their own common sense, examine the biblical testimony, and promptly believe it. Bypassing all the emotional paraphernalia of revivalism, they then could act on their faith and "obey the gospel," receiving immediately the full assurance and joy of salvation. In this way Campbell both rationalized and democratized the conversion process, removing its mystery and placing it at the initiative of the common person.

The preaching of the "ancient gospel" was dramatically successful in the 1820s and 30s. After observing this pattern of conversion at work for over fifteen years, however, Barton Stone voiced some concerns. Late in his life he warned that Campbell's ordo salutis was proving spiritually enervating because it tended to short-circuit the process of repentance and make conversion too quick and easy. To distressed believers who languished under conviction of sin, the charge to "obey the gospel" was certainly a great balm, but this pattern of conversion also easily swept people into the church who had not experienced deep sorrow for sin and true heart change. By the early 1840s this deficiency was reflected, he thought, in a growing coldness and nominalism in the churches.

Stone's complaint about Campbell's doctrine of conversion calls to mind Reinhold Niebuhr's complaint (in 1932) about Protestant liberalism. Niebuhr's problem with the liberals was that "they had exchanged the emotional fervor of Christianity, its deep and moving feeling for the terrible burden of human depravity, for a breezy faith in efficiency."[11] Campbell's faith in human efficiency was not quite "breezy"—he remained too much of a Presbyterian for that—but his new understanding of conversion partook somewhat of this later liberal spirit.

Campbell's doctrine of "baptism for remission of sins"—first set forth in his debate with the Presbyterian McCalla in Kentucky in 1823—played a key role in the appeal of his "ancient gospel." The trouble with the various "experimental" gospels, whether Calvinist or Arminian, he argued, is that they lack "an institution which gives a formal, sensible, and perfect remission of sins." One is left to rummage around in one's own inner experiences, deducing one's release from sin through a shaky "train of inferential reasonings." But the "ancient gospel" provides something more secure, Campbell proclaimed; God molded the gospel in "the form of a command" (baptism), thus enabling every believer "sensibly to feel" the divine forgiveness and "to remember the time and place in which he was justified and born into the family of God." Though Christ's blood "really washes away" sin, the institution of baptism "formally washes" it away. In this way baptism serves as a formal sign and seal of forgiveness, bringing an assurance and joy that the unimmersed simply cannot experience.[12]

As this message began to spread, the results were striking. One preacher of the "ancient gospel" told of baptizing a seventy-seven year old man. Asked why he had never become a Christian, the man replied that he had been waiting for God to make him a Christian. The preacher said that he promptly pointed the man to the testimony of scripture and asked him to obey it. The old man replied, "Sir, I will with all my heart." He was immersed within the hour and, according to the preacher, went home rejoicing. Another man, after discovering the "ancient gospel" in Campbell's writings, exclaimed that the "simplicity and tangibleness of primitive Christianity became irresistibly apparent to me—the nebulous mysticism which had hid the true gospel from me was dispelled." A Baptist minister testified that, since hearing the "ancient gospel," reading the New Testament had become "more delightful than ever" and that "I have enjoyed more peace than in all the rest of my life."[13]

Though Campbell first set forth the contours of "the ancient gospel" and developed its theoretical base, he credited his friend Walter Scott as "the first practical restorer of the ancient gospel." After being chosen as the itinerant evangelist by the Mahoning Baptist Association in mid 1827, Scott formulated a simple schema that proved enormously effective in his preaching on the Western Reserve. It contained five steps: (1) hear the biblical testimony to the grand proposition that Jesus was the Messiah; (2) believe the testimony; (3) repent of one's sins; and (4) be baptized for remission of sins; then (5) God would grant forgiveness and the gift of the Spirit. With this formula, Scott reported baptizing over one thousand people a year for many years. So heady were the results that by 1836 he could claim that "in 1827 the True Gospel was restored" and that he, not Campbell, had been the agent of its restoration.[14]

THE ANCIENT ORDER OF THINGS

Equally important to Alexander Campbell's restoration movement was the systematic reconstruction of "the ancient order of things." By this he meant the original pattern of church ordinances and order visible in the first apostolic communities and set down primarily in Acts of the Apostles and the Epistles. This "ancient order," he insisted, must not be separated from the "ancient gospel." Not only must one believe the gospel facts and be immersed, one must also seek a church "organized according to the Christian constitution." For the "ancient gospel and order of things" are inseparable, constituting "one divine system of remission, holiness, and happiness."[15]

Campbell's reconstruction of the "ancient order" rested squarely upon two important features of his "true and rational" approach to the Bible: (1) a dispensational arrangement of the Bible and (2) a constitutional view of the New Testament documents.

Making a sharp distinction between the old and new covenants, Campbell divided the Bible into three dispensations: the patriarchal, spanning from Adam to Moses; the Mosaic, spanning from Moses at Sinai to Peter on Pentecost; and the Christian, beginning at Pentecost and ending with the final judgment. This dispensational arrangement, in effect, divided the Bible into three blocks: (1) Genesis 1 through Exodus 19; (2) Exodus 20 through Acts 1; and (3) Acts 2 through Revelation 22. On this basis Campbell stressed time and again that only biblical texts reflecting the Christian dispensation (Acts 2 to Revelation 22) could authorize Christian faith and practice.

In his famous "Sermon on the Law," delivered before the Redstone Baptist Association on September 1, 1816, he argued that because Christians do not live under the old or Mosaic covenant they are not bound in any way by its laws and institutions. Thus, any arguments appealing to the Old Testament to support infant baptism, tithes, Sabbath observance, holy days, national covenants, or civil control of religion are illegitimate, indeed, "repugnant to Christianity" and entirely "ineffectual." Rather, "[Christ's] will published in the New Testament is the sole law of the church."[16]

In arguing this position Campbell drew sharp and frequent fire, especially from Baptists and Presbyterians who charged him with an heretical rejection of the Old Testament. In defending himself Campbell acknowledged that the Old Testament contained much important teaching, indeed that it was essential to understand the coming of the Messiah. But he flatly denied that it served in any way as a rule of life for Christians. He also rejected the view, common following the Reformation, that the preaching of the law prepares people to receive the gospel; the gospel itself, he argued, most effectively convinces people of sin. In these ways, Campbell departed sharply from the standard Reformed position promulgated in the Westminster Confession and its Baptist version, the Philadelphia Confession.

This dispensationalism formed a cornerstone of Campbell's new hermeneutic. Following the "Sermon on the Law," he gave it extensive systematic treatment and appealed to it regularly in his debates and polemical writings.[17]

Closely connected to this dispensationalism was a constitutional view of the New Testament documents. In the *Declaration and Address*, Thomas Campbell had written that "the New Testament is as perfect a constitution for the worship, discipline, and government of the New Testament Church, and as perfect a rule for the particular duties of its members, as the Old Testament was for the worship, discipline, and government of the Old Testament Church." Alexander picked up and developed this view. The kingdom of God, he said, consists of five elements: the constitution, the king, the subjects, the territory, and the laws. The constitution was the plan of salvation conceived by God before time began (and reflected in the New Testament); the king or "constitutional monarch" was Jesus Christ, whose reign began on the first Pentecost after his ascension; the subjects were all those who had been born again; the territory was the "whole earth"; and the laws were found in the New Testament (primarily in Acts and the Epistles), for the king made his apostles the legislators of the kingdom.[18]

This view of the kingdom, when combined with his dispensationalism, led Campbell to a striking conclusion: the teachings of Jesus before Pentecost do not possess the same authority for the church as do the teachings of the apostles after Pentecost. Jesus' life and teachings predated establishment of the kingdom and actually belong in the "old Jewish dispensation." The Gospels could not provide the "laws" for Christ's kingdom; rather, they "must be learned from what the Apostles published to the world, after the ascension and coronation of the King, as they are recorded in Acts of the Apostles and the Epistles." One should not seek these laws, he added, "antecedent to the day of Pentecost; except insofar as our Lord himself, during his lifetime, propounded the doctrine of his reign." As this last phrase indicates, Campbell did not simply lump the Gospels together with the Old Testament. One living under the Christian dispensation used the Gospels, particularly the miracle stories, to prove the supernatural fact of Jesus' messiahship. But once that purpose was achieved, the Gospels took a back seat to the rest of the New Testament. Campbell, in fact, sometimes used the phrase "Acts and the Epistles of the Apostles" as the functional equivalent of New Testament.[19]

In this way the New Testament, or more precisely Acts and the Epistles, became the "statute-book of Heaven," a precise and uniform legal code for the church. On this basis, Campbell set forth "the ancient order of things": congregational autonomy, baptism for remission of sins, weekly observance of the Lord's supper, a plurality of elders and deacons in each congregation, and a simple pattern of worship. This ancient order was specific and complete; any practice or institution lacking an apostolic command or example was simply an illicit novelty. Campbell over the years was not entirely comfortable with such a strict constitutional view, and basic inconsistency appears in his writings, but the logic of his kingdom theory pushed him and many of his followers in this direction.[20]

Taken together "the ancient gospel and order of things" presented an astounding and glorious prospect: the collapse of the many warring sects and the union of believers in the one true church established on the day of Pentecost (Acts 2). The "ancient gospel," Campbell exulted, would be "the instrument of converting the whole human race, and of uniting all christians upon one and the same foundation."[21]

THE ODD EMBRACE OF THE MODERN

This vision with which Campbell launched his restoration movement in the 1820s was grandiose and profoundly optimistic, enthralling by its very simplicity. But behind this vision, as we saw briefly in chapter one, lay a fundamental, over-arching irony. Put simply, Alexander Campbell's primitivism, from its very beginning, partook deeply of modernity. Though the early Disciples envisioned themselves as enacting a simple repristination of primitive Christianity, nothing more and nothing less, their repristination was neither simple nor thoroughly primitive. It was rather a complex mix of elements both old and new, deeply rooted in the early American ethos and reflecting Enlightened currents of thought.

The Enlightenment or Age of Reason brought a profound shift in how people viewed their world and their place in it. To put it simply, one could say that in this age the cosmos was mechanized. Scientists and thinkers like Galileo, Rene Descartes, and especially Isaac Newton began to picture the universe as a great machine operating according to unalterable natural laws which could be expressed with great mathematical precision. The workings of the natural world thereby became more intelligible and regular, more predictable and thus more controllable.

Along with this new mechanistic view of nature came a new view of human nature. The essence of human nature became the capacity for rational calculation and action. Reason and emotion, thinking and feeling, were thus placed in sharp opposition. As Stephen Toulmin put it, "Calculation was enthroned as the distinctive virtue of the human reason; and the life of the emotions was repudiated, as distracting one from the demands of clear-headed deliberation."[22]

Together, the new mechanistic view of nature and the new exalted view of human reason formed a powerful combination. Scientific and technological achievement exploded, soon giving rise to utopian visions of cultural progress. Throughout the eighteenth century more and more people became enthralled by the prospects of controlling nature's previously uncontrollable forces.

But for all its gifts the Newtonian view of nature exacted a costly price. The price was subtle but steady secularization. God gradually became more distant and impersonal. The traditional belief in "special providence"--the sense of God's immediate and personal involvement in human affairs--gradually gave way to the regularity of impersonal natural laws. As Newton and his successors described and praised the wonderful regularity of nature's laws, the need for divine interruptions seemed less and less necessary. So perfect, in fact, seemed the natural system that God's own self became bound to it. The committed Scottish churchman William Robertson, for example, in 1769 denounced as superstitious anyone who expected "particular and extraordinary acts of power under the divine administration." As many other Christians came to agree, the "providential world" of the seventeenth century gave way to the "observable world" of the Age of Reason. There arose a conception of general providence, often expressed in the principle of the "invisible hand," that left little or no room for present-day divine intervention in the world.[23]

In the new mechanistic worldview, God remained creator and first cause but, rather than guiding creation immediately and personally, worked only through secondary, natural causes. In this way the natural became sharply separated from the supernatural and, as a result, the modern conception of the natural world was born.

In eighteenth- and early nineteenth-century Britain and America, this new view of nature engendered a new mindset that James Turner calls "analytic-technical thinking." This new cast of mind held up the natural sciences, with their rigorously empirical method, as the model for all human knowing. It thirsted for precise knowledge, and harbored suspicion for whatever did not conform to the rule of computation and usefulness. In America one sign of the new mentality was the rage for statistics that emerged in the first two decades of the nineteenth century.[24]

This new mindset profoundly shaped Christian views of the Bible in America. Behind it was a long and varied lineage of American "Supernatural Rationalists," ranging from moderate Calvinists, Arminians, and Unitarians, to Episcopalians and Disciples of Christ like Alexander Campbell.[25] These Christian thinkers, concerned about the spread of unbelief, felt that they must reconcile the Bible with the new view of nature. Otherwise, people who now thought in more precise, scientific terms about the world might cast aspersions on the Bible as an irrational or unscientific authority. Christian apologists proceeded to adjust the Bible so that it fit with the physics of Isaac Newton and the epistemology of John Locke. They modernized the Bible so that people would find it more scientific, more "natural," and thus more believable.

This rationalization of the Bible took place through a complex and subtle process. A few people became exponents of "natural religion" or Deism, glorifying human reason and playing fast and loose with the Bible. The Supernatural Rationalists shunned such a radical step and clung to the Bible as divine revelation. But to varying degrees these devout Christian theologians aggressively fitted the Bible to the scientific model. Entranced by the "analytic-technical" view of things, they naturalized the Bible, turning it into a collection of facts analogous to the facts of nature.

Alexander Campbell partook deeply of this early modern, scientific worldview with its new approach to the Bible. His heroes were "Bacon, Newton, Locke, and all the great masters of science." The names and ideas of this triumvirate permeate his writings, and no person (except Jesus

Christ) receives higher honor and greater encomiums. "What have these mighty minds achieved for science, physical, mental, and moral—for the world!" he exclaimed. Under their ministrations science has "advanced society ten generations in a single century"; its triumphs are "inscribed upon ten thousand pillars." Besides "Bacon, Newton, and Locke," Campbell praised other stellar lights in the modern firmament: Joseph Butler, George Campbell, Samuel Clarke, Thomas Reid, Dugald Stewart, James Beattie, and others—all of them from the "modern schools of Britain." The greatness of all these men lay, Campbell said, in their devotion to scientific method and to the Bible—a happy combination for which God had blessed their efforts.[26]

With his way lighted by these British pioneers of modernity, Campbell claimed, as we have seen, to have restored the "true and rational" way of reading the Bible. But far from jettisoning all philosophical systems and predilections, as he often claimed, Campbell actually employed a hermeneutical method combining a strict Lockean epistemology with the Baconianism of the Scottish Common Sense philosophers. His method was in fact a "new hermeneutic."

THE RISE OF "SCIENCE FEVER"

For Campbell the basic source of this cluster of ideas was the moderate Scottish Enlightenment in its later phase (around the turn of the nineteenth century). This period, according to Richard Sher, was marked by an "epidemic of science fever" which grew out of a long Scottish tradition of respect for practical science. This end-of-the-century "rush to science," in turn, provided the backdrop for the rise and triumph of the "common sense" or realist school of philosophy fathered by Thomas Reid of Edinburgh and popularized in Dugald Stewart's lectures on moral philosophy at Edinburgh from 1785 to 1810.[27]

Reid and Stewart were conservative Lockeans who sought to preserve Locke's empiricism from the skeptical and deistic positions to which some had taken it. They affirmed a core of common sense beliefs shared by all people of all times and cultures: the existence of an external world, the continuity of the self from day to day, the reality of other minds, and the reliability of sense perception, memory, and testimony. On this basis, they believed, certain knowledge could be erected. To do this they turned to the method of inductive and experimental science that they attributed pre-eminently to Francis Bacon and secondarily to Isaac Newton. Indeed, as Dwight Bozeman put it, Reid and Stewart "considered their entire philosophical program to be an enactment of the inductive plan of research set forth in Bacon's *Novum Organum.*" For this reason their philosophy quickly was labeled the "Baconian Philosophy." It consisted of four principle emphases: a vigorous enthusiasm for natural science; a strict empiricism based on a "common sense" confidence in the senses; a deep suspicion of all "speculation" and abstraction; and homage to "Lord Bacon" as the pioneer of the inductive method.[28]

In the early nineteenth century this pattern of ideas was transferred as a whole into the mainstream of American thought where it maintained a dominant position until the Civil War. This transfer was mediated by the influence, since the late 1760s, of the Scottish Philosophy that had radiated from Princeton. By the early nineteenth century Scottish textbooks held sway in American colleges. In the culture at large the name of Bacon became an almost magic word, one invoked as the remedy for almost any intellectual or social ill. Presbyterian, Congregational, Episcopalian, and Disciple theologians all seized upon the Baconian philosophy as a ready ally, particularly as a means of restoring and reinforcing an essential harmony between natural science and Christian faith. Baconianism quickly became a major pillar in the edifice of nineteenth-century evangelicalism.[29]

In adopting the Baconian philosophy as his hermeneutical base, Alexander Campbell thus stood shoulder to shoulder with many evangelical theologians in America. But unlike most of his American colleagues, Campbell received his Baconian orientation directly from the Scots. His father Thomas had studied at the University of Glasgow (1783-86) and subsequently based young Alexander's home schooling on the Glasgow curriculum (which included careful study of Locke's *Essay on Human Understanding*). Later Alexander himself spent ten months at Glasgow in 1808-1809. There both men studied philosophy under George Jardine, a student and close friend of Thomas Reid. In the published outline of his course on logic, which Alexander purchased and used at Glasgow, Jardine argued that Bacon had revolutionized the art of reasoning by overthrowing Aristotle and establishing the inductive method. Further, he argued that Newton's great scientific discoveries rested squarely upon Bacon's *Novum Organum* (a work that Jardine frequently used as a textbook).

Jardine argued in short that the inductive method, established by Bacon and refined for nearly two centuries afterwards, was the only trustworthy approach to knowledge.[30]

The younger Campbell embraced Jardine's (and thus Reid's) views with great enthusiasm. Throughout his career in America, Campbell's writings reflected the direct influence of the Glasgow logic course (he called Jardine's lectures "the most useful series of college lectures, of which I have any recollection"). In his 1829 debate with the skeptic Robert Owen, he appealed numerous times to "Lord Bacon," asserting that he would "use the principles of the inductive philosophy [as his] rule and guide." In his opening address upon the founding of Bethany College in 1841, he drew upon Jardine's course outline to show the covenant between "philosophy and Common Sense." "We are in science and philosophy Baconians and not Aristotelians," he wrote late in his career. "We build on Bible facts and documents and not on theories and speculations."[31]

Part of the great appeal of Baconianism to theologians like Campbell lay in the simple fact that it provided a philosophical base for applying the day's scientific method to the Bible. Nature consists of facts, the thinking went, and so does the Bible. The natural scientist inductively gathers his or her facts from nature; the biblical "scientist" inductively gathers his or her facts from the Bible. The natural scientist, reasoning from the facts, reaches precise and certain knowledge; the biblical "scientist," likewise reasoning from the facts, also attains precise and certain knowledge. Both scientists use the same method because God created "two great volumes— the Book of Nature and the Book of Revelation."[32]

The Enlightenment's new mechanistic view of nature with its order and "system" deeply impressed Campbell. Therefore, like other Protestant theologians, he applied the same thinking to the Bible. "Order is heaven's first law, the Bible's first law, and the Christian preacher's first concern," he often insisted. "If nature be a system, religion is no less so. God is `a God of order,' and that is the same as to say he is a God of system." Campbell's student James Lamar essentially summarized his teacher's view in 1859. The Bible is "a record in all respects analogous to that of a competent scientific observer," Lamar wrote; as a result, one could "perceive the exact place and precise force of every fact, incident, precept, doctrine, and communication" and "assign every sentence its proper place, and give to every word its legitimate force."[33]

With their Baconianism, Campbell and his followers naturalized the Bible, construing it as a scientific book of "facts." They unwittingly modernized the Bible so that it fit with the new Newtonian world of natural laws. The scientific method had systematized, demystified, and brought nature under control; it did the same thing when applied to the Bible. In this way the Bible became a revelation well suited to an age characterized by "science fever."

THE MYTH OF PROGRESS

A close corollary to Campbell's scientific view of the Bible was a doctrine of cultural progress, as already noted briefly in chapter one. Campbell joined many English and Scottish intellectuals of the late eighteenth and early nineteenth centuries in sounding the trumpets of progress-in science and technology especially, but also in art, literature, morality, and religion. He reflects especially the Scottish Enlightenment's quest for a scientific understanding of the workings of society and morals, and thus the ability to engineer the way of cultural progress.

Key figures of the eighteenth-century British Enlightenment embraced a vision of history as moving from "rudeness to refinement."[34] These intellectuals saw their task as application of Newtonian science, with its emphasis on observation and experimentation, to the whole realm of social phenomena. In this way they expected to develop a "science of man," so that, just as natural science was bringing nature under control, they also could bring human society under control.

Here we see a fundamental feature of the Enlightenment vision: "the quest to duplicate outside the realm of physics the method and achievements of Newton."[35] The result was a powerful doctrine of cultural progress. Scottish Presbyterian minister Richard Price well stated the new doctrine: "One generation thus improved communicates improvement to the next, and that to the next, till at last a progress in improvement may take place rapid and irresistible, which may issue in the happiest state of things that can exist on this earth."[36] In this view human history consisted of a series of orderly stages by which virtually all peoples would eventually move "from rudeness to refinement."

In eighteenth and nineteenth-century England, such a doctrine of cultural progress was tied closely to the advance of science and technology.

It was not by accident that this profound optimism arose between 1760 and 1830, for this was the key period of the "first" Industrial Revolution in England (which brought things like the steam engine, steam boats, and a rush of remarkable new technology). It was a time of profound social, economic, technological, and intellectual transformation.[37]

Thomas Macaulay, an English contemporary of Alexander Campbell, expressed this exuberant progressive spirit in his famous essay on Francis Bacon. Reciting the marvelous accomplishments of the "Baconian Philosophy," he wrote:

> It has lengthened life; it has mitigated pain; it has extinguished diseases; it has increased the fertility of the soil; it has furnished new arms to the warrior;…it has lighted up the night with the splendor of the day; it has extended the range of human vision; it has multiplied the power of the human muscles; it has accelerated motion; it has annihilated distance,…it has enabled man to descend to the depths of the sea, to soar into the air, to penetrate securely into the noxious recesses of the earth, to traverse the land in cars which whirl along without horses, and the ocean in ships which run ten knots an hour against the wind. These are but a part of its fruits, and of its first fruits. For it is a philosophy which never rests, which has never attained, which is never perfect. Its law is progress.[38]

This enormous confidence in the possibilities of science contributed directly to the emergence of a new kind of millennialism in the eighteenth century. By 1750 William Whiston, for example, could proclaim that the "wonderful Newtonian philosophy" provided "an eminent prelude and preparation to those happy times of the restitution of all things." Late in the century, the Anglican Richard Clarke could envision an earthly paradise where the curses of the fall would "go away gradually, as the progressive restitution of all things comes on, and is ripening through this Millennial reign."[39] The Christian millennium came to be viewed as gradual, progressive, and natural, not as a sudden, cataclysmic, supernatural event. Many Englishmen of this period, including John Wesley, the father of Methodism, shared a similar view.

Alexander Campbell's millennialism must be viewed against this backdrop. His longest running journal, the *Millennial Harbinger*, was devoted to the "introduction of that political and religious order of society called THE MILLENNIUM, which will be the consummation of that ultimate amelioration of society proposed in the Christian Scriptures." "Things are in progress," he often said, "to another—a golden—a millennial—a blissful period in human history," a time when "society is perfectly civilized"; and toward this goal society has been moving "with a slow but steady pace, since the commencement of the sixteenth century."[40]

The new millennial world order, he believed was well under way by 1830, though still in the early stages. The Protestant Reformation represented a great leap forward, and the scientific revolution that followed had dramatically harnessed the engines of progress. Then the American democracy had appeared on the scene with its exhilarating atmosphere of liberty, further setting the stage. And finally the "ancient gospel and order" had been recovered in 1823, and it was quickly pushing back the tyrannies and confusion of sectarianism. Thus Campbell could report in 1830 that "No seven years of the last ten centuries, as the last seven, have been so strongly marked with the criteria of the dawn of that [millennial] period."[41]

For Campbell, as for the Christian intellectuals of the British Enlightenment, this new world order was emerging progressively through scientific and moral "means"-and it was evolving exponentially, not just through simple progression. "Tens now count hundreds, and hundreds thousands, in the progress of time and its manifold and sublime innovations and revolutions. The invention of gunpowder, the mariner's compass, the printing press, the discovery of America, the American Revolution-what have they wrought!!" And with the Baconian method now applied rigorously to biblical interpretation and with the "ancient gospel" once again in place, the world stood on a new and higher threshold of millennial breakthrough. "To introduce the last and most beneficial change in society," Campbell declared, "it is only necessary to let the gospel, in its own plainness, simplicity, and force, speak to men." Divested of all human philosophy and traditions, the "true gospel" will pass irresistibly throughout the whole earth and serve as "the mighty instrument by which this world is to be revolutionized."[42] The new millennial order will mean "the restoration of the Jerusalem church in all its moral and religious character" and "the extension of it through all nations and languages for one thousand years."[43] Human governments will be subverted and Jesus will govern the world by "religion only."

Behind Campbell's postmillennial fervor lay the myth of progress that emerged in eighteenth-century Britain, and especially the Scottish Enlightenment's quest for a scientific understanding of the workings of society and morals, and thus the ability to engineer the way of progress.

DIVINE AGENCY IN A SCIENTIFIC WORLD

This tendency in Campbell's thought appears strikingly in his strictures on divine agency in the world. God's power to affect people, he said many times, is "all contained in [revealed] words." Since the Bible already "contains all the arguments which can be offered to reconcile man to God, and to purify them who are reconciled," therefore "all the power of the Holy Spirit which can operate on the human mind is spent." To be filled with the Spirit thus meant little more than having the words and arguments of the Bible in one's mind. Thus the basic difference between the "natural man" and the "spiritual man" was that the first possessed only the five senses as an avenue to knowledge while the second possessed the Bible in addition. And in regard to prayer's petitions, one must not expect that "the laws of nature are to be changed, suspended, or new-modified, or that we are to become the subjects of any supernatural aid in obtaining these things." Campbell affirmed divine providence but defined it simply as the "power of circumstances"—"no new miracles are wrought, no new laws or impulses are created."[44] With such views Campbell reflected the Scottish Enlightenment's marked retreat from the older, traditional Christian supernaturalism.

When readers who caught the import of Campbell's modern world view on occasion asked him, in effect, "Why pray?" his answers were dense and convoluted, usually boiling down to the fact that the New Testament commands it. His strict Lockean epistemology, which limited all spiritual influences to the channel of the five senses, actually left little room for prayer (and, indeed, eliminated it as pointless for the unconverted). In practice, however, Campbell could break out of this philosophical framework and at least point toward a larger view of divine agency in the world.[45]

CONCLUSION

Campbell's thought represents an odd embrace of the modern-odd because he claimed to reject the modern with its traditions and philosophies and to embrace only the primitive and apostolic. But his reverence for Newtonian order and system, his adulation of scientific empiricism, his postmillennial eschatology, and his view of divine agency in the world reveals the profoundly modern character of his thought. The primitivist impulse, however, veiled this modernity. It served as an enormous screen, masking the cultural forces and intellectual currents that remained always and profoundly at work in the movement.

Behind this odd embrace of the modern lay the sense of historylessness that characterized much American religion in this period and that often has marked restorationist movements. The Stone/Campbell movement arose out of a profound disenchantment with the past. The past had bequeathed only spiritual confusion, moral decay, sectarian wrangling, and a deadening traditionalism. And so Campbell and his colleagues in reform sought, not to filter the dirty stream, but to abandon it for the pure spring. "On the subject of religion," Campbell could write in one of his more iconoclastic moods, "I am fully persuaded that nothing but the inspired scriptures ought ever to have been published"-though he himself would publish many thousands of pages on the "subject of religion."[46] Nineteen centuries of Christian reflection and writing, he seemed to say, served only to inhibit the practice of true Christianity. Reforming such a tradition would accomplish little, he thought; only a radical restoration of the original institution would avail.

Campbell's historylessness, however, was not a simple ignorance of the past or an untutored scorn of it. As one of the last in a long and distinguished line of American scholar-preachers, Campbell stood far removed from the historical naiveté of the unschooled frontier evangelist. Considerable erudition, historical breadth, and intellectual sophistication marked his thought. Though his training in historical theology was notably deficient, he knew the broad outlines of the Christian tradition fairly well, especially the Reformation, often citing its creeds and confessions in his polemics. Campbell's historylessness lay not so much in glaring ignorance of the past but rather in the pervasive assumption that one can transcend it, indeed, that with the "ancient gospel and order of things" he had done so. A fundamental premise underlying the movement was the bold claim that "We brought no [traditional] doctrines with us at all into the...proposed Reformation."[47]

In this assumption Alexander Campbell joined company with many intellectuals of the moderate British Enlightenment. Whether in religion or science, these Enlightenment thinkers assumed that the newly discovered powers of reason made possible a "clean slate"; one could entirely let go of the past and start all over again.[48] The fact that they stood some where, some time in particular was beside the point; their ideas, they assumed, arose directly from nature, unsullied by the effluvium of culture and tradition. The irony was that the very notion that one could escape history and culture altogether was itself a notion given force by the particular history and culture of the time. And the irony remains that one must draw heavily upon circumstantial factors to account for the rise of movements assuming that they had risen above the taint of all circumstances.

With their "ancient gospel and order of things," Alexander Campbell and the early Disciples claimed to occupy only primitive ground, nothing more or less. Yet at the same time, they held profoundly modern assumptions about the Bible and the world. In this odd embrace of the modern lay great power and vitality, as the movement's growth attests. But it also contained the roots of the deep tensions that quickly emerged and that have plagued the movement ever since.

Notes

1. See Jonathan Edwards, *Religious Affections* (New Haven, CT: Yale University, 1959), pp. 197-239, and John Wesley, *John Wesley's Fifty-Three Sermons*, ed. Edward H. Sugden (Nashville, TN: Abingdon, 1984).

2. B. F. Hall, "The Proud Preacher: The Autobiography of B. F. Hall" (typescript in Disciples of Christ Historical Society), pp. 7-19.

3. Alexander Campbell, "Mr. Lynd on the Influence of the Holy Spirit," *Millennial Harbinger* new series 1 (September 1837), 410; ibid. 2 (1831), 215.

4. Campbell, "Letter to William Jones. No. VI," p. 353; *Christian System*, pp. 90-100; "The Confirmation of the Testimony," *Millennial Harbinger* 1 (January 1830), 8-14.

5. See Carisse Mickey Berryhill, "Alexander Campbell's Natural Rhetoric of Evangelism," *Restoration Quarterly* 30 (1988), 111-24. Between 1808 and 1820 Alexander

Campbell probably read nearly all of the Scot's work. For a catalog of his extensive citations and quotations of George Campbell, see Berryhill, "Sense, Expression, and Purpose: Alexander Campbell's Natural Philosophy of Rhetoric" (Ph.D. diss., Florida State University, 1982), pp. 32-54.

6. Alexander Campbell, "Foundation of Christian Union," in *Christian System* (1839), pp. 85-100; see also "Supernatural Facts," in *Popular Lectures and Addresses.*

7. Alexander Campbell, *Millennial Harbinger* 4 (July 1833), 333; "Foundation of Christian Union," . Cf. Campbell, "Reply," *Christian Baptist* 2 (April 4, 1825), 178-82; and "Dialogue on the Holy Spirit," in *Christianity Restored* (1835, reprint ed., Rosemead, CA: Old Paths Book Club, 1959), pp. 343-79. See also Pat Brooks, "Alexander Campbell, the Holy Spirit, and the New Birth," *Restoration Quarterly* 31 (Third Quarter 1989), 149-64.

8. Campbell, "Confirmation of the Testimony," pp. 8-9; "Christian Experience— No. I," *Millennial Harbinger* 1 (June 7, 1830), 260. For fuller treatment, see D. Newell Williams, "The Gospel as the Power of God to Salvation: Alexander Campbell and Experimental Religion," in *Lectures in Honor of the Alexander Campbell Bicentennial, 1788-1988* (Nashville: Disciples of Christ Historical Society, 1988), pp. 127-48.

9. Campbell, "Confirmation of the Testimony," p. 9.

10. Alexander Campbell, "An Address to the Readers of the Christian Baptist. No. IV," *Christian Baptist* 1 (March 1, 1824), 148.

11. R. Lawrence Moore, *Selling God: American Religion in the Marketplace of Culture* (New York: Oxford University, 1994), 220. See Niebhur's *Moral Man and Immoral Society* (1932).

12. Alexander Campbell, "Incidents on a Tour of Nashville, TN. No. IV," *Millennial Harbinger* 2 (February 7, 1831), 50-51; *Campbell-McCalla Debate* (1823), p. 144. See also Campbell, "Ancient Gospel—No. II," *Christian Baptist* 5 (February 5, 1828), 167; *Christian System*, pp. 39-42, 161-71, 232-33.

13. *Millennial Harbinger* 4 (1833), 325; "Renunciation of Sectarianism," ibid. 6 (July 1835), 330; ibid. 6 (April 1835), 180.

14. Alexander Campbell, "Reply to Epaphras-No. 7," *Millennial Harbinger* 4 (April 1833), 173-74; Walter Scott, "From the Minutes of the Mahoning Association Report," *Christian Examiner* 1 (November 1829), 5-8; Scott, *The Gospel Restored* (Cincinnati, 1836), p. v. B.F. Hall disputed Scott's priority, claiming that he had "converted and immersed over one hundred persons for the remission of sins, before Scott first opened his lips and lifted up his noble voice in pleading the ancient gospel." (Hall, "Proud Preacher," p. 69). Furthermore, Campbell himself acknowledged that John Secrest of Ohio had baptized over 300 "for the remission of sins" by mid 1827 ["Miscellaneous Letters-No. 1," *Christian Baptist* 5 (October 1, 1827), 71-72]. Scott did not begin his "experiment" in preaching the "ancient gospel" until the last week of January 1828.

15. Alexander Campbell, "Reformation and Restoration," *Millennial Harbinger* 6 (January 1835), 25; ibid. 3 (December 3, 1832), 609.

16. Alexander Campbell, "Sermon on the Law," in *Familiar Lectures on the*

Pentateuch, ed. W. T. Moore (St. Louis: Christian Publishing, 1867), pp. 266-304; *Christian Baptist* 1 (November 3, 1823), 72. See also Everett Ferguson, "Alexander Campbell's `Sermon on the Law': A Historical and Theological Examination," *Restoration Quarterly* 29 (Second Quarter 1987), 71-85; and Elmer Prout, "Alexander Campbell's Attitude Toward and Use of the Old Testament" (MA thesis, Pepperdine University, 1962).

17. Alexander Campbell, "Essays on Man in his Primitive State and Under the Patriarchal, Jewish, and Christian Dispensations," *Christian Baptist* 6 (August 4, 1828), through 7 (July 5, 1830), sixteen articles; *Christian Baptism with Its Antecedents and Consequents* (reprint, St. Louis: Christian Board of Publication, 1882), pp. 89-115; *Christian System*, pp. 107-52; *Debate on Christian Baptism Between Mr. John Walker...and Alexander Campbell* (Pittsburgh, 1822), pp. 153-74.

18. *Declaration and Address* (Washington, PA, 1809), p. 16; *Christian System*, pp. 125-35. In this view Campbell was influenced significantly by the "social compact" theory of John Locke. See William D. Howden, "The Kingdom of God in Alexander Campbell's Hermeneutics," *Restoration Quarterly* 32 (Second Quarter 1990), 87-104.

19. Campbell, *Christian System*, pp. 133, 59.

20. See Campbell's long series, "A Restoration of the Ancient Order of Things," beginning in the *Christian Baptist* 2 (February 1825), and especially No. VII (September 5, 1825), 29: "Whatever the disciples practiced in their meetings with the approbation of the apostles, is equivalent to an apostolic command to do the same. Apostolic example is justly esteemed of equal authority with an apostolic precept."

21. Alexander Campbell, "Millennium—No. I," p. 58.

22. Stephen Toulmin, *Cosmopolis: The Hidden Agenda of Modernity* (New York: Free Press, 1990), 134. For an admirably clear account of these philosophical developments see William Barrett, *Death of the Soul: From Descartes to the Computer* (Garden City, NY: Doubleday, 1986), esp. pp. 11-27.

23. See David Spadafora, "Secularization in British Thought, 1730-1789: Some Landmarks," in *The Secular Mind: Transformations of Faith in Modern Europe*, ed. W. Warren Wagar (New York: Holmes and Meier, 1982), pp. 35-56 (Robertson citation, p. 49); J. H. Plumb, "Reason and Unreason in the Eighteenth Century: The English Experience," in *In the Light of History* (New York: Allen Lane, 1972), p. 324.

24. James Turner, *Without God, Without Creed: The Origins of Unbelief in America* (Baltimore, MD: Johns Hopkins University, 1985), pp. 132-40; Patricia Cohen, "Statistics and the State: Changing Social Thought and the Emergence of a Quantitative Mentality in America, 1790-1820," *William and Mary Quarterly*, 3rd series, 38 (1981), 35-55.

25. Conrad Wright, "Rational Religion in Eighteenth-Century America," in *The Liberal Christians: Essays on American Unitarian History* (Boston, MA: Beacon, 1970), pp. 1-21.

26. Alexander Campbell, "Evidence of the Gospel—No. III," *Millennial Harbinger* 6 (October 1835), 472; "A Word to Neutrals and Partial Reformers," ibid. 3 (January 2, 1832), 40; "The Millennium—No.I," ibid. 5 (November 1834), 549; Robert Owen and

Alexander Campbell, *Debate on the Evidences of Christianity* (Bethany, Va., 1829), 1:260-63, 2:5; Campbell, "Address, Delivered at New Athens College," *Millennial Harbinger* new series 2 (November 1838), 507, 513.

27. Richard B. Sher, *Church and University in the Scottish Enlightenment: The Moderate Literati of Edinburgh* (Princeton, NJ: Princeton University, 1985), pp. 309-14. See also J. R. R. Christie, "The Rise and Fall of Scottish Science," in *The Emergence of Science in Western Europe*, ed. Maurice Crosland (London, 1975), pp. 111-26.

28. Paul Wood, "Thomas Reid: Natural Philosopher" (Ph.D. diss., University of Leeds, 1985); S. A. Graves, *The Scottish Philosophy of Common Sense* (Oxford: Oxford University, 1960); Theodore Dwight Bozeman, *Protestants in an Age of Science: The Baconian Ideal and Antebellum American Religious Thought* (Chapel Hill, NC: University of North Carolina, 1977), pp. 7, 4-21. See also J. Charles Robertson, "A Bacon-Facing Generation: Scottish Philosophy in the Early Nineteenth Century," *Journal of the History of Philosophy* 14 (1976), 37-49.

29. See William R. Brock, *Scotus Americanus: A Survey of Sources for Links between Scotland and America in the Eighteenth Century* (Edinburgh, Scotland: University of Edinburgh, 1982); Sydney Ahlstrom, "The Scottish Philosophy and American Theology," *Church History* 24 (1955), 257-72; Bozeman, *Protestants in an Age of Science*, esp. pp. 71-131; Herbert Hovenkamp, *Science and Religion in America, 1800-1860* (Philadelphia: University of Pennsylvania, 1978), pp. 19-36; George H. Daniels, "The Reign of Bacon in America," in *American Science in the Age of Jackson* (New York: Columbia University, 1968), pp. 63-85; George Marsden, "Everyone One's Own Interpreter? The Bible, Science, and Authority in Mid-Nineteenth-Century America," in *The Bible in America*, ed. Nathan Hatch and Mark Noll (New York: Oxford University, 1982), pp. 79-100; and Mark A. Noll, "Common Sense Traditions and American Evangelical Thought," *American Quarterly* 37 (Summer 1985), 216-38, esp. 222-25.

30. On the Campbells' schooling see Lester McAllister, *Thomas Campbell: Man of the Book* (St. Louis: Bethany, 1954), pp. 24-9, and Robert Richardson, *Memoirs of Alexander Campbell*, 1:28-36, 131. On Jardine's Baconianism, see George Jardine, *Synopsis of Lectures on Logic and Belles Lettres Read in the University of Glasgow* (Glasgow, 1804), pp. 78-84. For Alexander's notes on this course, see "Lecture Notes at Glasgow University," John Barclay Family Papers, Disciples of Christ Historical Society. Some of Campbell's compositions for Jardine have been published in *Alexander Campbell at Glasgow University, 1808-1809*, transcribed with an introduction by Lester McAllister (Nashville, TN: Disciples of Christ Historical Society, 1971).

31. Alexander Campbell, *Memoirs of Elder Thomas Campbell*, p. 267; *Evidences of Christianity*, 1:248-49; *Introductory Addresses Delivered at the Organization of Bethany College, November 2d, 1841* (Bethany, VA, 1841), pp. 64-65; Campbell, "Bethany College," *Millennial Harbinger* (April 1858), 213.

32. James S. Lamar, *The Organum of Scripture: Or, the Inductive Method of Biblical Interpretation* (Philadelphia, 1859), pp. 187-91. For a brief survey of the long history of the "two books" idea, see Roland M. Frye, "The Two Books of God,"

Theology Today 39 (1982), 260-66.

33. Alexander Campbell, "On Prayer and Special Influence," *Millennial Harbinger* 4 (May 1833), 233; *Christian System*, pp. 2, 6; Lamar, *Organon of Scripture,* pp. 193, 196, 197. See also C. Leonard Allen, "Baconianism and the Bible among the Disciples of Christ: James S. Lamar and The Organum of Scripture," *Church History* 55 (March 1986), 65-80, and Thomas H. Olbricht, "The Rationalism of the Restoration," *Restoration Quarterly* 11 (1968), 77-88.

34. David Spadafora, *The Idea of Progress in Eighteenth-Century Britain* (New Haven, CT: Yale University, 1990), 255-84.

35. Ibid., 265.

36. Richard Price, *The Evidence for a Future Period of Improvement in the State of Mankind, with the Means of Promoting It* (London, 1787), 36, cited by Spadafora, p. 353.

37. See Landes, *The Unbound Prometheus,* 52 ff.; J. H. Plumb, *The Birth of Consumer Society: The Commercialization of Eighteenth-Century England* (Bloomington, IN: University of Indiana, 1985), 316.

38. Thomas Macaulay, "Lord Bacon," in *The Miscellaneous Works of Lord Macaulay,* ed. Hannah Trevelyn (New York, 1897), 4:131-32.

39. *Memoirs of the Life and Writings of Mr. William Whiston,* 2d ed, (ca. 1749), 1:34; Richard Clarke, *A Series of Letters, Essays, Dissertations, and Discourse on Various Subjects* (London, 1790?), 258, cited by Spadafora, 124-25. This view was popularized by Whitby's *Treatise of the True Millennium.*

40. Alexander Campbell, "An Address on the Amelioration of the Social State," *Millennial Harbinger* new series, 4 (July 1840), 326, 312; Campbell, "The Millennial Character of the Harbinger," ibid., 4 new series (December 1840), 561-2.

41. Alexander Campbell, "Prefatory Remarks," *Millennial Harbinger* 1 (January 1830), 3-8.

42. Alexander Campbell, "An Oration in Honor of the Fourth of July," *Millennial Harbinger* 1 (July 5, 1830), 309, 308.

43. Alexander Campbell, "The Millennial Character of the Harbinger," 561. On the emergence of postmillennialism as a dominant outlook in early nineteenth-century America, see James W. Davidson, *The Logic of Millennial Thought* (New Haven, CT: Yale University, 1977), 269-76; see also James H. Moorhead, "Between Progress and Apocalypse: A Reassessment of Millennialism in American Religious Thought, 1800-1880," *Journal of American History* 71 (December 1984), 524-42.

44. Alexander Campbell, "Dialogue on the Holy Spirit—Part 1," *Millennial Harbinger* 2 (July 4, 1831), 295, 296; ibid. (August 1831), 369; "Incidents on a Tour to Nashville, TN. No. 1," ibid. 1 (December 6, 1830), 560; "Prayer—No. 1," ibid. (October 1831), 471; "Mr. Lynd on the Holy Spirit," p. 409. On occasion Campbell could speak of daily divine superintendence of creation (and not simply through "secondary causes") [e.g., ibid. (1833), 186], but his strict empiricism usually pushed him in the opposite direction.

45. Alexander Campbell, "On Prayer and Special Influence," *Millennial Harbinger*

4 (May 1833). See Winfred E. Garrison, *Alexander Campbell's Theology: Its Sources and Historical Setting* (St. Louis: Christian Publishing, 1900), pp. 255-81, and Thomas H. Olbricht, "Alexander Campbell's View of the Holy Spirit," *Restoration Quarterly* 6 (1962), 1-11.

46. Alexander Campbell, "Prefatory Remarks," *Christian Baptist* 4 (August 7, 1826), 3.

47. Thomas Campbell, *Millennial Harbinger* 4 (August 1833), 421.

48. See David Gross, *The Past in Ruins: Tradition and the Critique of Modernity* (Amherst, MA: University of Massachusetts Press, 1992), pp. 20-39.

CHAPTER FOUR

UNEARTHING THE "DIRT PHILOSOPHY": BACONIANISM, FAITH, AND THE SPIRIT

At the Bethany College commencement exercises of 1856 a young man named Walter Scott Russell delivered an address entitled "The Real and the Ideal." The student address was so impressive that it was published in *The Millennial Harbinger* in August 1856. But at least one reader of the *Harbinger* was not impressed. When Tolbert Fanning, editor of the *Gospel Advocate* and president of newly-founded Franklin College in Nashville, read the article he called it "one of the most infidel productions we have seen...." In the same series of articles, Fanning also attacked Russell's teacher, Dr. Robert Richardson, calling one of Richardson's articles "purely metaphysical" and designed to "introduce novelties among the brethren."[1]

These attacks provided the occasion for Richardson to write a series of ten articles entitled "Faith versus Philosophy," to which Fanning replied in a series of six articles. The controversy that erupted around these articles was complex, damaging, and deeply revealing. It was damaging to Richardson and Russell personally and to the movement collectively. It was also deeply revealing of the theological tension that had long been at work in the movement and that, joined with the powerful sectional and social tensions surrounding the Civil War, would lead to open division. The controversy, in effect, was the clash of two incompatible theologies.

At its heart was the exposure and critique of the Baconian philosophy that had been deeply woven into the theological fabric of the movement since its early days.

As we saw in the previous chapter, Alexander Campbell, near the inception of his reform movement, adopted the cluster of ideas termed "Baconianism" as the philosophical undergirding for his recovery of the "ancient gospel and order of things." Because this philosophy was an anti-philosophy philosophy, that is, claimed to reject all philosophical "speculation" and to admit only the hard data of sensory experience, it was easy for its proponents to imagine themselves free of all philosophy and in possession of unadorned truth. Thus in Campbell's polemics the Protestant theologians by and large remained ensnared in "mystical" and "speculative" schemes of human invention, while his own position had nothing to do with such things. Campbell of course could acknowledge his indebtedness to "Bacon, Newton, and Locke," but only in that these men recovered the proper and necessary rules of all correct thinking. To learn from them, therefore, was to embrace no philosophical theory at all but simply to learn the correct way to gain truth. In this way the Baconian philosophy could remain essentially invisible throughout the first generation of the movement—and indeed for much of its subsequent history.

The controversy that erupted around Robert Richardson and his student Walter Scott Russell for several years in the late 1850s resulted from their direct exposure of and challenge to this philosophy. They sought not only to expose the irony of embracing a philosophical system while claiming all the while to have none but also to correct what they saw as the debilitating spiritual effects of this particular philosophy. This chapter unfolds this controversy in three episodes, the first involving Richardson, the second centering on Russell, and the third featuring James Lamar who was not involved in the upheaval but who unwittingly brought it to an oddly fitting conclusion.

BACONIANISM REVEALED: ROBERT RICHARDSON

When Richardson began his "Faith versus Philosophy" series in March 1857 he had been living in Bethany and working closely with Campbell for 21 years. He was a medical doctor by training (and the Campbell's family physician), professor of chemistry at Bethany College, associate editor of the *Harbinger* (for which he had written regularly since its beginning in 1830), and a close friend of Campbell. A somewhat quiet and retiring man, he was deeply respected throughout the movement and widely viewed as one of its most eloquent and thoughtful writers.[2]

Though the 1857 series seems to have been provoked by Fanning's attacks, the basic issues Richardson addressed were long-standing concerns. For him one of the most basic was spirituality—the "real communion" with God made possible by the indwelling Holy Spirit. Fifteen years earlier in 1842 and 1843 he had published a series of seven articles on "The Spirit of God" where he had voiced concern. He noted four current positions. (1) At one extreme were those who denied the Holy Spirit, and at the other (2) those who made everything depend upon the reception of the Spirit. In between these two extremes were two intermediate positions: (3) those who affirmed the presence of the Spirit in Christians but supposed the Spirit to be only "the influence which the Scriptures produce upon the mind of the believer"; and (4) those who believe in "the reception of the Spirit in his own person, character and office." Against Campbell and the tide of the movement's thinking, which was clearly running in the third category, Richardson affirmed the fourth position, that the "Holy Spirit of God is imparted to the believer, really and truly, taking up his abode in his person, as a distinct guest." He believed that Campbell and others, in rightly opposing the extremists of the second group, had overreacted and been driven into a practical denial of the Spirit's real presence and power. Certainly they talked of both the Spirit and the word, Richardson said, but they put THE WORD in capital letters and (the Spirit) in parentheses, thus advocating in effect the false position that "the Spirit works only through the word of truth."[3]

At the very time in 1842 and 1843 when Richardson was publishing these articles, he and Campbell—close friends and co-workers—were having heated discussions over these very issues. Campbell was preparing for his debate with N. L. Rice (which began in November 1843) and had agreed to defend the proposition that "in conversion and sanctification the Spirit works only through the word of truth." Richardson had tried to persuade him not to defend such a proposition or at least not to limit God's working by attaching the word "only."[4]

Such a view, Richardson believed, chilled spiritual vitality and replaced it with a doctrinal formalism, thus arresting the full restoration of pure Christian faith. Throughout the 1840s and 50s he continued to address these issues in his many writings. By 1857, with the movement's theology hardening and thus his concern of many years unabated, Richardson decided to take a bold step. He determined to address explicitly and openly what he believed to be the underlying root of the spiritual concerns he had been addressing over the years.

There are "earnest and thoughtful individuals," he began, "who fear that the true temple of God has not yet been restored to these foundations; or that, if built, it has not, as yet, been filled with the Divine presence." Richardson made it very clear that he counted himself among this group. Something had gone awry in the movement, and the problem lay in one of three things: (1) there was some defect in the basic principles of the movement; (2) the principles have not been applied properly; or (3) "some system of human philosophy has insidiously intruded itself, and, like the serpent in Eden, seduced the unwary, by the charms of forbidden knowledge."[5] The basic principles—scripture the only guide, rejection of tradition, freedom of conscience—contained not the slightest flaw, he concluded, and in their application to the preaching of the gospel and the ordering of the church there had been no deficiency. Indeed, he claimed that theirs was the only body professing these principles "in their primitive purity and simplicity." The problem in fact lay in the third possibility: "the introduction of theories and speculations in direct violation of the very fundamental principles of this Reformation."[6] Pure faith had been adulterated by human philosophy, not openly, not in formal propositions or creeds, but subtlety and insidiously in the very foundation of the edifice, with the result that the basic principles operated with a "want of power."

Tolbert Fanning provided Richardson with a ready and irresistible example of this very tendency. Fanning had just written a series of articles in the *Gospel Advocate* denouncing all philosophy as inherently destructive to Christian faith and in the process charging Richardson and Russell with "infidelity" for embracing speculative philosophy.[7] But in his very denunciation of all philosophy, Richardson shows, Fanning had employed the philosophical theories of John Locke. Fanning holds, like Locke, that the human mind at birth is a blank slate, that all knowledge comes through the five senses, and that, since God and spiritual things cannot be experienced by the senses, we are entirely dependent upon the Bible for any knowledge of or contact with God. In short, the Bible and the five bodily senses provide the only pathway into the human soul. This system, Richardson noted, has appropriately been called the "dirt philosophy" due to its "materialistic tendencies."[8]

Given Fanning's bold rejection of all philosophy, it was not difficult for Richardson to make him look silly. "President Fanning maintains, as we have shown, these propositions: 1st. That man is incapable of learning the being and attributes of God from the works of nature. 2nd. That he is incapable of deriving knowledge from his own inward spiritual nature. And now, gentle reader, what is all this but President Fanning's own philosophy; his adopted theory of human nature; his approved speculative view of man's powers and capacities."[9] Richardson concludes that Fanning, though unconscious of it, is "a philosopher of the School of Locke, or, what is usually termed a sensualistic dogmatist." Indeed, the case of Fanning shows "that it is entirely possible for an individual to be thoroughly imbued" with a human philosophy "without having the slightest suspicion of the influence by which he is directed."[10]

In this stark expose of Fanning as one "thoroughly imbued" with the Lockean or Baconian philosophy, Richardson found himself in the awkward and delicate position of opposing Mr. Campbell. For as we have seen it was Campbell, far more than Fanning, who was responsible for the Baconian cast of the movement's theology. Campbell was in fact the great purveyor of the "dirt philosophy" in the movement. Richardson could say that bluntly in private,[11] but in public his critique had to be indirect, for he was in a double bind. He deeply admired Mr. Campbell, saw him as a great and good pioneer of restoration, agreed with the foundational principles upon which he had set the movement—and on top of that, was his junior colleague and office manager for the *Harbinger*. But he had long been convinced that Campbell's philosophical stance was deeply compromising the very plea he had so effectively pioneered. It was a sharp and troubling irony, and Richardson seems to have endured it with considerable grace. But by 1857 he felt compelled to offer a more open critique of Campbell's Baconianism—to unearth the "dirt philosophy"—and since he could not or would not direct it to Campbell himself chose Fanning as a stand in.

The "dirt philosophy" or "sensualistic philosophy" was insidious, Richardson believed, because it struck at the heart of Christian faith, distorting its essential nature, sapping its power, and diminishing the enjoyment it brings. By its very nature this particular philosophy "constantly seeks to resolve everything into sensation, or into mere words." Its effect is "to unfit men's minds to receive anything that is not merely outward and formal," and it is thus "naturally and directly antagonistic to everything spiritual in religion." "It gradually dries up the fountains of spiritual sympathy, and creates in the heart a species of impiety towards the spiritual and invisible which doubts its presence and denies its power."[12] The practical effect, in short, is spiritual debilitation: God's presence is not allowed to fill God's temple.

Richardson spelled out the specific ways this philosophy worked itself out: it exaggerates the power of facts, endows the words of the Bible with "unwonted efficacy," distorts faith by improperly tying it to material things, denies the personal indwelling of the Spirit (which is the very source of spiritual life), destroys belief in "special providence," and finally undermines belief in the efficacy of prayer.[13]

The backdrop for this critique was Campbell's understanding of divine agency in conversion and sanctification. As we saw in chapter two, near the heart of Campbell's movement (as a theological movement) was a particular understanding of the nature and order of conversion (*ordo salutis*). Drawing upon the theory of George Campbell, he argued that conversion results from an unbreakable chain of cause and effect. It begins with "gospel facts," then testimony to those facts, belief of testimony, obedience, then appropriate feelings or "affections." On this basis, a staple of his polemics for many years had been the argument that where factual testimony begins, faith begins, and where testimony ends, faith ends. He had said it dozens of times: the amount of faith depends upon the amount of testimony one has received. "No testimony, no faith; strong testimony, strong faith; weak testimony, weak faith; little testimony, little faith." Campbell could occasionally link faith to trust or confidence in a person, but the momentum of his thinking was strongly toward faith as acceptance of factual testimony. "Faith is neither testimony nor reason," he wrote in a typical remark, "but reason receiving testimony."[14]

With this view of faith, Campbell came close to Locke's definition of faith: "Faith is the assent to any proposition not made out by the deductions of men, but upon the credit of the proposer as coming from God, in some extraordinary way of communication."[15] When Fanning quoted this definition with hearty approval, Richardson was quick to point out that such a definition makes faith little more than an intellectual assent to the truthfulness of facts rather than trust in a person-part of the very problem that Richardson believed was paralyzing the movement's spiritual progress.

Campbell had developed this view of conversion and faith thirty years earlier in opposition to what he considered extreme and damaging views of "spiritual operations." Word and Spirit had been driven apart among the various "sects," he believed, so he sought to stress the foundational role of the word with its hard and secure "facts." The Lockean or Baconian philosophy proved a ready and effective weapon in this struggle. There are two, and only two, types of power that can operate upon human beings, he theorized: physical power which operates upon matter, and moral power which operates upon the mind or will. Moral power consists of arguments or motives. The only way the human spirit can exert power over another spirit is through arguments and motives all of which are expressed in words. By analogy the same is true for God's Spirit. "As the spirit of man puts forth all its moral power in the words which it fills with its ideas," Campbell wrote in 1831, "so the Spirit of God puts forth all its converting and sanctifying power in the words which it fills with its ideas." Indeed, it is impossible to imagine that the divine Spirit's influence upon our spirits "can consist in anything else but words and arguments."[16]

This theory, developed in the late 1820s, had long been a staple of Campbell's aggressive attacks on the "mysticism" of the "sects," and by the 1850s it was deeply entrenched in the movement's theology. Campbell could neither admit that it was a "theory" nor entertain the possibility of a competing theory. All other views were destructively "speculative"; his was simply "the doctrine of the Apostles upon this subject." In mid-1857, even as Richardson was writing, Campbell again expressed scorn for those "philosophists" who attempted to "teach Christ or preach his gospel with Plato, Locke, or Cousin in their head or hearts," proclaiming boldly that "We have no human philosophy of spiritual operations in us, or spiritual operations by us, or spiritual operations through us."[17] Richardson knew otherwise, and proceeded to say so at great length in his series.

The view of faith and the faithful life produced by the Baconian theory was Richardson's main concern. He argued that if "faith was the direct result of testimony…then the degree of faith would depend upon the amount of testimony." But such is not necessarily the case, for often testimony does not produce faith or much testimony produces only a little faith. Belief of testimony or of gospel "facts" is certainly necessary as a foundation for faith-and here Baconian principles could serve an important though limited function; but the setting of a foundation, Richardson argued, does not necessarily mean the erection of a proper building upon it. Factual testimony provides only the foundation of faith's house, and it is absolutely vital, to be sure; but faith itself is nothing more or less than "a trusting in Jesus, a personal reliance." Indeed, when Jesus commended people for their faith it was "because with a very moderate amount of evidence, there was exhibited a ready and confiding trust." Certainly growth in faith requires an increase in knowledge but it depends primarily upon the deepening of the heart's "affections" where one "enter[s] into fellowship with Christ, into the nearest and most intimate spiritual relations."[18] Thus the normative act of faith is not accepting the gospel facts but rather entering into a trusting relationship with Christ.

But the "dirt philosophy" distorts the nature of faith and arrests its proper growth. It exaggerates the power of facts, endows the words of the Bible with "unwonted efficacy," and improperly ties faith to material things. The strict Baconian cannot get beyond "facts" and arguments to an intimate and personal communion with God. He cannot get beyond the "letter" to the Spirit, or we might say that for him the "letter" is the only means of contact with the Spirit. Indeed, the reflex of this philosophy is "to resolve, so far as possible, everything into words, propositions, arguments, and to reduce all spiritual phenomena to the forms of the ordinary understanding."[19] Richardson did not disparage the material, the phenomenal, and the factual, but he insisted that faith, properly speaking, involves much more. Faith, he insists,

> does not terminate on the facts recorded, but these are recorded that our faith might reach forward to something else—to something which is not recorded; to something which could not be recorded; to something which passes wholly beyond this wretched objective philosophy under view, even to the power, the love, the personal and official character of our blessed Redeemer himself, realized subjectively in the inner consciousness and affections of the soul.[20]

To stop short of this and content oneself with the question, "Are the facts true?" is to stay "wholly destitute of the Christian faith."

With this view of faith Richardson was identifying with the heritage of great Christian thinkers like Augustine, Anselm, Luther, and Kierkegaard. Faith is prior. The role of philosophy is to aid the understanding and perfecting of faith. From the "Divine stand-point," Richardson says, the philosophy or "reasons for things" precedes faith. But from the "merely human stand-point" we must reverse the order and say that "it is faith alone that can introduce us to this loftiest reason and philosophy…the possession of which is at once the fruit and the confirmation of our faith." Indeed, he asserts that "it is impossible that [one] should attain to faith through any philosophy, even the true one, much less by any system of mere human philosophy."[21]

This classic view of faith was connected closely to a doctrine of the Spirit's illumination and personal indwelling. Strict Baconian faith, in contrast, logically moved toward a "Word only" doctrine of the Spirit's presence, illustrating the fact that one's doctrine of the Spirit tends to coordinate with one's doctrine of faith. If divine agency is limited to the channel of the five senses and faith in essence is reason accepting testimony, then the Spirit must work only through revealed words. If on the other hand, faith in essence is a trusting relationship, then the Spirit must be God's personal presence.

This was precisely at issue between Richardson and Fanning (and Campbell): Does the Spirit comfort, guide, and sustain Christians through means other than biblical words?[22] Fanning gave an emphatic no, and in the course of their exchanges finally revealed openly his strict Baconian commitments: "We profess no religious belief beyond what is written or 'verbal.' Words limit our confidence in religious truth. We also freely admit that we acknowledge none but a 'formal' religion,' and we can with good conscience call men infidels and profane scoffers at spiritual truth who profess anything beyond 'verbal truth taught in words' or beyond the 'formal religion of the Bible.'"[23] To the same question Campbell said no most of the time. In 1860 he wrote for example: "We affirm that the Holy Spirit works through or by the gospel upon saint and sinner, and upon neither but through or by the word, preached and believed."[24]

Richardson answered the question with an emphatic yes. For him the indwelling Spirit was the very source and power of the trustful relationship with God that one entered by faith. The Spirit was the real presence of God returned to indwell his temple, and that temple was the human heart and the church. Campbell's argument that the Spirit's work is analogous to the change one's words or arguments make on the mind or spirit of another person was a serious error, he judged, for with such a view one is actually affirming that "there is no Spirit of God literally and really imparted, but merely a change effected in the human spirit."[25] To the contrary, the Spirit is a real and abiding presence to guide, comfort, and renew. Further, though many admit the indwelling of the Spirit as a fact of Christian life, they do not know what it means in practice—it is "granted by words to the ear, but denied by Philosophy to the heart." And a gospel that comes in "word only" is not the gospel preached by Paul and the apostles.[26]

Richardson closed his series by affirming what he believed were the original ideals of the movement. The "current reformation" was built on the rejection of human opinions, creeds, and philosophies. We constantly attack and expose the "mystical philosophy" so entrenched among the various denominations, he said, yet ironically the Baconian philosophy has quietly and almost imperceptibly and without protest entrenched itself in our theology. This philosophy, to be sure, is the opposite of the mystical one but is no less damaging to spiritual growth and progress, for it numbs the spiritual sensibilities, leaving people content with mere doctrines and forms of the faith. To uphold the foundational principles of the movement the philosophy that has blindsided them and compromised those principles must be exposed. "It will not do," he said, "to stop with baptism for remission of sins and leave the convert deprived by false philosophy of all true faith in the actual indwelling of the Holy Spirit, the impartation of which is the great end of gospel ministration, and which is the true source of spiritual life and power."[27]

Beginning with Richardson's fourth article, Fanning wrote a series of six sharp replies. To the charge that he was "deeply imbued" with the Lockean philosophy, Fanning's response was contradictory and at times incoherent. Though he had earlier praised Locke as the "real author of the Baconian philosophy, and all correct thinking in England since his day," he now asserted that Locke "was, strictly speaking, no philosopher"—a claim one could make only by first accepting Locke's radical empiricism.[28] Fanning vociferously denied being a disciple of Locke, but toward the end of his reply states more openly his Lockean commitments. He embraced Locke's definition of faith and though he denied holding a "Word only" view of the Spirit's indwelling could make no coherent argument against it.[29]

To Fanning's mind, Richardson's position was "unblushingly infidel," for he had abandoned the solid ground of revealed truth and embraced "modern spiritualism." Claiming direct access to a higher spiritual realm, the "spiritualist" soon ends up discounting Christ as the savior, renouncing the church as a saving institution, and rejecting the efficacy of Christ's ordinances. Richardson's response was that Fanning appeared to be "too deeply imbued with sensualistic philosophy to receive or comprehend the spiritual things of Christianity"; as a result, he was "unable to distinguish between modern spiritualism and ANCIENT SPIRIT-UALITY."[30]

Midway through the series tension began to mount between Campbell and Richardson as controversy over this issue spilled out in the movement. Campbell disapproved of Richardson's articles, and in September issued a rebuke: "we do not approve of philosophical disquisitions of any sort being presented to our readers in our monthly bills of fare. And as little do we approve of placing faith and philosophy in any real or formal antagonism." The tension deepened when a Baptist editor picked up on the controversy and wrote an article asking, "On Which Side Is Alexander Campbell?" In response Campbell attempted again to explain his view of faith; and he accused Richardson of being "infelicitous" in two things: his "choice of a subject" and "his manner of treating it."[31] Campbell basically assumed the awkward position of siding with Fanning, and this stance opened up a flood of attack upon Richardson. Richardson noted in a letter that Campbell "quietly suffered this to go on for months with only one or two slight and very imperfect corrections." He later commented that the "Faith versus Philosophy" series had brought him "the most bitter and unrelenting hostility in the form of misquotation, misrepresentation, and personal and professional distraction."[32]

Deeply distressed by these developments, Richardson in late 1857 resigned his editorial position with Campbell's journal and in February 1858 accepted a faculty position at the new Kentucky University. Campbell apparently was shocked. He urged Richardson to reconsider, and also printed an apology for supporting Fanning's charge that Richardson advocated a "Spirit-alone" theory. Affirming that Richardson's views were in keeping with those he had always promoted, Campbell rebuked Fanning, calling his effort to paint Richardson and others as heretics and infidels an "outrage" and the "grossest injustice." Fanning has become "super-excited," he said, and lost the ability to judge properly in these matters. By January 1859 Richardson had accepted Campbell's offer to resume his editorial duties.[33]

BACONIANISM REJECTED AND REPLACED: WALTER SCOTT RUSSELL

Richardson's theology had created something of a school of thought among graduates of Bethany College. In the mid-1850s several of these young men were writing for the *Christian Sentinel* published in Illinois. They were joined in 1857 by Walter Scott Russell, who proved to be the most talented and outspoken among them. After leaving Bethany he had ministered briefly with a church in Missouri then moved to Jacksonville, Illinois, where he preached and served as president of Berean College. Together with I. N. Carmen, another Bethany graduate who moved to Illinois in 1857, he would take a step beyond his teacher Richardson and further test the firmly set boundaries of Disciples orthodoxy.[34]

Russell's views first appeared in his 1856 commencement address at Bethany. Taking cues from Richardson, Russell spelled out an explicit Christianized idealistic philosophy as a means of rejecting the "sensualistic philosophy" that he thought—and which his teacher thought—was sapping the spiritual vitality of the movement. "Phenomena cannot hold the relation of cause to us," Russell wrote. "No word, no action, no external existence can be the cause of our having knowledge. Spirit, either our own or that of God, acting within us, is the only cause of the effect which we call intelligence." Sensory experience provides only the occasion for human knowing; it serves to awaken the soul which, "when awakened, soars far beyond the mere occasion of its awakening."[35] Here, in short, was an explicit rejection of the movement's Baconian empiricism—the very point that provoked Fanning's charge of "infidelity."

In Illinois the controversy began with an article by I. N. Carmen. In it he described the Baconian method: one gathers facts, classifies them, and makes inferences from the classes of facts. "But alas!" he exclaimed, "for its barrenness of truth—its positive separation of the Real from the Ideal!" The problem is that while one may well grasp the "facts," "the reason, which is ever looking at truths, is left shut up in the dark chambers of the mind; and the glorious power of those truths—bright mirrors of the Eternal One-is forever lost." Russell approved Carmen's essay and elaborated upon it. Locke's epistemology—that knowledge comes only through the five senses—dangerously curtails what we can know. The five senses can grasp only "the show of things" or appearances and cannot grasp spirit which is "the only substantial cause in the universe." We must rise above "sensuous images" in order that "the divine light may shine into the dark places of the heart."[36]

Russell proceeded to expound his views at length in five essays on the "Doctrine of the Holy Spirit." He set out his working hypothesis in the form of four postulates. First, the soul or mind contains a "higher reason" or intuition given by God. Second, this "intuitive reason or conscience" provides the avenue through which all divine revelation must come. Third, the soul in addition possesses a "will and understanding or reflective power" which gives each person a unique personality. In this way, "the oracles of impersonal reason...are given with the coloring of a person clinging to them." Fourth, the soul is made so that it "needs the excitement of outward occasions, reflectively appropriated, to arouse it into activity." These occasions vary from place to place, giving rise to a great variety of intellectual and moral achievements.[37]

From these four postulates Russell stated his hypothesis about "spiritual operations": in inspiring prophets and apostles God did not violate the constitution of the soul or mind but worked in harmony with it; God acted and spoke in the "objective occasions" and through those occasions prophets and apostles "received subjectively the inspiration of the Spirit." God thus did not violate their individuality and responsibility.

To test his hypothesis Russell turned to three groups of data from the Bible. First, he observed how, from Moses to David to Paul and the Gospel writers, the unique personalities of the writers are always preserved. Second, he showed how the biblical prophets and apostles, even when spoken of as being under compulsion, still retained their freedom and moral responsibility. So when Paul was under "necessity" to preach the gospel he was under "a moral, not a physical or mechanical, necessity." Third, he showed that those who received the Spirit's revelation always required "objective occasions" to "arouse the spiritual capacities of the soul and awaken desires for truth." Thus the specific revelation can be correlated with the specific situation in which the one receiving it lived.[38]

Russell next proposed to test his view of the Spirit's agency by examining the period following the close of New Testament history." Scripture declares, he said, "the continuance of the Spirit as an efficient agent for the propagation of Christianity." The question is "how?" and to this question there are only two possible answers: either the Spirit works the same way as in biblical history or "there is some express and authoritative declaration in Scripture, saying that the mode of influence was to be changed after the Apostolic age." Russell concluded that there is no such declaration in the New Testament, and proceeded to set forth the case that the same Spirit continues to work (or at least can work) in the same way.[39]

Surveying numerous New Testament passages, Russell found a general rule about the Spirit in the "primitive churches": "Every genuine Christian was enabled to give evidence of his being in the truth by exhibiting some one of the various effects (*charismata*) of the inworking Spirit." Drawing evidence from Eusebius and Neander, he concluded further that these diverse phenomena continued well beyond the New Testament period. Miraculous power gradually disappeared, "not by a withdrawal of the Savior's promise," but rather because "the chilling influences of the world began to resume their power." Spiritual vitality and passion waned. Clearly, he argued, the Spirit's work does not continue in "the same degree of fullness as at first" yet the Spirit still operates in "the same manner" and produces "some of the same effects." Given similar "outward occasions" and similar responsiveness to God, the same signs and wonders are, in principle, still possible.[40]

The fundamental objections to these conclusions, he argued further, come not from the Bible but from the Lockean philosophy of mind which denies any "immediate [divine] influence upon the soul." In a manner very much like his teacher, Russell rejected the "word only" view that this philosophy produced. It is a "superficial and destructive" position, making salvation hinge on "the logical power of the understanding in weighing premises and conclusions" and tending to produce "dead churches and prayerless Christians." "Oh, let us come out from under this dark cloud of shallow rationalism," he urged, "and stand in the broad glare of heaven's own light!"[41]

Word and Spirit, he made clear, stand in close relationship but not in the way the "word only" advocates supposed. "The written or spoken word is the indirect method of reaching man, through the lower understanding, in order that the direct means—the Spirit—may be able to come into action." Scripture is the external means by which the soul or mind is aroused to seek after and receive the Spirit's life. Thus through word and

Spirit the Lord provides "an outward and an inward standard, which recip-rocally regulate each other," thus guarding "against an ignorant and false mysticism on the one hand, and a hollow formalism on the other."[42]

Russell completed his series by noting briefly the practical fruit of rely-ing upon the indwelling Spirit. First, reliance upon the Spirit empowers prayer. Let a Christian "grow skeptical in regard to the direct and powerful influences of God's Spirit," Russell said, "and prayer will become a tasteless and irksome duty....But if the christian feels that when he goes into his clos-et the true Shekinah—the real God's presence—is in his soul, he can not but pray with a joyful confidence." Second, faith in an indwelling Spirit brings more trust in the "special Providences of God." Believers are "led by the Spirit," receiving "special communications of the will of the Lord" to guide them through the complex circumstances of life. Third, reliance upon the Spirit "gives reality to divine communion." Through the Spirit Christians become "partakers of the divine nature" and drink from the streams of liv-ing water. This communion is the heart and highest joy of Christianity.[43]

Russell's essays immediately grabbed attention. Campbell noted "some strange reports concerning our much beloved Bro. Russell"; after reading the essays, he judged them "in good keeping with Calvinism in its hale and unregenerate days." Fanning of course used the essays to step up his attacks on Richardson who, he charged, was guilty of the same "infidelity" but was simply not willing to state his views so openly or clearly.[44]

In late 1857 Richardson took note of Russell's argument that miracu-lous powers would still exist if not for the spiritual decline in subsequent Christian tradition. In itself it is a "harmless opinion," he stated, "but given the theory behind it, it reveals a tendency to go beyond what is safe." He quipped that he did not object to these ardent young men performing mir-acles, indeed if they do "I most sincerely hope that the very first miracle they perform will be to cast out of the church the demon of philosophi-cal speculation, for I really begin to fear that nothing less than a miracle will accomplish it." Richardson's basic concern was that, in Russell's eager-ness to seek a (needed) higher spirituality, he seemed too eager to con-struct a system of human philosophy (Idealistic in this case) through which to interpret scripture. Richardson expressed confidence in Russell but also the wish that he would put his essays away for a decade and let them ripen into maturity.[45]

But it was already too late. Russell had already violated the Disciple "creed" and in this had moved a step beyond his teacher. Though Richardson argued for the direct indwelling of the Spirit in Christians, he held generally to Campbell's view that the Spirit does not directly impact or illumine unbelievers in any way but works only through the word in conversion.[46] Against this position, Russell argued that "we cannot have one theory of spiritual influence for the Christian and another for the sinner." Rather, God uses both his word and Spirit to influence unbelievers and Christians alike. He quoted 1 Thessalonians 1:4-5: "For our gospel came not unto you in word only, but also in power, and in the Holy Spirit, and in much assurance." Campbell and others charged him with holding the view that the non-Christian must simply wait passively for the Spirit to quicken and illumine. "Nothing is further from my real position and practice in preaching the gospel," Russell insisted; rather, God's saving power flows in upon those who earnestly seek the Lord and who go "forward in the line of active and trustful obedience to the commands of Christ."[47] Thus as one begins to trust God and struggles to obey God the Spirit aids the process of trusting and obeying.

Throughout 1858 criticism of Russell intensified. Scores of writers attacked his views in the brotherhood journals. E. L. Craig, a member of Russell's own congregation and editor of the *Bible Advocate*, repeatedly called for Campbell to denounce Russell. Many others put pressure on him. Finally in 1859 Campbell responded with a full frontal assault. Russell's basic heresy, he charged, was the claim that the Spirit of God can work directly upon the human spirit without "means." "He will have the Spirit to work upon man—sinful, fallen man—not through the word, but without the word; that is, by positive impact and contact or impression of the Spirit." On this most fundamental point, Campbell concluded, "Brother Russell seems to be at sea without compass or pilot."[48]

In a response letter Russell protested (correctly) that he was charged with a teaching that he did not hold. Russell quoted his original words: "Many secondary instrumentalities are employed by God in reaching man—as his word, with all its facts, promises, and urgent appeals—but these no more exclude the direct and purely spiritual agency of the Holy Spirit, in addition, than they do the personal agency of Christ in redemption."[49]

Though Campbell was wrong on this point, he was right about one thing: the bright young man from Illinois had passed beyond Disciple orthodoxy. He had in fact violated the deeply entrenched Disciple stance against "spiritual operations," and he had done so by employing a philosophical idealism sharply at odds with the reigning Baconian empiricism. For this, he and his friend Carmen were expelled from the movement. As Campbell put it, Russell has "turned aside into vain janglings and cannot legitimately be regarded as one of us." As W. K. Pendleton, who did much of the polemical work, put it, "we will have no fellowship with this work of flesh. We leave them to the world, and whatever of notoriety or of glory, it may afford them." Richardson finally stood against them only with great reluctance and sadness; he agreed that Russell and company had gone somewhat too far but thought that responsibility for the controversy should be laid at the feet of the "semi-materialists" (like Fanning) who insisted that the Spirit indwells only by "ideas" or "influences."[50]

In Illinois John S. Sweeney, a young preacher and co-editor of the *Bible Advocate*, apparently played a decisive role in the crusade against Russell. At the Illinois State Convention of 1860 he delivered a forceful speech that, according to his younger brother, turned the tide against the Russell supporters.[51] Russell himself joined the Union army as a chaplain and died of disease at Vicksburg, Mississippi, in 1863.

BACONIANISM REAFFIRMED: JAMES S. LAMAR

In light of subsequent history it seems oddly fitting that in 1859, right at the height of this controversy, James S. Lamar of Augusta, Georgia, should publish a book entitled, *The Organon of Scripture, or, The Inductive Method of Biblical Interpretation*. For this work was nothing less than an erudite and full-fledged systemization of the Baconian philosophy as it applied to biblical interpretation—the very philosophy that Richardson had exposed as entrenched in the movement and that Russell had explicitly rejected and replaced with a theory drawing from philosophical idealism.

Lamar was converted in his early twenties and enrolled in Bethany College where he graduated as valedictorian in 1855. Upon Campbell's recommendation he accepted a position with a congregation in Augusta, Georgia, and for the rest of his life ministered to churches in Georgia. When *The Organon of Scripture* was published in 1859 it received favorable review and strong recommendation from both Campbell and Fanning as well as others. "Lamar takes the true ground in regard to reading the scriptures of truth," Fanning remarked, but then proceeded to criticize the phrase "biblical interpretation" in the title. It "seems to imply," he wrote, "that the Bible needs interpretation; whereas, in strictness, the book of God is but a transcript of the mind of our Heavenly Father, and the New Testament particularly, is a full and complete will of our Lord Jesus Christ." "The Scriptures fairly translated," he concluded, "need no interpretation." Lamar almost would have agreed with him but would have insisted that a true method needs to be found and used to dispel the "fogs of mystical or metaphysical obscurities."[52]

Central to the discovery of the true method, he began, was exposure of the false methods people have pursued over the centuries. These he grouped into two categories: the "Mystic Method" and the "Dogmatic Method." By mysticism he meant "any system which professes to see more in natural and revealed phenomena than is cognizable by common sense." A stream of mysticism poured into Christianity in the Middle Ages, he argued, and after the Reformation it continued among a host of "spiritual-ists." And though Protestants attempted to reject mysticism, it continues to lurk just beneath the surface of Protestant hermeneutics. It surfaces when-ever Protestant theologians attempts to reconcile the Bible with their pre-ferred system of philosophy; whenever the literal meaning of scripture fits the system they accept it but when it does not they resort to the "Mystic Method" of spiritualizing.

Even more widespread, Lamar argued, was the "Dogmatic Method," which uses mysticism as a tool. This method was governed by ecclesias-tical authority and tradition. The Reformation had begun with two basic principles: the Bible as the only standard of faith and the right of private interpretation. But these principles were seldom carried out in practice. Creeds were written and imposed as tests of orthodoxy. People began looking to "great names" and to the creedal traditions produced at Geneva, Augsburg, and Westminster. Through the "Dogmatic Method" interpretation of the Bible served to uphold a particular tradition.

Over against these two false methods was the "true method" of inter-pretation—the "Inductive Method" pioneered by "Lord Bacon." Bacon had wrought wonders in scientific method when he persuaded people to "abandon their theories…and consult nature for truth, not for proof." With this method "ten thousand subjects of controversy" have all been settled because "everything is reduced to one single point-Are these the facts?"[53] Equal wonders could be wrought, the same number of disputes settled, if this inductive scientific method could be applied to biblical interpretation.

Using this method, Lamar proclaimed, every person will find truth easily accessible. Indeed, whenever people have worked "strictly upon the inductive method" they have without exception "perfectly agreed." The application of the method is certain because "it is founded upon the eternal principles of common sense."[54]

Lamar repeatedly illustrated the Baconian method using the doctrine of conversion. To find the truth on this subject one must first use the rules of common sense to collect the relevant biblical facts. Then the facts must be classified according to their bearing on the topic. Biblical conversion, Lamar said, is a generalization made from a certain class of facts—"the cases of actual conversion in the New Testament (and especially Acts). When these cases are studied inductively, they all agree on one basic point: "the exhibition of an obedient faith." The same analysis will also show that the degree of faith is "measured by the amount of testimony" received, and further, that baptism is a vital part of this obedient faith. Lamar concluded: "every human being who has the capacity to enable him to appreciate the force and meaning of ordinary language, will reach precisely the same conclusion as to what is scriptural conversion."[55]

With this foundation for "precise" agreement on all aspects of biblical teaching, the path was now clear for the overthrow of all human sects and the creeds around which they rallied. The stranglehold of the "Mystic" and "Dogmatic" methods could be broken and Francis Bacon's great revolution in method completed. Through strict use of the inductive method the simple truth of scripture would at last prevail. The vision for Christian unity pioneered by Campbell could be brought to a glorious fulfillment.[56]

Lamar's book was quite an intellectual production for a young man. But contrary to his claims, it actually contributed little that was new to the movement; it was rather a systematizing of the theological method that Campbell had developed over thirty years earlier and that had long since become standard. What was new in 1859 was not the method itself or its application to doctrinal issues but rather the explicit, full-blown exposition of and identification with the Baconian philosophy. The book borrowed heavily from leading theoreticians of Baconianism (like Sir John Herschel), and the title itself was drawn from Bacon's famous work (*The Novum Organum*).

The timing of the book was strangely fitting. On the one hand, for those who had eyes to see, it provided profuse supporting evidence for

Richardson's basic contention that the Baconian philosophy had indeed been plowed deeply into the soil of the movement. If that fact had remained obscure before 1859, it could remain so no longer. But on the other hand, because the book was a paean to the Baconian method, praising it as the triumphant key to all truth and the healing of all division among Christians, it served to reinforce the very mindset that Richardson and Russell decried.

James Lamar himself, interestingly enough, moved away from the Baconianism he had articulated so elaborately in 1859 and closer to Richardson's vision. Twenty years later, for example, he wrote that the Christian faith can be presented "simply as logical propositions" and as "mainly intellectual," and in the early years of the movement such an approach was needed to dislodge the exorbitant claims and emotionalism of the competing Christian groups. But what was once the right way has become "distasteful, jangling, and rasping." Churches are tired of our "cold, heartless, clamping, clinching, invincible logic," he said; what they want is "the primitive gospel with the sweet fragrance of the primitive Spirit." A bit later he expressed doubts that "highest truth can ever be indubitably brought home to the mere intellect"; rather, there must be "an intuition of the soul-a deep sympathetic feeling so that with his inner eyes he can see God."[57] Richardson would have understood—and said "amen."

The fact is that Fanning's view, not Richardson's, overwhelmingly carried the day among Churches of Christ. Richardson's concerns became an obscure footnote. The Baconian philosophy became—despite James Lamar's unabashedly open systematizing of it—more and more invisible, embedded in the unquestioned assumptions grounding the theology of the movement. The prevailing view was expressed tersely by David Dungan in 1888: "nothing more respecting the Scripture method need be said, for it is everywhere apparent that when the Lord would conduct an investigation on any subject, He did it by the inductive method."[58] Such simplistic and misguided Baconianism made it possible for several generations of leaders to read the Bible thinking that they were drawing out of it only "simple," "natural" facts untainted by any tradition or personal predispositions. It also perpetuated, as Richardson and Russell already saw so clearly in their time, a diminished understanding of how Christians become partakers of the divine nature through faith.[59]

BACONIANISM AND THE QUENCHING OF THE SPIRIT

Tolbert Fanning was the undisputed leader of thought among southern churches up to the Civil War. His stand on these issues would set a dominant theological pattern. Not all of those who followed him down this path after 1857-58 were as starkly rationalistic in their views of faith and the Spirit, but the general emphasis and ethos represented by Fanning would characterize the southern churches for over a century.[60]

Two examples from the twentieth century serve to show how enduring was this theological legacy. First is an influential book by Z. T. Sweeney entitled *The Spirit and the Word*, published in 1919. Sweeney argued that all of the work of the Comforter or Paraclete (as stated by Jesus in John 14-16) applied only to the twelve apostles, not to Christians in general. The Spirit as Comforter, he said, was a "private and peculiar" gift to the twelve for their one-time work of establishing the foundations of the church and producing inspired writings. Once this work of the Spirit was completed in the original apostles, "no man has been guided, shown and directed personally by him since." "God does no unnecessary work, and the work of the Paraclete is not necessary now. His work remains [only] in the teachings and lives of the apostles."

Sweeney echoed Campbell's (Lockean) theory that there are only two possible means by which one spirit (or the Spirit) can influence another spirit: one is physically or "immediately" through the five senses, the other is rationally or "morally" through words and arguments. After the apostles and the inspiring of the New Testament, God's Spirit no longer works immediately but only mediately through words and arguments.

This assumption led Sweeney to a remarkable conclusion: many of the New Testament admonitions regarding the Spirit simply do not apply to Christians living after the first century. Some examples:

"You were sealed with the Holy Spirit of promise, which is an earnest of our inheritance" (Eph. 1:13, 14).
"Be filled with the Spirit" (Eph. 5:18).
"He saved us through the washing of regeneration and the renewing of the Holy Spirit" (Titus 3:5).
"He has given us of his Spirit" (1 Jno. 4:13).

All of these verses, together with a long list of others, Sweeney insisted, must be interpreted as applying to first-century believers in whom God was "manifesting his presence by supernatural demonstrations"; but now that God works only through the words of scripture these verses "lack meaning" for Christians since that era.[61] Sweeney's book became a standard among Churches of Christ. It was reprinted by a major publisher serving Churches of Christ and went through many editions well past mid-century.

The second example is an episode that occurred in 1966 and 1967. Several speakers at the annual Abilene Christian University Bible Lectures in 1966 began to call for a renewed emphasis on the dynamic (though "non-miraculous") influence of the Spirit in the Christian life. One said that "our lack of spiritual emphasis has dried up for many the spring of living water provided by the Holy Spirit, and people are thirsty." "One of the greatest weaknesses in our fellowship," said another, "has been our lack of understanding of the Holy Spirit."[62]

This raising of the "Spirit question" quickly touched a nerve, provoking an outburst of reaction that continued throughout 1966 and 1967. Reuel Lemmons, a prominent thought leader and editor of the *Firm Foundation,* wrote several editorials warning about the dangers of raising such issues and reaffirming the traditional "Word only" view. Others wrote in a similar vein.

J. D. Thomas, of the ACU Bible faculty, responded, noting the unacceptable worldview implied in such a doctrine of the Spirit: "We must discount the idea of 'biblical Deism,' which assumes that God started the Christian system and left the Bible down here to do what it could, but meanwhile, He, Christ, and the Spirit have all retired to heaven and have nothing to do with the world until the end, when they will come back and check up to see how it all worked out."[63] Thomas proceeded to lay out in a long series of articles a very modest, cautious treatment of the Spirit in the life of the Christian. He affirmed the Spirit's personal, actual indwelling, rejecting the "Word only" view. He firmly rejected any new revelatory or miraculous activity of the Spirit. And he affirmed that we know of the Spirit's personal indwelling, not from any physical effects the Spirit may produce, but only because the Bible teaches it. Indeed, this position retained the Lockean or Baconian assumption that all our knowledge is gained empirically through the five senses.

Yet even so cautious an exposition of the doctrine of the Spirit as this provoked strong and alarmed response from prominent leaders. Reuel

Lemmons feared that such a view meant that the Spirit can work in "an independent instantaneous, miraculous way unconnected with the word of God." Another writer, also fearing that direct influence or indwelling would open Pandora's "pentecostal box," insisted that the Spirit works only in "an indirect, mediate, natural, understandable manner." He set forth the remarkable conclusion that both the Spirit and Satan no longer affect us supernaturally but are both "restricted to the use of 'natural means.'" Foy Wallace, Jr., long a garrulous defender of the "Word alone" theory, entered the fray and starkly restated Campbell's (and Fanning's and Sweeney's) position: "Apart from the inspiration of the apostles and prophets, it is impossible for spirit to communicate with spirit except through words. God and Christ never personally occupied anyone; and for the same reason the Holy Spirit does not personally occupy anyone."[64]

This 1960's debate was in several ways a rehash of 1857's "Faith versus Philosophy" exchange. Behind this traditional doctrine of the Spirit lay the Enlightenment world view shaped by the Lockean epistemology, as mediated by Campbell, Fanning, Sweeney and others. Indeed, the spirit of Locke haunts—or should we say "indwells"—the whole episode from beginning to end. What is missing in Sweeney's book of 1919 and in the 1960s reprise is any explicit discussion of this fact. So deeply entrenched had this philosophy become that the sources of it had long been forgotten or lost; indeed, it had long functioned behind the scenes, at an unconscious, ideological level.

The fact that in 1966 an extremely cautious and unremarkable treatment of the Spirit's indwelling could call forth such painstaking and vigorous refutation provides a telling sign of the road taken by Churches of Christ. Certainly there had been a very modest lineage of leaders who had affirmed a personal, immediate indwelling of the Spirit-twentieth-century leaders like Charles Roberson, G. C. Brewer, K.C. Moser, and J. D. Thomas. But even there, as J. D. Thomas' 1966 exposition shows, the Lockean constraints had remained strong.

The issue of the mode of the Spirit's indwelling surfaced time and again in the tradition, and provides perhaps the clearest and most direct sign of the hidden heritage of the "dirt philosophy." But this issue is only one piece of a whole theological mindset. Closely related, as Richardson pointed out in 1857, are issues of the nature of faith, the nature and source of the Spiritual life, and the character and purpose of prayer.

Behind these doctrinal issues (as Richardson only implied) lies the central Christian doctrine of the Trinity. The doctrine of the Trinity speaks of the character of God and of the way God enters into relationship with his creation. It proclaims, not the passionless deity of Hellenized faith or the remote god of Enlightened theism, but a God who is dynamic, demanding, immediate, personal, and present. The chief problem with the hidden Baconian theology among Churches of Christ, as we will see more fully in chapter nine, lies precisely here: in its weak and hobbled doctrine of the Trinity.

Only in the present time—some 125 or so years later—is this theology beginning to play itself out, as more and more ordinary Christians among Churches of Christ restlessly and often uneasily renew the search for a more personal and immediate relationship with God.

Notes

1. Tolbert Fanning, "Metaphysical Discussions-No. 5," *Gospel Advocate* 3 (February 1857), 35; Fanning, "Metaphysical Discussions-No. 2," ibid. 2 (1856), 328.

2. See Cloyd Goodnight and Dwight Stevenson, *Home to Bethphage: The Life of Robert Richardson* (St. Louis, MO: Christian Board of Publication, 1949).

3. Robert Richardson, "The Spirit of God," *Millennial Harbinger* (1842-43).

4. Benjamin L. Smith, *Alexander Campbell* (St. Louis, MO: Bethany Press, 1930), 328.

5. Richardson, "Faith versus Philosophy—No. 1," *Millennial Harbinger* 4th ser. 7 (1857), 135.

6. Richardson, "Faith versus Philosophy—No. 3," 255

7. Fanning, "Metaphysical Discussions—No. 1-4," *Gospel Advocate* 2-3 (1856-57), 314-15, 326-29, 1-5, 31-38.

8. Richardson, "President Fanning's Reply," *Millennial Harbinger* 4th ser. 7 (1857), 433-34.

9. Richardson, "Faith versus Philosophy—No. 4," 270.

10. Ibid., 274.

11. In a letter to Isaac Errett on July 16, 1857, Richardson could write: "The philosophy of Locke with which Bro. Campbell's mind was deeply imbued in youth has

insidiously mingled itself with almost all the great points in the reformation and has been all the while like an iceberg in the way-chilling the heart and numbing the hands, and impeding all progress in the right direction." Cited by Goodnight and Stevenson, *Home to Bethphage*, 123.

12. Richardson, "Faith versus Philosophy—No. 5," 329.

13. Richardson, "Faith versus Philosophy—No. 8," 560.

14. Campbell, "Opinionisms—No. 1," *Millennial Harbinger* 5th ser. 2 (1859), 434; Campbell, "Kingdom of Satan—No. 2," *Millennial Harbinger* new ser. 2 (February 1838), 70.

15. Locke, *An Essay Concerning Human Understanding*, ed. A. D. Woozley (New York: New American Library, 1964), 424; Fanning, "Fourth Reply to Professor Robert Richardson," *Gospel Advocate* 3 (1857), 281.

16. Alexander Campbell, "The Whole Work of the Holy Spirit in the Salvation of Men," *Millennial Harbinger* 2 (July 1831), 293-95; see also Campbell, "Mr. Lynd on the Influence of the Holy Spirit," *Millennial Harbinger* new ser. 1 (September 1837), 408.

17. Campbell, "Whole Work of the Holy Spirit," 289; Campbell, "Spiritual Influence—No. 1," *Millennial Harbinger* 4th ser. 7 (October 1857), 543, 546.

18. Richardson, "Faith versus Philosophy—No. 5" [actually No. 6], 405, 404, 402.

19. Richardson, "Faith versus Philosophy—No 5 (6)," 396-97.

20. Ibid., 400.

21. Richardson, "Faith versus Philosophy—No. 9," 297-98.

22. The same issue, with its philosophical undergirding, was being debated at this time between Benjamin Franklin and H. T. Anderson in the pages of the *American Christian Review*.

23. Fanning, "Sixth Reply," 339.

24. Campbell, "Philosophy, Dogmatism, Schism. No. 1," *Millennial Harbinger* 5th ser. 3 (1860), 20. "All the illuminating, purifying, sanctifying, regenerating influences of the Spirit have been through the instrumentality of his own word....Naked spirit working upon or manipulating naked spirit, is no where affirmed in the inspired annals of the universe" (15, 17).

25. Richardson, *Millennial Harbinger* (1843), 509-10.

26. Richardson, "Doctrine of the Spirit," ibid. 5th ser. 1 (April 1858), 203, 204.

27. Richardson, "Faith versus Philosophy—No. VII," 551.

28. Fanning, "Metaphysical Discussions-No. 4," *Gospel Advocate* 3 (January 1857), 3; "President Fanning's Reply," 445.

29. Fanning, "Fourth Reply to Professor Richardson," *Gospel Advocate* 3 (1857), 281; "Second Reply to Professor Richardson," 204.

30. Fanning, "Fifth Reply to Professor Richardson," 317, 313-17; Richardson's note in "President Fanning's Reply,'" 448. Behind Fanning's charges was his painful break with Jesse Ferguson, a co-worker in Nashville, who did in fact embrace "spiritualism" and caused much discord in the Nashville church.

31. Campbell, "Christianity the True Philosophy—No. 1," *Millennial Harbinger* 4th ser. 7 (1857), 481; Campbell, "The Religious Herald and Prof. Richardson," ibid., 577.

32. Goodnight and Stevenson, 176; Richardson, "Doctrine of the Spirit," *Millennial Harbinger* 5th ser. 1 (April 1858), 200.

33. Campbell, "A Correction," *Millennial Harbinger* 5th ser. 1 (1858), 289; Campbell, "President Fanning," ibid., 353. In his apology Campbell said: "I know not how this misstatement could have occurred, unless that my writing the article away from home I had not an opportunity of examining Bro. Richardson's essay, and had probably before my mind some of those misquotations and misrepresentations of which he has complained." Campbell at this time also recognized the fact that this controversy was rooted in a struggle for power in the movement. The "truthful heading of the whole controversy, in spirit and form," Campbell wrote, would be "the 'Gospel Advocate' versus the 'Millennial Harbinger' and Franklin College versus Bethany College." "Faith versus Philosophy," ibid., 86.

34. I am indebted to an unpublished paper by Walter Sikes (located in the Disciples of Christ Historical Society) for first introducing me to the Russell controversy.

35. W. S. Russell, "The Real and the Ideal," *Millennial Harbinger* 4th ser. 6 (August 1856), 423.

36. I. N. Carmen, "Conscience," *Christian Sentinel* 4 (1857), 72-73; Russell, "The Doctrine of Conscience," ibid., 84-85.

37. Russell, "Doctrine of the Holy Spirit—Number I," *Christian Sentinel* 4 (1857), 168-69.

38. Russell, "Doctrine of the Holy Spirit—Number II," 193-98.

39. Russell, "Doctrine of the Holy Spirit—Number III," 225.

40. Ibid., 227-28, 230, 226.

41. Russell, "Doctrine of the Holy Spirit—Number IV," 270; Russell, "The Holy Spirit," 80, 81.

42. Russell, *Two Discourses on the Father, Son and Holy Spirit Delivered before the Christian Congregation at Jacksonville, Ill.* (1859), 28; Russell, "Doctrine of the Holy Spirit—Number IV," 274.

43. Russell, "Doctrine of the Holy Spirit—Number V," 292-95.

44. Campbell, "Brother W. S. Russell," *Millennial Harbinger* 4th ser. 7 (1857), 594; Fanning, "Fifth Reply to Professor Richardson," 317.

45. Richardson, "Faith versus Philosophy—No. 8," 563-64, 565. Richardson repeated the standard argument that "direct inspiration, tongues, and miracles" were discontinued since their purpose was "the successful introduction of Christianity" and the production of scripture. "Doctrine of the Spirit," *Millennial Harbinger* 5th ser. 1 (April 1858), 203.

46. Richardson however did hint at another view on at least one occasion: "That there are various obstacles and hindrances which often prevent the gospel from reaching the heart of the sinner; and that there are, on the other hand, various agencies, ministerial and providential, human and Divine, general and special, which tend to remove

these obstacles, and thus enable the gospel to exert its power, we freely admit." *Principles and Objects of the Religious Reformation Urged by A. Campbell and Others* (Bethany, 1853), 80. But Richardson sought to distinguish clearly between God's "providential" power aiding the unbeliever and the Spirit's power given only to Christians.

47. "Letter from W. S. Russell," *Millennial Harbinger* 5th ser. 3 (March 1860), 138-40.

48. Campbell, "Philosophy, Dogmatism, and Schism—No. 1," *Millennial Harbinger* (1860), 14; Campbell, "Opinionisms—No. 1," 436.

49. "Letter from W. S. Russell," 137-38.

50. Campbell, "Philosophy, Dogmatism, and Schism—No. 1," 17; W. K. Pendleton, "W. S. Russell and I. N. Carmen," *Millennial Harbinger* 5th ser. 3 (1860), 11; Richardson, "Personal Indwelling of the Spirit," ibid. 5th series, 2 (August 1859), 423-28.

51. See Z. T. Sweeney, "The Walter Scott Russell Crisis," *Christian Standard* 63 (January 13, 1923), 443.

52. Fanning, "A New Book on 'Interpretation,'" *Gospel Advocate* 6 (1860), 30; Lamar, *The Organon of Scripture, or, The Inductive Method of Biblical Interpretation* (Philadelphia, 1859), v.

53. Lamar, *Organon of Scripture*, 174-75.

54. Ibid., 197.

55. Ibid., 256-7, 239.

56. For a fuller treatment of Lamar, see C. Leonard Allen, "Baconianism and the Bible among the Disciples of Christ: James S. Lamar and The Organon of Scripture," *Church History* 55 (March 1986), 65-80. The preceding summary of the book has been adapted from this article.

57. Richardson, "The Veiled Heart,"

58. David R. Dungan, *Hermeneutics: A Text Book* (Cincinnati, 1888), 101.

59. For a similar critique of such misguided Baconianism in the Fundamentalist Movement of the late nineteenth and twentieth centuries, see Mark A. Noll, *The Scandal of the Evangelical Mind* (Grand Rapids, MI: Eerdmans, 1994), 126-29, 196-200.

60. Earl West, in *The Search for the Ancient Order* (Indianapolis, IN: Religious Book Service, 1952), 1:125ff., uncritically accepts Fanning's account of the exchange and clearly embraces Fanning's theological position. So also James Wilburn, *The Hazard of the Die: Tolbert Fanning and the Restoration Movement* (Austin, TX: Sweet, 1969). These works reflect the virtually complete triumph of Fanning's theological stance in the twentieth-century Churches of Christ.

61. Sweeney, *The Spirit and the Word: A Treatise on the Holy Spirit in Light of a Rational Interpretation of the Word of Truth* (1919; reprint ed., Nashville, TN: Gospel Advocate, 1950), 67-79, 95-97, 99.

62. *Abilene Christian College Bible Lectures, 1966* (Abilene, TX: ACC Bookstore, 1966), 175-76, 185.

63. J. D. Thomas, *The Spirit and Spirituality* (Abilene, TX: Biblical Research Press), 19.

64. Reuel Lemmons, *Firm Foundation* 83, 722; ibid., 757; Foy Wallace, Jr., *The Mission and Medium of the Holy Spirit* (Nashville, TN: Wallace Publications, 1967), 7.

CHAPTER FIVE

"THE STONE THAT THE BUILDERS REJECTED": BARTON W. STONE'S LOST LEGACY

In a 1928 biographical sketch in the *Gospel Advocate*, editor H. Leo Boles stated as well as anyone the dominant view of Barton Stone among Churches of Christ in the twentieth century. Boles spoke in reverent tones. He recounted how Stone broke from Presbyterianism, how he took the name "Christian," how he adopted baptism for remission of sins soon afterwards, and how he formed churches after the New Testament order. Then when Stone came into contact with Alexander Campbell, Boles asserted, the two movements "had so much in common and so little difference" that they naturally began to converge. Stone emphasized "the New Testament idea and spirit of unity" and Campbell emphasized "exact conformity to the primitive faith and practice." "It was not difficult to unite these two," Boles concluded, "as both were New Testament teachings." J. W. Shepherd made essentially the same point in 1929: Stone and Campbell found their differences "more imaginary than real, and they joined hearts and hands and God blessed them with the most important work since the apostolic age."[1]

Behind both of these views lay the work of John F. Rowe, *A History of Reformatory Movements Resulting in a Restoration of the Apostolic Church*, rev. ed. (Cincinnati, 1884), a work that did much to set the historiographical pattern for twentieth-century Churches of Christ. Rowe says very little about Stone, basically noting that Stone and Campbell "sought and accomplished the same ends by the same means."[2]

The other slight and scattered references to Barton Stone among twentieth-century Churches of Christ tell basically the same story. N. B. Hardeman noted in 1928 that Stone and Campbell, in their first meeting, discovered "almost perfect agreement between them." In 1939 another historian wrote that the two men discussed certain issues for a time but soon realized that they held "practically the same" views. In 1945 another wrote that Stone's plea provided "the beginning of the way out of confusion into the light of gospel truth." He said that Stone's movement could unite with Campbell's because the two groups were "so nearly in perfect agreement." Such harmony was "simply the result of studying the same book" and desiring to restore the New Testament pattern. In 1957 still another historian wrote that Stone and Campbell "discovered that they were both teaching the same thing" and "standing on the same foundation."[3]

The other modern histories give a few more nuances but paint essentially the same picture. One cites Stone's own 1831 assessment of his similarities to Campbell—anti-creedal, faith based on evidence, and "baptism as a means"—but shows little first-hand awareness of Stone's thought. Two other accounts list basic differences between the two (the name "Christian," frequency of the Lord's Supper, the emphasis on immersion, evangelistic methods, and the contrast between Spirit and reason), but they emphasize that the "similarities far outweighed the differences" and note the "ease" with which the union occurred.[4]

In short, the picture of Barton Stone among twentieth-century Churches of Christ looks something like this: Stone pioneered the rejection of creeds and the call to unite on the Bible alone; he met up with Campbell and both were struck by the similarity of their agendas; they easily ironed out a few minor differences and united in 1832, forming the great platform of truth on which the Churches of Christ have stood ever since.

One should not get the impression from this quick survey that Barton Stone occupies a prominent position in the memory of Churches of Christ. Far from it. Alexander Campbell stands as the great champion of restoration, and several of the historians explicitly date the movement's beginnings either to Thomas Campbell's *Declaration and Address* of 1809 or to the founding of the Brush Run Church by the Campbell's a short time later.

Stone stands far back in the shadows. He often gets a couple of paragraphs or pages right before a chapter or two on Campbell.

But the basic problem is not that Stone stands back in the shadows in undeserved obscurity. It is not that he has been slighted and simply deserves somewhat more credit. It is rather that the Barton Stone standing back there in the shadows bears only a minor resemblance to the man himself. To put it differently, one could say that the memory and legacy of Stone has been almost entirely lost among Churches of Christ in the twentieth century—even though his name remains known by many and his memory revered by some.

To outsiders this conclusion might at first sound simply curious or unsurprising. To insiders it may sound rash or perhaps a bit shocking. The point in such a conclusion, however, reaches far beyond arousing curiosity or producing discomfort. The point rather is this: when Churches of Christ lost the memory and legacy of Barton Stone by the early twentieth century they lost the theological soil in which they were first rooted and the theological legacy that deeply shaped their identity throughout much of the nineteenth century. This chapter attempts to explain what was lost—and perhaps why.

THE STONITE ROOTS OF CHURCHES OF CHRIST

For many years R. L. Roberts argued that Churches of Christ owe their first and primary debt to Barton Stone and his "Christian" movement, not to Alexander Campbell.[5] In a groundbreaking article published almost forty years ago, Roberts traced the growth of the Stone movement from 1804 to 1832. He traced details of Stone's extensive evangelistic work, which centered in Kentucky, Ohio, and Tennessee, and chronicled the host of preachers under his influence who labored in small, mostly backwoods churches across the Ohio, Tennessee, and Mississippi valleys—men like Samuel and John Rogers, John Mulkey, Ephraim Moore, James Matthews, B. F. Hall, W. D. Jourdan, Tolbert Fanning, and Reuben Dooley.

Roberts located the strength of the Stone movement in the Cumberland Plateau region of Kentucky and Tennessee. He compiled a list of about 200 Stonite preachers in the Cumberland region who were establishing what they called "Churches of Christ" long before Campbell was ever known there. Stone himself lived just above Nashville, Tennessee, for two or three years beginning in 1812. By 1832 there were as many as 380 Stonite churches in Tennessee and northern Alabama, most of them established by men who were largely unaware of Campbell's work. In addition, there were reports by 1824 of Stonite preachers in Texas, and in 1835 several families—assisted by Davey Crockett—led a whole Stonite church from West Tennessee to East Texas, from which the movement spread further west.[6]

As the Churches of Christ emerged as a separate movement somewhat later in the century, their geographical center and strength lay precisely in the Cumberland Plateau region where the Stone movement had been dominant well before Campbell's influence. The Disciples of Christ, on the other hand, found their strength in a line stretching across the upper Midwest to Kentucky—the areas where Campbell's influence was most pronounced. Such regional alignments resulted not simply, or even primarily, from the sectional tensions associated with the Civil War, as some historians have tended to assume. As Richard Hughes has shown, they were rooted, in fact, in a much earlier divide—in the two sharply differing theological worlds of Barton Stone and Alexander Campbell.[7]

By the mid-1820s Campbell's "ancient gospel and order of things" began to spread throughout Stone's "Christian" movement. Stone himself embraced Campbell's new *ordo salutis*, though with some reservation. As the Stonite "Christians " gradually adopted Campbell's new theology of conversion and church order they underwent a subtle but significant transformation. Their spirit of freedom and openness diminished, giving way to a growing certainty that they had restored the ancient order.[8] But behind this shift remained the worldview of Barton Stone: an apocalyptic worldview marked by cultural pessimism, an outlook very different from Campbell's. This apocalyptic worldview, overlaid with Campbell's biblical patternism, endured in some form among a significant segment of southern Churches of Christ throughout the nineteenth century.

TWO THEOLOGICAL WORLDS

Near the heart of Stone's theological outlook lay a solidly Calvinistic assessment of human nature. Though Stone reacted against some features of traditional Calvinism, especially the doctrines of election and predestination, he retained a profound sense of human sinfulness. Joined to that was an understanding of conversion rooted deeply in the Reformed tradition and reshaped in the revivalism of the Second Great Awakening. Though he turned away from the standard view of faith as infused by God, Stone continued to view conversion as a profound spiritual transformation wrought in the believer by the power of the Holy Spirit.[9] For this reason he always looked favorably on revivalism and, as late as 1832, was willing to retain the mourner's bench—if such a practice, he said, was "contrary to the letter and spirit of the gospel," then "we cannot conceive how God should have blessed so many in the practice of it."[10]

Campbell, on the other hand, held a much more modern view of the conversion process, as we saw in Chapter 3. He viewed revivals with their experimental conversions as dangerously unbiblical. The gospel, he insisted, "makes no provision for despondency" or the dramatic display of emotion; people can simply examine the biblical testimony, promptly believe it and "obey the gospel," receiving immediately the full assurance of salvation. Conversion did not involve, as in classical Protestantism, a sudden and radical change of affections; rather, one entered a new state or legal standing before God—change of affections then gradually followed the acceptance of the gospel "facts."[11] Campbell, in short, rationalized conversion, turning it into an ordered, educational process that followed certain inviolable natural laws.

In these contrasting views of conversion or God's work in the individual we find an important clue to Stone and Campbell's contrasting views of God's work on the larger stage of history. James Davidson and others have argued that in the eighteenth and early nineteenth centuries the way people viewed God's work in history often paralleled their view of God's work in individuals. Put another way, the millennial views of the period often were models of conversion writ large.

This meant that if one viewed conversion as arising out of seasons of affliction, then one's view of redemptive history tended to reflect apocalyptic images of overturning and catastrophe. Evil would appear more deeply entrenched and intractable. Human effort would seem weak and insufficient. The heralds of progress would sound hollow and deluded. But if one viewed conversion as pre-eminently rational, quick, and largely free of "humiliation" or affliction, then one tended to see a progressing world, one surging forward to a brighter future. Evil would appear to be in retreat or at least being successfully repelled. Progress would appear all

but certain before a conquering rationality. Optimism about human potential would soar.[12]

James Moorhead points to an "afflictive model of progress" in this
period in which one cannot neatly oppose an optimistic progressivism to
a pessimistic apocalypticism. With this model one hears two seemingly
opposing claims: things are getting better and better, yet evil is rising.
Resolution lay in the fact that, as God's kingdom progressed, Satan's opposition would mount. Progress thus took place through periods of affliction.[13] Campbell (along with other advocates of a more rational religion)
moved beyond the afflictive model, though he could fall back on it at
times as his movement encountered unexpected obstacles.

Here then we find two worldviews, the one more culturally pessimistic and apocalyptic, the other more progressive and postmillennial.
One was Stone's world, the other Campbell's. The difference between
these two worlds was not simply a difference over the prospects for Christ's
imminent return, that is, over precise pre- or post-millennial issues. Such
a focus misses the important issues. As Hughes points out, the differing
millennial views, rather, provide a window into a cluster of theological
issues that, taken together, mark out two strikingly different theological
visions. These visions involved differing views of divine agency in the
world, of the Holy Spirit, of conversion, of the kingdom of God, of the
stance toward culture, and of the nature of Christian discipleship.

The sharp difference in Stone and Campbell's view of divine agency
can be seen clearly in the issue of miracles. Stone remained open all of
his life to God's direct, even "miraculous," working in the world, while
Campbell taught that God worked presently only through secondary channels like natural law and the Bible. "I see no authority in scripture," Stone
wrote in an open letter to Walter Scott in the 1830s, "why we should draw
the conclusion, that the miraculous gift of the Holy Spirit, is, according to
the will of God, withdrawn from the church." Responding to Scott's assertion that Christians do not work miracles now, Stone asked: "Why do not
some christians work miracles now? You answer correctly, because God
has not given them that power. And why does he not give that power? I
answer because of unbelief. If you say, because God designed that miracles should cease with the Apostles, I pray you to convince us by the testimony of the scriptures."[14]

Near the end of his life Stone wrote a long article answering what, by that time, had become standard objections to miracles. Miracles were done to confirm scriptural truth, it was said, and thus were not necessary since the apostles' time. Stone did not agree. "What is it but a miracle to be born of God—to be made new creatures?" he exclaimed. "What but stupendous miracles will end the present dispensation?" Furthermore, "we pray God daily to perform miracles, but in unbelief of them. We pray him to protect us from our enemies, to ward off threatening casualties....If we believe he will not interpose for our deliverance, why pray for it?" Stone concluded that "the denying of miracles leads to the denying of divine Providence and interposition—and this destroys the spirit of prayer and thanksgiving." Stone then said he had written so pointedly in order to "wake up my brethren to re-examine this subject." Because it is "a subject long neglected, and cast among the rubbish of useless divinity," he admonished, "it will require time to undo our unbelief, and the unbelief of our forefathers." "I acknowledge my faith in the doctrine is very weak," he confessed, "but my judgment declares in its favor."[15]

Alexander Campbell emphatically rejected any place for miracles in the modern world. Once miracles had validated the Bible as God's word and testified to the founding events of the Christian church their role was complete. Since that time God worked only through natural law and the "moral" power of words in the Bible.

Campbell's vision partook deeply of the early modern, scientific worldview. Beginning with the Protestant Reformation, he said, "the march of mind has been onward and upward"; in that momentous age "learning awoke from the slumber of centuries; science assumed her proper rank."[16] And its march had continued at an ever-quickening pace. As we saw in Chapter 3, it was just such enormous confidence in scientific advancement that had given rise in the late eighteenth century to postmillennial views. Postmillennialism emerged not simply with the view that Christ would return *after* the millennium (that was common by the eighteenth century), but when Christians came to view history as a series of gradual, ordered, progressive steps toward a perfect or near perfect world order. Such thinking thereby instilled in believers the confidence that, using scientific and moral "means," they could establish the kingdom on earth.[17]

In this regard Campbell's primitivist theology was profoundly modern and profoundly optimistic. Campbell was brimming over with Enlightened optimism when, in 1833-36, he engaged a man named Samuel McCorkle in a lively exchange. McCorkle was an ardent apocalypticist and he struck hard at Campbell's basic assumptions. Those who sought "a gradual millennium," he said, were nothing more than "silly dreamers of the age." The world was too full of corrupt tradition and "spiritual drunkenness" to be "wafted by the gentle gales of prosperity into the Millennium." Despite the best human exertions, the world was growing steadily worse—only God could restore the divine government of the world to its "primitive rectitude."[18]

Such an apocalyptic scenario Campbell found unreasonable, fanciful, and downright aggravating. It represented the disillusioned dreamings of the disaffected or ignorant; it flew in the face of an enormous amount of hard evidence to the contrary. "Almost every common newspaper," he said, "presents insuperable difficulties to such a preposterous opinion." Science was on the march. And as science runs its inexorable course, he said, it will "exalt man above himself, and raise a generation of intellectual and moral giants from the pygmies of the present day." Indeed, science is "preparing the world for some great, and...most salutary and happy change." Already its path was strewn with remarkable accomplishments, all of which served to refute such an outlandish apocalyptic forecast.[19] With such rhetoric Campbell fully embraced the ebullient assumption of progress that had already emerged with the industrial revolution.

ESCHATOLOGY AND ETHICS

If Campbell dismissed such apocalyptic views with a wave of the hand, Barton Stone was deeply sympathetic to them. Though not agreeing with McCorkle in every particular, he held a similar apocalyptic outlook. This outlook took shape to some degree early in Stone's career, and was not simply the result of millenarian excitement in the late 1830s and early 40s as some historians have supposed. His youth was a time when the new American nation witnessed an enormous outpouring of literature on prophetic themes. So radical appeared the democratic revolutions that people on every hand turned to apocalyptic imagery to explain what was happening. The old, hierarchical structures of authority were breaking down, many sensed, and a "new order of the ages" was arising. The majority envisioned this new order in nationalistic and optimistic terms, while a minority saw it more in pessimistic and millenarian terms.[20]

Not surprisingly, apocalyptic expectations ran high at the Cane Ridge Revival and in the early Stonite movement. "We confidently thought that the Millennium was just at hand, and that a glorious church would soon be formed," wrote participants Robert Marshall and John Thompson. And David Rice, a critic of the revival, noted the revivalists "high expectation of the speedy approach of the Millennium."[21] The old order, dominated by creeds, traditions, and the clergy, was passing away, they felt, and a whole new order of Spirit-formed holiness and unity was fast approaching.

Between the revival and 1827 we know little of Stone's eschatological views, but by the late 1820s the early apocalypticism had become an explicit premillennialism. In 1829 Stone wrote that "popular establish-ments...must fall in order to prepare the way of the Lord." God will "over-turn, and overturn, and overturn, till Messiah shall reign alone." A short time later he spoke explicitly of Christ's thousand-year reign on earth. "In his first coming he abode but a few years on earth," Stone wrote; "in his second coming he will abide 1000, and not leave the world, till he [has]...assigned to each one his eternal portion."[22]

By 1836 he could write that "the grand revolution has commenced, which will close at the coming of the Lord." The Great Revival had "loos-ened the shackles," liberating many from the bondage of creeds. And soon, he said, all remaining obstacles to unity "will be cast to the moles and bats." Evil clouds are gathering, but out of it "God will bring good-the union of Christians."[23] While Campbell viewed unity as the means of ushering in the millennium, Stone here envisioned a divinely wrought mil-lennium as the only way to any lasting unity.

To grasp the import of Stone's apocalyptic eschatology, we must see its close connection to his ethics. Throughout his career Stone issued the call to radical discipleship and separation from the fashions, preferments, and allures of the world. The Christian must be willing to surrender all "worldly gain," and even to see his family suffer hardship and persecu-tion. The great spiritual snares, he warned time and again, are "the love of money,...the love of ease and the dread of persecution." "To make reli-gion wealthy, and honorable in view of the world," he said, "and to con-fer on it worldly ease and comfort, were among the first causes of its ruin and fall."[24] Such warnings and such calls to separation from the world make up a constant theme throughout all of Stone's writings.

Closely linked to this call to separateness was Stone's conviction that

Christians should not participate in human governments. Human govern-ments, he believed, had arisen when human beings rebelled against God's government. All human governments, therefore, remained as vestiges of human revolt against the divine sovereignty. But Christians, who are now citizens of God's kingdom, acknowledge and submit to the true and right-ful sovereign, and therefore, Stone said, we "must cease to support any other government on earth by our counsels, co-operation, and choice."

For Stone this meant no political office-holding, complete pacifism, and even refusal to vote. It also meant rejecting all religious societies beyond the church. Christians "have no divine right," Stone wrote in 1829, "to build colleges for educating pious young men for the ministry, nor for Sunday Schools, nor tract societies, nor bible societies, nor rag societies, nor mite societies, nor any such money institutions."[25] For the same rea-son that Christians stood aloof from civil government they also drew back from such humanly-devised institutions.

Many people, of course, continued to refuse the "government of Jesus," and Christians "should not aid them in rebellion against the right-ful sovereign." But the time is coming, Stone concluded, when the "law-ful king, Christ Jesus, will shortly put them all down, and reign with his Saints on earth a thousand years, without a rival." Only then shall "the unity of Christians take the place of strife and discord."[26] Here we see, in sharp relief, the close link between eschatology and ethics in the Stonite movement.

Campbell's postmillennial eschatology, in contrast, gave his ethics a dif-ferent shape and tenor. Campbell had little basic sense of alienation from his culture. Though in his early years as a leader he mercilessly ridiculed fashionable church buildings and opposed religious societies, he eventual-ly left such rhetoric well behind. In 1853, for example, he could congratu-late the church in St. Louis on its expensive new building, saying it would "attract the attention and allure the ears of a large class of that community who otherwise would never listen to the ancient apostolic gospel."[27]

For Campbell the church was identified primarily by its apostolic forms and ordinances, not so much through the visible marks produced by the Holy Spirit in the lives of believers. Though he was a pacifist and could at times express his disillusionment with politics, he by and large embraced the myth of progress, as we saw in Chapter 3, and the belief in the triumph of Anglo-Saxon civilization that so captivated the intellectuals of the moderate British Enlightenment. Campbell's thought in general reveals an ethic of accommodation to American democratic culture that contrasts sharply to that of Stone.[28]

STONE'S LEGACY

When in 1832 the two movements united, this fundamental difference in worldview lay deep and obscure. Controversy focused on things like the name "Christian," fellowship with the unimmersed, the frequency of the Lord's supper, ministerial authority, and evangelistic methods. As a result, the far larger difference was hardly ever articulated or perhaps even recognized. It was obscured by certain commonalties—by the common rejection of creeds and "human invention," by the common rhetoric of restoring primitive Christianity, and by the common goal of Christian unity. The two groups could unite in 1832 believing that they shared the same basic assumptions and goals. But the underlying difference in worldview remained—and it lay like a deep geological fissure hidden for a time beneath a somewhat placid landscape, its presence betrayed only by occasional tremors.

The deep fault line soon began shifting. And as it did the Churches of Christ and the Disciples of Christ slowly emerged as two distinct groups. The Churches of Christ tended to retain the Stonite worldview and to cling to the primitivist elements of Campbell's thought, particularly his "ancient gospel and order of things" and his early opposition to all human "innovations." The Disciples of Christ embraced the Campbellite worldview with its cultural optimism and retained a few elements of Stone's thought, particularly his concern for unity.

Among the emerging nineteenth-century Churches of Christ, the memory of Barton Stone and familiarity with his writings faded fairly quickly. But his influence and legacy remained strong, especially in the South. The most important bearer of that legacy was David Lipscomb of Nashville, Tennessee, editor of the *Gospel Advocate* for fifty years and unquestionably the most influential leader of the southern Churches of Christ in the second half of the nineteenth century. Though Lipscomb imbibed much of Campbell's rational and common sense theology, his writings also reveal an apocalyptic worldview remarkably similar to Barton Stone's.[29]

Lipscomb's earliest religious influences came out of the Stonite movement. By 1831, the year of Lipscomb's birth, his father and uncles had been expelled from the Baptist church and had united with a Stonite church. According to Lipscomb, the first preacher of the reform movement he remembered hearing was Thacker V. Griffin at the Salem Church on Bean's Creek in Franklin County, Tennessee (a church established by the Stonite preacher James Matthews). Griffin's name appears in the lists of "Christian" preachers in the early issues of the *Christian Messenger*. Lipscomb's mentor was Tolbert Fanning, who had been deeply influenced by several Stonite preachers in his youth.[30] Campbell's influence, of course, also figured prominently; Lipscomb indicates something of the extent of it when he reported that he had read every issue of the *Millennial Harbinger* since he was ten years old.

Lipscomb published his apocalyptic views in many articles and in a little book entitled *Civil Government* (1889). Like Stone before him, he believed that all human government represented the rebellion of humankind against God's sovereign rule and the transferring of allegiance to the kingdom of Satan. Due to this rebellion, the earth, which was once a paradise, became "a dried and parched wilderness" where sin and suffering permeated everything. Christ came, Lipscomb said, to rescue this world and to restore it to its "primitive and pristine allegiance to God." Christ mightily engaged Satan's rule and succeeded in re-establishing God's kingdom. But this kingdom in its present churchly form was not the "everlasting kingdom," but the kingdom in "a lower state of growth and development." But the time will come, Lipscomb believed, when that kingdom "shall break in pieces and consume all the kingdoms of earthly origin." Jesus will come again and then "the will of God will be done on earth as it is in heaven, and all things in the world will be restored to harmonious relations with God."[31] Lipscomb clearly envisioned a restored millennial kingdom on the earth, though he refused to speculate about Jesus reigning on the earth for a literal thousand years.

For Lipscomb, as for Stone, this apocalyptic outlook deeply shaped his ethics. Christians should stand aloof from civil government, refusing to hold political offices, to participate in war, and even to vote. They should live lives of simplicity, sacrifice, and service, expecting as a matter of course the misunderstanding and scorn of the world.

STONE'S LEGACY LOST

This apocalyptic outlook characterized a sizable segment of Churches of Christ throughout the nineteenth century. In the early twentieth century, however, Churches of Christ cast off the apocalyptic worldview with its calls for radical discipleship. Some openly denounced Lipscomb's apocalypticism as heresy. One of the most influential men among twentieth-century Churches of Christ, for example, charged that Lipscomb had cultivated the seedbed for premillennialism; and he charged that Lipscomb's book, *Civil Government*, was "about as rank with false doctrine as one book of its size could be."[32] Among most people, however, Lipscomb's apocalypticism was simply ignored or forgotten. And so it remains to the present day.

Two episodes epitomize the rejection of the Stone/Lipscomb worldview in the twentieth century. In 1922 a young preacher came to work for a congregation in Memphis, Tennessee. His main purpose in coming, he said, was to build a new church building. He threw himself into the task and by 1925 the building was completed. In a lengthy report to the *Gospel Advocate*, the preacher estimated the building's value at $125,000—an enormous sum in a time when a new Ford cost around $300.

A sharp and lengthy response from James A. Allen, a protégé of Lipscomb and editor of the *Advocate*, followed the preacher's report. He wrote that a building costing that much money was "a satire on the spirit and genius of Christianity." He said it was "a sin that cries to heaven and will continue to so cry until it is sold and that huge amount of money given to the poor or used to have the gospel preached." Such a building, he continued, breeds "a spirit of worldliness that is incompatible with the true worship and service of God." Allen concluded with words that could just as well have been written by his mentor David Lipscomb. "In the age when the church grew most rapidly," he wrote, " most of its members were common laboring people; and while some few of its members were men of wealth, they were taught to preserve their wealth by giving it away. They were taught to give to two objects—to help the poor and to have the gospel preached."[33]

The other episode epitomizing the rejection of the Stone/Lipscomb worldview occurred during World War II. By this time the apocalyptic worldview of Stone and Lipscomb, with its dim view of all human governments and its sole allegiance to God's kingdom, had eroded badly.

With the war fever raging, the strict pacifist stance which had predominated in Lipscomb's time made little sense to many people. A preacher named O. C. Lambert expressed the prevailing attitude. "I lose faith in the Lipscomb Lion and Lamb story!" he proclaimed. Indeed, Lambert stated that Churches of Christ should call in all copies of "the Lipscomb book [*Civil Government*]" and burn them. So dangerous was its message, he was convinced, that it "would be outlawed now if the FBI knew its contents."[34]

With the apocalyptic theology of Barton Stone and David Lipscomb left behind, the theology of Churches of Christ lost whatever eschatological dynamism it had retained. It became more rigid and doctrinaire, harder-edged and exclusive. Churches of Christ could now view themselves unabashedly and without hesitation as the One True Church, as the kingdom of God restored to the earth.[35] At the same time that the theology became more rigid and exclusive, the ethical rigor and sense of separateness from the "world" declined. Churches of Christ became ever more content with conventional moral standards, more taken with the American civil religion, and increasingly concerned with respectability.

It is not surprising, then, that in 1928 H. Leo Boles and N. B. Hardeman, both prominent and very influential leaders, could speak of the "almost perfect" agreement between Stone and Campbell, and that the other twentieth-century Church of Christ historians could follow suit. For, in the first place, the actual memory of Stone and his writings had disappeared well back in the nineteenth century; and, in the second place, his legacy that had been born under the name of David Lipscomb recently had been cast off. But Stone's was a name too distant and too heroic to be branded a heretic—as some did Lipscomb. And so Stone, still left well back in the shadows, received a new and more appropriate persona, one fitting more easily into what Churches of Christ had become.

Churches of Christ are presently facing a period of considerable disorientation and change. Many members are questioning their recent theological heritage and reacting against it. In such a time, it may be that some members will discover again the counter-cultural, apocalyptic vision of Barton Stone and find it an encouraging resource for renewing spiritual life. That itself presents no small challenge, however, for it will mean, among other things, rediscovering the Stone that the builders of the tradition resoundingly rejected.

Notes

1. H. Leo Boles, "Barton W. Stone," *Gospel Advocate* (July 12, 1928), 654-55; J. W. Shepherd, *The Church, the Falling Away, and the Restoration* (1929, reprint ed., Nashville: Gospel Advocate, 1961), p. 251.

2. John F. Rowe, *A History of Reformatory Movements Resulting in a Restoration of the Apostolic Church*, rev. ed. (Cincinnati, 1884), p. 175.

3. N. B. Hardeman, *Tabernacle Sermons* (Nashville: Gospel Advocate, 1928), 3:121; E. M. Borden, *Church History, Showing the Origin of the Church of Christ, and Its History from the Days of the Apostles to Our Time* (Austin, TX: Firm Foundation, 1939), p. 348; Homer Hailey, *Attitudes and Consequences in the Restoration Movement* (Rosemead, CA: Old Paths Book Club, 1945), pp. 43, 46, 47; Robert W. Brumback, *History of the Church through the Ages: From the Apostolic Age, through the Apostasies, the Dark Ages, the Reformation, and the Restoration* (St. Louis: Mission Messenger, 1957), pp. 323, 341; on Stone see pp. 291-99, 319-20, 323-24, 341-43. See also Leslie G. Thomas, *Restoration Handbook: A Study of the Church, the Falling Away, and the Restoration* (Nashville: Gospel Advocate, 1941), pp. 74-75.

4. Earl I. West, *The Search for the Ancient Order: A History of the Restoration Movement, 1849-1906* (Nashville: Gospel Advocate, 1949), 1:18-35; Bill J. Humble, *The Story of the Restoration* (Austin, TX: Firm Foundation, 1969), pp. 31-32; F. W. Mattox, *The Eternal Kingdom: A History of the Church of Christ*, rev. ed. (Delight, AR: Gospel Light, 1961), pp. 341-47.

5. R. L. Roberts, "The Influence of B. W. Stone vs. A. Campbell in the History of Churches of Christ in America" (unpublished paper); R. L. Roberts and J. W. Roberts, "Like Fire in Dry Stubble—The Stone Movement, 1804-1832 (Part I)," *Restoration Quarterly* 7 (1963), 148-58, and "Like Fire in Dry Stubble—The Stone Movement (Part II)," ibid. 9 (1965), 26-40.

6. Roberts, "Like Fire in Dry Stubble (Part II)," pp. 26-40; Roberts, "Early Tennessee and Kentucky Preachers" (unpublished paper).

7. Richard T. Hughes, "The Apocalyptic Origins of the Churches of Christ and the Triumph of American Progress," *Religion and American Culture: A Journal of Interpretation* (1992). The argument that follows depends upon Hughes' article for its general direction and shape.

8. See Richard T. Hughes and C. Leonard Allen, "From Freedom to Constraint: The Transformation of the `Christians in the West,'" in *Illusions of Innocence: Protestant Primitivism in America, 1630-1875* (Chicago: University of Chicago, 1988), pp. 102-32.

9. See Newell Williams, "Barton W. Stone's Calvinist Piety," *Encounter* 42 (1981), 409-17; Williams, "The Theology of the Great Revival in the West as Seen Through the Life and Thought of Barton Warren Stone" (Ph.D. diss., Vanderbilt University,

1979), pp. 78-96.

10. Barton Stone, *Christian Messenger* 6 (1832), 86; cf. Stone, "Revivals of Religion," ibid. 5 (July 1831), 164-67.

11. Alexander Campbell, "An Address to the Readers of the Christian Baptist. No. IV," *Christian Baptist* 1 (March 1, 1824), 148; Campbell, *Millennial Harbinger* 4 (July 1833), 333; *Rice Debate*, pp. 629-33, 638, 643, 674-5.

12. James West Davidson, *The Logic of Millennial Thought* (New Haven: Yale University, 1977), pp. 129-41, 161-63.

13. James H. Moorhead, "Between Progress and Apocalypse: A Reassessment of Millennialism in American Religious Thought, 1800-1880," *Journal of American History* 71 (December 1984), 524-42.

14. Barton Stone, [Letter to Walter Scott], *Christian Messenger* 7 (1836), 13-14.

15. Stone, "Missionaries to Pagans," ibid. 14 (1844), 362-67.

16. Alexander Campbell, "Extract of the Opening Speech...at the Commencement of the Late Debate," *Millennial Harbinger* new series 7 (Dec 1843), 530.

17. See Chapter 3, pp. 60-62. On millennialism and the idea of progress, see David Spadafora, *The Idea of Progress in Eighteenth Century Britain* (New Haven: Yale University, 1990), esp. pp. 366-70. On the emergence of postmillennialism as a dominant outlook in early nineteenth-century America, see Davidson, *Millennial Thought*, pp. 269-76. Though Jonathan Edwards is sometimes called the first postmillennialist in America, a full postmillennialism developed only in the 1790s through early 1800s.

18. Samuel McCorkle, "The Signs of the Times," *Millennial Harbinger* 4 (February 1833), 64; "Signs of the Times (2)," ibid. (March 1833), 101, 105; "Signs of the Times (9)," ibid. (October 1833), 483.

19. A Reformed Clergyman, "The Millennium—No. 3," *Millennial Harbinger* 5 (October 1834), 550; Alexander Campbell, "M'Corkle Reviewed—No. 4," ibid. 7 (April 1836), 159-61.

20. On millennialism in America at the end of the eighteenth century, see Ruth Bloch, *Visionary Republic: Millennial Themes in American Thought, 1756-1800* (Cambridge, England: Cambridge University, 1985), and Nathan Hatch, "Millennialism and Popular Religion in the Early Republic," in *The Evangelical Tradition in America*, ed. Leonard I. Sweet (Macon, GA: Mercer University, 1984), pp. 113-30. On the crisis of authority, see Hatch, *The Democratization of American Christianity* (New Haven: Yale University, 1989), pp. 17-46. The 1790s saw a spate of premillennial interpretations of Christ's second coming, which paradoxically arose at the same time that postmillennial optimism was emerging as dominant. See Davidson, *Millennial Thought*, pp. 272-75.

21. R. Marshall and J. Thompson, *A Brief Historical Account of...the Christian, or as it is commonly called, the Newlight Church* (Cincinnati, 1811), in *The Biography of Elder David Purviance* (Dayton, 1848), p. 255; David Rice, *An Epistle to the Citizens of Kentucky, Professing Christianity* (1805), quoted in Bishop, *An Outline of the*

History of the Church in the State of Kentucky (Lexington, 1824), p. 335.

22. Barton Stone, *Christian Messenger* 3 (February 1829), 91; Stone, "The Millennium," ibid. 7 (October 1833), 314. Cf. Stone, ibid. (December 1833), 365-67, and Stone, "To Elder William Caldwell," ibid. 8 (May 1834), 148. For a fuller treatment of Stone's eschatology, see Hughes, "Apocalyptic Origins of the Churches of Christ."

23. Barton Stone, "Desultory Remarks," *Christian Messenger* 10 (December 1836), 181-83.

24. Barton Stone, "An Humble Address to the Various Denominations of Christians in America," *Christian Messenger* 2 (January 1828), 50, 51.

25. Barton Stone, "Sectarianism," *Christian Messenger* 3 (June 1829), 194.

26. Barton Stone, "Reflections of Old Age," *Christian Messenger* 13 (August 1843), 123-25. Cf. Stone, "Civil and Military Offices Sought and Held by Christians," ibid. 12 (May 1842), 201-205. On such views among the Stonite churches, see John T. Jones, John Rigdon, M. Elder, D. P. Henderson, "Report," ibid. 9 (November 1835), 250.

27. Alexander Campbell, *Millennial Harbinger* (1853), 138-9.

28. We must be careful in accepting the ethical consequences that pre- and post-millennialists assigned to one another. Premillennialists sometimes charged that making the millennium metaphorical and postponing it would cause complacency, while postmillennialists sometimes charged premillennialism with causing withdrawal and despondency. But in this period both groups fail to fit the stereotypes that developed (and which historians have tended to perpetuate). On the nineteenth-century premillennialists' efforts to reform American culture and evangelize the world, see Ernest Sandeen, *The Roots of Fundamentalism: British and American Millenarianism, 1800-1930* (Chicago: University of Chicago, 1970).

29. Establishing this theological linkage between Stone and Lipscomb is a key contribution of Hughes' "Apocalyptic Origins of the Churches of Christ."

30. *Christian Messenger* 1 (November 25, 1826), 21. On Fanning and his early influences, see James Wilburn, *The Hazard of the Die: Tolbert Fanning and the Restoration Movement* (Dallas: Sweet Publishing, 1969), esp. pp. 13-16.

31. David Lipscomb, "The Ruin and Redemption of the World," in *Salvation from Sin* (1913, reprint ed., Nashville: Gospel Advocate, 1950), pp. 109-28; Lipscomb, *Civil Government: Its Origin, Mission, and Destiny and the Christian's Relation to It* (Nashville: McQuiddy, 1889), 44-93; Lipscomb, "The Kingdom of God," *Gospel Advocate* 45 (May 21, 1903), 328; Lipscomb, *Queries and Answers,* ed. J. W. Shepherd (1910, reprint ed. Cincinnati: F. L. Rowe, 1942), p. 360.

32. Foy Wallace, Jr., "The Lipscomb Theory of Civil Government," *Bible Banner* 6 (October 1943), 5, quoted by Hughes, "Apocalyptic Origins," p. 36.

33. John Allen Hudson, "My Work with the Union Avenue Church," *Gospel Advocate* 67 (December 3, 1925), 1158; James A. Allen, response to Hudson, ibid., pp. 1158-59. For an analysis of this episode, see Don Haymes, "The Road More Traveled: How the Churches of Christ Became a Denomination," *Mission Journal* (March 1987), 4-8.

34. O. C. Lambert, "The Lipscomb Theory of Civil Government," *Bible Banner* 6 (October 1943), 3; Lambert, "The David Lipscomb Book," ibid. 7 (September 1944), 15; and letter from Lambert in Foy Wallace, "The Lipscomb Theory of Civil Government," ibid. 6 (October 1943), 3.

35. On Church of Christ exclusivism, see Chapter 9, pp. 194-96.

CHAPTER SIX

THE "NEW WOMAN" IN A MODERN WORLD: SILENA M. HOLMAN AND THE QUEST FOR WOMAN'S PLACE

"Shall the sisters pray and speak in public?" Throughout 1888 and for several years that followed that question was one of the most pressing among Churches of Christ. It aroused controversy and debate across the pages of the *Gospel Advocate* and other periodicals.

In March of 1888 a man wrote to David Lipscomb, editor of the *Gospel Advocate*, suggesting that the command, "Let your women keep silence in the churches" (1 Cor. 14:34), prohibited women even from teaching children in the Sunday school. Lipscomb responded that they could teach children and even their husbands but only in a "modest deferential manner," not in "an assuming, authoritative way." And certainly, he added, women must never stand "before promiscuous [or mixed] assemblies" but rather teach only in private.[1]

Silena Moore Holman (1850-1915), an elder's wife from Fayetteville, Tennessee, and mother of eight children, responded to Lipscomb and the question of woman's place. She boldly challenged some of the traditional assumptions, provoking sharp and lively exchanges with Lipscomb that continued on and off for many years. These exchanges provide an

extraordinary glimpse into the tensions in church and society in the late
nineteenth century—tensions that have much to say as Churches of Christ
face similar tensions today.

THE "TRUE WOMAN"

Silena Holman was born on July 9, 1850 on a farm near Lynchburg in
Moore County, Tennessee. Her father served in the Confederate Army and
died when she was fourteen from a battle wound. Her family lived in
poverty following the war. At age fourteen she began teaching school to
supplement the family's meager income. In January 1875 she married T. P.
Holman, a young physician who had attended her during an illness. In the
1880s, in the midst of raising her eight children, she began a public career
that would span nearly thirty-five years.

Her response to David Lipscomb in 1888 on the question of woman's
place in church and society was a sign of things to come. In an article entitled "Let Your Women Keep Silence," published in August 1888, Holman
admitted that there would be little doubt about Paul's view of women in
the church if all we had was his injunction in 1 Corinthians 14:34-35. But
there are other passages indicating that women were prominent workers
in the early church, "and others still, seeming to teach differently from 1
Cor. 14:34." It is these passages, she said, that raise doubts about the traditional view of Paul's meaning.[2]

In several lengthy articles she examined these passages, underscoring
the active and public ministries of women like Deborah the judge of Israel
(Judges 4-6), Anna the prophetess (Lk. 2:37-38), Priscilla who taught
Apollos (Acts 18:26), the women assembled with the apostles on Pentecost
(Acts 2), and Phillip's four daughter's who prophesied (Acts 2:8-9). All of
these provided biblical examples, she thought, of a public role for women
that did not "usurp authority" over men.

She made clear her agreement with Lipscomb on one thing: "the man
is the head of the woman, and should take the lead, most especially in
the family relation." But she strongly disagreed that women were thereby
completely removed from public leadership roles and confined entirely to
the private and domestic sphere. The home was a woman's primary focus,
she agreed, and public activity should never displace that; but women
who possessed the God-given gifts should be allowed "to go out in the

world and tell of the unsearchable riches of the gospel" and to combat the social evils that threatened the home.[3]

Holman in fact rejected the distinction between private and public spheres that Lipscomb and most others sought to maintain. A woman could teach a man privately, they insisted, but not publicly, in her parlor but not in the assembly. Such a distinction, she argued, was much more cultural than scriptural. "Suppose a dozen men and women were in my parlor and I talked to them of the gospel and exhorted them to obey it? Exactly how many would have to be added to the number," she asked, "to make my talk and exhortation a public instead of a private one?"

She made her own answer to that question very clear. "I believe that a learned Christian woman may expound the scriptures and urge obedience to them," she stated, "to one hundred men and women at one time, as well as to one hundred, one at a time, and do much good, and no more violate a scriptural command in one instance than the other."[4]

In numerous articles, Holman developed her views with considerable skill and verve. She dealt extensively with biblical passages, and often affirmed her commitment to biblical authority. Lipscomb's responses were usually sharp, sometimes patronizing, and occasionally marked by exasperation. Her responses to him—and to other male critics—were firm, carefully reasoned, and respectful.

Lipscomb's basic response was that God assigned woman to the domestic sphere and when she oversteps that realm she rebels against God and threatens the stability of society. By nature and temperament, Lipscomb believed, woman was suited to this realm and no other. God had made her more emotional and less rational than man. As a result, she was wonderfully suited for nurturing children but not for public teaching or leadership. Eve's attempt to instruct Adam in the Garden of Eden provided proof. In that story, Lipscomb asserted, the Holy Spirit was saying, "I suffered you to take the lead once; your strong emotional nature led you to violate God's word and to shipwreck a world, I cannot again trust you to lead." God gave woman "heart-power" to fit her for being a wife and mother. But this very trait unfit her for leadership in society and church, Lipscomb stated, for it tends to "blind her to facts, shut out reason and lead her headlong where her emotions prompt her."[5]

Silena Holman's own writings, Lipscomb charged, provided a case in point. "When she wants a thing so, her strong emotional nature and intense love will see and have it that way any how." She can no more see the plain teaching of scripture regarding woman's place than "mother Eve could see death in the goodly fruit that pleased her." In this way, Lipscomb concluded, Holman "thoroughly vindicates her womanly nature," offering living proof why God forbids women to teach and lead in the church.[6]

In his exchanges with Holman, Lipscomb revealed clearly his deep allegiance to what historians of the period have called the "cult of true womanhood" or the "cult of domesticity." This vision of the ideal woman emerged in America between 1820 and 1860 and remained dominant until near the end of the century.[7] As America became industrialized, fathers steadily left the home or the farm for the workplace. With men newly caught up in careers, women were left with the chief responsibility for maintaining the home and providing spiritual and moral training for the children. As a result, the roles of wife, mother, and homemaker were heightened and idealized, and the model of "true womanhood" emerged.

This ideal permeated the women's magazines, popular books, and religious literature of the period. Four attributes stood out: purity, piety, submissiveness, and domesticity. With their superior moral purity and spiritual sensibilities, women were to restrain the natural lust and aggressiveness of husbands and sons. They were to make their homes havens of stability and nurture.

At the same time, the ideal woman was passive, dependent, deferential, and childlike. As one Christian woman put it in 1870, "God has so made the sexes that women, like children, cling to men; lean upon them as though they were superior in mind and body." Women could exert an enormous leavening, uplifting, and nurturing influence, but only by remaining properly submissive. Indeed, by remaining strictly within their ordained sphere, women served as the backbone of society.[8]

David Lipscomb and many other leaders of the Churches of Christ in the 1880s held this ideal of "true womanhood" without question. It deeply shaped their interpretation of biblical teaching about the role of women. On this basis, for example, Lipscomb, his co-editor E. G. Sewell, and most other leaders condemned the "strong-minded women" who sought the right to vote. Women voting, Sewell wrote, was based on "a principle which, if allowed to spread, threatens to destroy the most sacred of all institutions, and make America a homeless nation." Women who sought the vote, he warned, would "break the `bond of subjection' divinely laid upon them and assert their independence; vote, hold office, electioneer, and, if necessary, fight their way to the ballot box."[9]

By stepping beyond their divinely ordained sphere, women threatened the whole moral order of things. When women entered the public sphere, Lipscomb proclaimed, chaos resulted: "loose marriage, easy divorce, indisposition to bear children, and…attendant social impurity."[10]

THE "NEW WOMAN"

Silena Holman also assumed the cultural ideal of "true womanhood" in certain ways but begged to differ with Lipscomb at major points. Against Lipscomb, she denied that women were unfit for leadership due to their emotional nature. "The Bible nowhere intimates," she retorted, "that the mind of woman is inferior to that of man (and it is the mind that makes the leader)." Indeed, in the fields of science, the arts, education, literature, journalism, business, and the professions, "woman has come to the front and proven her ability to cope with man, in anything she may undertake."[11]

Further, when Lipscomb charged that much of the moral disarray of American society was to be laid at the feet of women who neglected their domestic duties and sought public roles, Holman took sharp exception. "My dear sister," Lipscomb had written, "man is what his mother makes him. The great and good men are always conceded to be the work of their mothers. The bad men [too] are just as much the work of their hands." Preposterous, replied Holman; women do not possess all the goodness in the world, and neither should they "shoulder the responsibility for all the bad." Man is the head of the woman, she argued, and he has an obligation to keep her on the right path. When she fails in her duty, he cannot excuse himself by blaming her.[12]

With such critique, Silena Holman stood among those who in the 1890s promoted the ideal of what they called the "new woman." Proponents of the "new woman" accepted neither the passivity of the "true woman" nor the militancy of the emerging "women's rights" movement. They supported women's suffrage, women's reform societies (like the Women's Christian Temperance Union), higher education for women, and a more public role for women in the churches. They stressed loyalty to home and family and did not reject male headship. They did not promote a feminist rejection of the domestic sphere, but rather believed that more opportunities for women would make better wives and mothers.[13]

In 1895 the *Gospel Advocate* printed an attack on the "new woman." Six months later Holman published a spirited reply. "The days of the 'clinging vine woman' are gone forever," she proclaimed. In her place a "husband will find walking by his side the bright, wide-awake companion,...a helpmeet in the best possible sense of the term." The "new woman" is well educated, and her education has not "impaired her feminine grace or lovable qualities in the slightest degree." She will probably marry, but will not have to "marry for a living." She knows the world around her and takes an active part in it. And she will vote when that right is granted her (only three states gave full suffrage to women at the time). "When the 'new woman'...comes into her kingdom, wide-awake, alert, thoughtful, and up to date," Holman wrote, "she will not depreciate, but...magnify and glorify the profession of motherhood."[14]

David Lipscomb and the *Advocate* remained a staunch foe of this "new woman." She was a "usurper" of male prerogatives and dangerous to society, he said in 1897. As for Silena Holman, he wrote: "It gives a body the blues to read Sister Holman's article[s]."[15]

Holman herself modeled the "new woman" in many ways. Besides raising seven sons and one daughter and serving as the wife of a physician, she worked faithfully in her church, wrote hundreds of articles for publication, and served for almost sixteen years as president of the Tennessee Women's Christian Temperance Union. Her work with the WCTU became perhaps the central commitment of her life outside of her family. Understanding that commitment helps explain her progressive views on the role of women in society and church.

The Women's Christian Temperance Union was established in 1873. It was a response to the social ills arising in late nineteenth-century America from rapid urbanization and industrialization. In addition to combating alcohol abuse, it worked for improved police forces and prisons; sought to aid indigent children, unwed mothers, and working women; supported the women's suffrage movement; and attended to problems of public health. It did not confine itself to the single issue of temperance but rather saw temperance as part of a complex of related social issues. By the 1890s the WCTU had become the largest women's organizations in America. By 1897 its membership stood at over two million.[16]

Through the WCTU thousands of church women gained both a heightened social awareness and a sense of new possibilities for their role in society. In the WCTU women served as fund-raisers, lecturers, organizers, lobbyists, and writers. Through traveling and speaking to organize union chapters, many women discovered their hidden talents for public speaking. They exercised all sorts of local, state, and national leadership roles. And in these new roles many women experienced awakening and transformation. They became no longer willing to leave such roles to men in the churches.[17]

The WCTU thus played a key role in the rising movement calling for the equal status of women in society. This new status, WCTU leaders insisted, should begin in the woman's own family. A woman was entitled to a share of her husband's income, and a dollar value should be placed on her homemaking chores. Women should possess the right to refuse sex in marriage and the right to legal possession of her own children [in 36 states in 1890, a married mother was not the legal "owner" of her children].[18]

In general the WCTU occupied the front ranks of those calling for the enlargement of "woman's sphere." As Ann Scott put it, the WCTU "provided a respectable framework in which southern women could pursue their own development and social reform without drastically offending the prevailing views of the community about ladylike behavior."[19]

THE TEMPERANCE CRUSADE

Silena Holman's temperance involvement began in the early 1880s when she joined the Band of Good Templars. In 1887 she joined the WCTU and served for ten years as state reporter for the national WCTU publication, *The Union Signal*. In 1899 she was elected the fifth president of the Tennessee WCTU and served in that position until her death in 1915. Under her dynamic leadership the membership of that organization grew from less than 200 to over 4,000.[20]

The issue of prohibition became a frequent point of discussion and debate in the pages of the *Gospel Advocate* in the 1880s and 1890s. Just as with the issue of woman's role, Holman and Lipscomb squared off on this issue too.

Some of their differences were focused by the question as to whether wine or grape juice ought to be used in the Lord's supper. In a May 1885 issue of the *Advocate*, Holman wrote: "I come with an humble plea to the Christian churches scattered abroad through our country to abandon the use of the drunkard's drink in the celebration of the Lord's Supper." Her argument, developed at great length, centered around three points: first, that people of Bible times knew how to make both intoxicating and non-intoxicating wines; second, that Jesus and the early Christians would have used only non-intoxicating wine since Jesus would not have sanctioned anything that was harmful; and third, that grape juice should be used for the sake of reformed alcoholics who might have the old desire revived at the taste of alcohol.[21]

In his response Lipscomb would not admit that use of fermented wine was wrong, though he did not object to grape juice. He also would not concede that Jesus and the earliest disciples used only unfermented wine. And in response to Holman's argument that wine might tempt reformed alcoholics, Lipscomb wrote: "God does not propose to raise hot-house plants on earth and transplant them to heaven. A man that cannot learn to endure and resist temptation, is not fit for heaven. The earth is a scene of trial and probation to test the worthy and separate the worthy from the unworthy." Lipscomb did not think that people were actually tempted to drunkenness at the Lord's table. But even if they were, he argued, many temptations will indeed come in this life, "and the removal of one temptation will not make the world Christian. God intends temptation to meet us; those who love the flesh rather than the Spirit, will find other ways then to gratify it."[22] Under Lipscomb's influence, Churches of Christ in Tennessee never entirely gave up the use of wine at the Lord's supper during this period.

Holman also argued vigorously for outlawing the sale and manufacture of alcoholic beverages in Tennessee. She put forward her arguments in extensive writings for the secular press. But she also pressed them in the pages of the *Advocate*, where she urged members of Churches of Christ to join in the crusade. The liquor traffic, she argued, is the greatest enemy the church has ever known; "intemperance more than anything else stands in the way of the evangelization of the world." She wrote: "give us the prohibition of the liquor traffic, give the universal practice of abstinence among the followers of Jesus, and, with the blessing of God, we predict a speedy revival of religion in the church and a rapid extension of it over the world." Christians should take the lead in this struggle because the church could not "do without the temperance reform if she wishes to convert the world to Christianity."23

Holman's views found favor with many Christians, but not with David Lipscomb. He practiced abstinence (except for medicinal purposes) and believed all Christians should follow suit, but he often criticized the cause of prohibition. He thought the evils of whiskey were exaggerated and rejected the frequently heard argument that "all ungodliness comes from intoxicating liquor, and if we destroy it, the world will become Christian." He saw Christians exercising a "one-sided zeal" which often let the temperance cause overshadow the teaching of faith in God. Most basically, Lipscomb denied that Christians should take part in political activities, and affirmed that the church was "sufficient as a sphere for all Christian work." God could take care of the evils of liquor, he thought, without Christians mounting political crusades.24

In October 1907 the Tennessee Anti-Saloon League and the Tennessee chapter of the WCTU began an ardent drive for state-wide prohibition. Baptists, Methodists, Presbyterians, and many heirs of the Stone-Campbell movement joined the fight. Silena Holman became an outspoken and widely-respected figure in the front ranks of this drive. As president of the Tennessee chapter, Holman closely monitored the intense political battles. She endorsed prohibitionist officeholders and candidates, and often wrote letters to state newspapers expressing her views.

For example, when the prohibitionist candidate for governor was defeated by a narrow margin in June 1908, Holman charged that the winner had misled the public regarding his position and that his supporters had stuffed ballot boxes and engaged in repeat voting.25 A few months later when the losing prohibitionist candidate Edward W. Carmack was murdered, Holman wrote to a national WCTU audience that the "bullet that ended Carmack's life will write prohibition on the statute books of Tennessee." In early 1909, as the state legislature was debating a new state-wide prohibition law, Holman placed on each prohibitionist senator's desk a letter admonishing that "as we sit in the galleries looking down upon you we are praying that every man may stand true in the hour of trial."26

During her long tenure as WCTU state president, Holman wrote thousands of letters each year promoting temperance and other social concerns. After her death a co-worker judged that the achievement of prohibition in

Tennessee was "due more to her wise, brave, untiring efforts than to those of any other one human being."[27]

Silena Holman's broad-ranging work with the WCTU and her ardent concern for larger roles for women in society and church were closely connected. In 1913, two years before her death, she was still addressing "The Woman Question" in the *Gospel Advocate*, still arguing for a woman's rights to teach publicly before "mixed audiences." "Men may change with the changing conditions of modern life," she wrote; "but when women find themselves trying to keep step with their fathers, brothers, and husbands in the new order of things, the brethren stand in front of them with a drawn sword and demand a halt, because, they say, the Bible forbids, when it does nothing of the kind."[28]

Silena Holman died on September 18, 1915. According to one report, her parting words to her children were: "Always stand by the Women's Christian Temperance Union and lose no opportunity to help the work." Her funeral was held on the lawn of her Fayetteville, Tennessee home. Over 1,000 people attended, among them many prominent people from throughout the state.

Well-known evangelist T. B. Larimore preached her funeral. She had requested Larimore, she said, because "I want no man to apologize for my work, and I know he will never do that." Larimore did not apologize. He praised her "honorable and industrious life," mentioning both her devotion to her family and her "wonderful intelligence" as a public leader. "In her last conversation with me," he concluded, "she spoke of men who had been bitter foes of her work, speaking not unkindly, but in the spirit of charity, and I want to commend that spirit to all who are here."[29]

Two years later, on May 10, 1917, a portrait of Silena Holman was unveiled at the State Capitol and hung in the Capitol Library. It was only the second time a woman had been granted that honor.[30]

CHURCHES OF CHRIST AND THE QUEST FOR WOMAN'S PLACE

Silena Holman, were she living, would be almost as controversial and troublesome a figure among present-day Churches of Christ as she was in the late nineteenth century. Indeed, between about 1900 and the 1970s there was virtually no quest for woman's place among Churches of Christ. Though some major changes in woman's role in society—women's suffrage and higher education for women, for example—were accepted by Churches of Christ during this period, the question of woman's role in the church was not an open question. An hierarchical view similar to David Lipscomb's remained almost uniformly in place.[31]

The only possible exception was the issue of deaconesses. Though this question received significant attention in the nineteenth century, it was being raised only slightly by the early twentieth century.

Two distinct positions favoring the appointment of deaconesses had emerged in the nineteenth-century movement. One position argued for an official order of deaconesses (Alexander Campbell, W. K. Pendleton, Robert Milligan, and Moses Lard).[32] In 1848, for example, Pendleton wrote that it was "generally regarded, among our brethren, as an essential element in the restoration of primitive order, to ordain, in every church, both deacons and deaconesses." The other position insisted that there was no official order of deacons or deaconesses but that anyone—male or female—could be appointed by the church for a specific work (Lipscomb, E. G. Sewell, and others).[33]

Neither position carried the day among Churches of Christ in the late nineteenth century. Lipscomb and Sewell's position was steadily supplanted by what they called "officialism." The office of elder and deacon solidified rapidly. But the office of deaconess—practiced by some in the early movement and advocated by a good many—vanished.

One basic reason, as we have seen, was that the churches in the South almost totally accepted the domestic role assigned to women by Victorian culture. The ideal of "true womanhood" demanded woman's submissiveness and domesticity. It placed strong taboos on women in any public leadership roles and drew a tight fence around the home, her God-given sphere.

In the early twentieth-century Churches of Christ a few male leaders spoke out in favor of deaconesses. One was C. R. Nichol, an influential Texas preacher. "It should be known in every congregation," he wrote in 1938, "that Sister Phoebe, Sister Priscilla, and Sister Dorcas are deaconesses in the congregation, and that when their assistance is needed they are to be called." He added that "Many congregations are falling short of the work that should be done, because they do not have women appointed to do certain work for the church….As there was a need for the deaconess in the early days of the church, so there is now."[34]

Though a few like Nichol spoke out, few congregations seem to have considered appointing women as deacons, and virtually no congregations actually did so. Women of course continued doing much of the serving, as they always had. In general there was essentially no "quest" for woman's place until recent years.

In the 1970s a few sharp voices of protest against the traditional role of women were raised, most all of them published in two small magazines practicing an "open" editorial policy. In 1973 *Integrity* magazine published the first major article, "Set Our Women Free," where the author leveled two major indictments against Churches of Christ: first, they had "impoverished the church by wasting the creative energies of the majority of every congregation"; and second, they had "done grave psychological damage to the psyche of untold numbers of potential Marys, Priscas, and Joannas of our time."[35] In a 1974 article in *Mission* magazine entitled "Putting Woman in Her Place," another writer charged that "the church has persisted in being a resistant stronghold of male superiority."[36] Using these two "radical" magazines as a forum, a small cadre of writers attempted to push the issue.

But not until the 1980s and 90s did a significant "quest" for woman's place in the church get underway. By 1995 a sizable group of Church of Christ biblical scholars, all of them trained in historical-critical methods, could produce an extensive collection of essays attempting to reframe the whole issue.[37] One writer, for example, concluded that "the faith, testimony, and discipleship of women is equal to that of men and is equally as important to the Christian community. The value of women's discipleship and influence has been tremendously overlooked." Another concluded that "when we insist that women cannot lead, we follow a restrictive tradition rooted in Greco-Roman patriarchal culture and Constantinian-established Christianity....Women in church leadership is biblical."[38] In general this collection of essays sought, through rigorous and extensive re-examination of Scripture, to open the way for Churches of Christ to a larger—and more biblical—view of woman's place in God's Kingdom.

But as yet that larger view remains embryonic and mostly theoretical. Even among the more progressive congregations that have begun this quest, the very reopening of the question has proved deeply unsettling if not explosive. And the visible results remain negligible, though significant changes have been made in a small number of congregations. The experience of one large suburban congregation in Mississippi is typical: "At the

Meadowbrook congregation, we have engaged in serious discussions, but no significant changes have yet been introduced. The present leadership is not of one mind on the matter, which precludes any major behavioral change within the congregation."[39]

Despite the profound changes that have already revolutionized the status of women in American culture, the journey down this road will be long and hard for Churches of Christ. In this sphere, Silena Holman was not only ahead of her time, she was ahead of this time.

Notes

1. David Lipscomb, "Woman's Work in the Church," *Gospel Advocate* 30 (March 14, 1888), 6-7.

2. Silena Moore Holman, "Let Your Women Keep Silent," *Gospel Advocate* 30 (August 1, 1888), 8.

3. Silena Holman, "Woman's Scriptural Status Again," *Gospel Advocate* 30 (November 21, 1888), 8.

4. Ibid.

5. David Lipscomb, "Woman's Station and Work," *Gospel Advocate* (October 10, 1888), 6.

6. Ibid.

7. Barbara Welter, "The Cult of True Womanhood, 1820-1860," *American Quarterly* (1966), 151-74; Rosemary Ruether, "The Cult of True Womanhood and Industrial Society," in *From Machismo to Maturity: Woman-Man Liberation*, ed. Eugene C. Bianchi and Rosemary Ruether (New York: Paulist, 1976), 39-53.

8. Fred Bailey, "Disciple Images of Victorian Womanhood," *Discipliana* 40 (Spring 1980), 7-12.

9. E. G. Sewell, "Woman and Politics," *Gospel Advocate* 26 (October 22, 1884), 674.

10. Lipscomb, "Woman's Station and Work," 6.

11. Holman, "Woman's Scriptural Status Again," 8.

12. Silena Holman, "A Protest," *Gospel Advocate* 34 (November 17, 1892), 729.

13. On the "new woman" see Anne Firor Scott, *The Southern Lady: From Pedestal to Politics, 1830-1930* (Chicago: University of Chicago, 1970), 212-231.

14. Silena Holman, "The 'New Woman,'" *Gospel Advocate* 38 (July 9, 1896), 438,

and "The New Woman, No. 2," ibid. (July 16, 1896), 452-53.

15. David Lipscomb, "Response to 'The New Woman,'" *Gospel Advocate* 38 (July 9, 1896), 438.

16. Ruth Bordin, *Woman and Temperance: The Quest for Power and Liberty, 1873-1900* (Philadelphia: Temple University, 1981), 95-116.

17. See Nancy Hardesty, *Women Called to Witness: Evangelical Feminism in the Nineteenth Century* (Nashville: Abingdon, 1984), and Glen Zuber, "The Gospel of Temperance: Early Disciple Women Preachers and the WCTU, 1887-1912," *Discipliana* 53 (Summer 1993), 47-60..

18. Bordin, *Woman and Temperance*, pp. 114-116.

19. Scott, *Southern Lady*, 147.

20. *Standard Encyclopedia of the Alcohol Problem* (1926), 1239.

21. Silena Moore Holman, "Wines of the Bible and of the Ancients. Communion Wine—No. 1," *Gospel Advocate* 27 (May 27, 1885), 326; Holman, "Communion Wine—No. 2," ibid. (June 10, 1885), 360.

22. David Lipscomb, "Bible Wine," *Gospel Advocate* 27 (June 24, 1885), 386.

23. Silena Holman, "Communion Wine—No. 3," *Gospel Advocate* 27 (June 17, 1885), 378; Holman, "The Church and the Temperance Question," ibid. (December 30, 1885), 818.

24. David Lipscomb, "Bible Wine," 386; Lipscomb, "Reply to Sister Holman," *Gospel Advocate* (July 8, 1885), 422. See also Paul E. Isaac, *Prohibition and Politics: Turbulent Decades in Tennessee, 1885-1920* (Knoxville: University of Tennessee, 1965), 24-27.

25. Silena Holman, "The Situation in Tennessee," *Union Signal* 34 (August 27, 1908), 3; Isaacs, *Prohibition and Politics*, 153-4.

26. Silena Holman, *Union Signal* 34 (December 3, 1908), 2; ibid. 35 (February 11, 1909), 3.

27. Mary B. Bang, "A Marvelous Leader—A Comrade Beloved," *Union Signal* (September 30, 1915).

28. Silena Holman, "The Woman Question, Again," *Gospel Advocate* 35 (April 10, 1913), 338.

29. "Brother Larimore's Tribute to Mrs. Silena Moore Holman," *Gospel Advocate* 57 (October 14, 1915), 1027-28.

30. Mattie Duncan Beard, *The W.C.T.U. in the Volunteer State* (Kingsport, TN: Kingsport Press, 1962), 122-27.

31. The more progressive Disciples of Christ, beginning in the late nineteenth century, gradually embraced evangelical feminism. In 1888 Clara Babcock became the first female evangelist among the Disciples. See Fred Bailey, "The Cult of True Womanhood and the Disciple Path to Female Preaching," in *Essays on Women in Earliest Christianity*, ed. Carroll Osburn (Joplin, MO: College Press, 1995), 2:485-517, and Sandra Hull, *Christian Church Women: Shapers of a Movement* (St. Louis, MO: Chalice Press, 1994).

32. Alexander Campbell, "The Deacon's Office," *Christian Baptist* 4 (May 1827), 212; W. K. Pendleton, "Deacons—Should the Church Have Them?" *Millennial Harbinger* 41 (1870), 50; Robert Milligan, *The Scheme of Redemption* (1868); Moses E. Lard, *Commentary on Paul's Letter to the Romans* (1875; Des Moines, IA: Eugene Smith, 1914).

33. E. G. Sewell, *"Diakoneoo,"* *Gospel Advocate* 34 (June 16, 1892), 377.

34. C. R. Nichol, *God's Woman* (Clifton, TX: Nichol, 1938), .

35. Norman L. Parks, "Set Our Women Free," *Integrity* 4 (January 1973), 114-22. See also Hoy Ledbetter, "Women and Slaves," ibid. 2 (September 1970), 50-52, and Parks, "Integrity and the ERA," ibid. 6 (March 1975), 156-59.

36. Thomas Kemp, "Putting Woman in Her Place," *Mission* (May 1974), 328. A 1975 issue of *Mission* was devoted to the theme of "Women in Christ Today"; the lead article was Bobbie Lee Holley, "God's Design: Woman's Dignity," *Mission* 8 (March 1975), 264-70.

37. Carroll D. Osburn, ed., *Essays on Women in Earliest Christianity*, 2 vols. (Joplin, MO: College Press, 1993, 1995). Of the 41 contributors to these two volumes, four were women. See also Osburn, *Women in the Church: Reclaiming the Ideal* (Abilene, TX: ACU Press, 2001).

38. Frank Wheeler, "Women in the Gospel of John," *Essays on Women*, 2:224; Frederick Norris, "Women Ministers in Constantinian Christianity," ibid., 2:374.

39. David Jackson, "Reflections on the 'Women's Issue' at the Meadowbrook Church, Jackson, MS," ibid., 2:592.

CHAPTER SEVEN

ARE CHURCHES OF CHRIST REALLY PROTESTANTS AFTER ALL?

In the tract rack of the church in which I grew up there was always a tract entitled "Neither Catholic, Protestant, nor Jew." Indeed, I saw that tract or one like it in almost every Church of Christ building I entered up through the 1970s. I had read the tract by the time I was ten or eleven, but by then its basic claim that we were neither Catholic nor Protestant had already become a fixture in my Christian identity. People commonly "classify the church of Christ," said the tract, "as just another denomination of the Protestant group. We would like to convey to them that the category does not fit." Though we "may possess some of the characteristics of Catholics, Protestants, and Jews," it insisted, "we are not members of any ecclesiastical group. We are just Christians only, members of Christ's church."[1] This claim was fundamental to how Churches of Christ understood themselves; indeed such a claim helped form the identity of the movement from its inception.

Were all those tracts fundamentally wrong? Was this claim to be neither Catholic nor Protestant only the claim of naive and misguided restorationists? With all the talk about being nothing but New Testament Christians, had Churches of Christ become blind to the Protestant character of their theology and to the Reformed tradition that had given it to them? Were they, despite the rhetoric, basically Protestants after all?

Or is there another possibility? Is there a "third way" that is indeed neither Catholic nor Protestant? If so, where do Churches of Christ stand in relation to it? And what difference does it make? In this chapter I will attempt to answer these questions and show their significance for how Churches of Christ think about the church at this juncture in their history.

THE BELIEVERS' CHURCH AS A THIRD WAY

Until recently most church historians divided western Christianity into Catholic and Protestant types. As a subcategory of the Protestant type they would talk about "radical" or "left wing" Protestants made up of an array of sectarian-type groups. These historians recognized divisions within Protestantism and recognized the Eastern Orthodox Churches as distinct from Latin Catholicism. But generally Protestant and Catholic remained the basic categories. The radicals, such as the Czech Brethren and the early "baptists" (or "anabaptists"), were viewed as Protestant variations, what some called "impure Protestants." Only in the last fifty years or so—and mainly among scholars—has the Believers' Church come to be viewed as a separate stream with its own distinct and coherent theological vision. The name "Believers' Church" became common in the 1960s as a way of identifying "that segment of the Christian heritage which is distinct both from Classical Protestantism and from Catholic—Roman, Eastern, Anglican, et. al.—understandings of the church."[2]

A basic reason that the Believers' Church tradition has been obscured in mainline historical scholarship is that these Christians were, at least early on, mostly on the run. That is, they did not have the leisure to write theology, and when they did it was often destroyed or lost. Indeed, these churches often existed only by hiding their beliefs. They did not have the status to be heard or the influence to shape historical scholarship. The magisterial Catholic and Protestant traditions defined orthodoxy, constructed theologies from their dominant positions, and wrote the church histories. Those we have come to call the Believers' Churches were, especially for much of the first two centuries of their existence, dissenters and outsiders, viewed by the Christian establishment as heretics, schismatics, fanatics, and rebels against the social order.

Near the beginning of the twentieth century this historical picture began to change somewhat through the work of Ernst Troeltsch and his now famous distinction between the "church" type and the "sect" type of Christian body. Today "sect" has become primarily a pejorative term applied to those who adopt an exclusivist stance—who regard their group as the only true church; but Troeltsch's original usage was nonpejorative: "The sect is a voluntary society, composed of strict definite Christian believers bound to each other by the fact that all have experienced 'the new birth.'" The "sect" stood in sharp contrast to the "church" which sought to "receive the masses" and "adjust itself to the world."[3]

And then just prior to and after World War II a generation of scholars, many of them Mennonite, began a massive project of historical recovery and theological articulation that still continues today. Harold Bender, perhaps the father of this scholarly movement, argued that the Believers' tradition was neither Catholic nor Protestant but a third way characterized by focus on discipleship, peacefulness, and brotherly love in community.[4]

Another noteworthy contribution was Franklin H. Littell's book, *The Anabaptist View of the Church* (1952), where he argued that the distinctive feature of this third way was its understanding of community. The Anabaptists, he said, were "those in the radical Reformation who gathered and disciplined a true church upon the apostolic pattern as they understood it." He contrasted the "Church of the Reformers" with the "Church of the Restitution," going so far as to suggest that "the Anabaptist revolution within Christian history was so thoroughgoing as to be *sui generis.*"[5] A sizable corp of scholars has sharpened and developed these views in the last generation. The effect has been fundamentally to revise the standard understanding of church history. It has become clear that the Believers' tradition is not just an aberration from the Catholic and Protestant theological traditions but in fact represents a distinct and coherent vision (though with diverse and broken historical expression).[6]

Harold Bender and John Yoder marked the beginning of the modern Believers' Church tradition among the sixteenth-century Swiss Brethren, particularly at the moment Conrad Grebel refused to accept the jurisdiction of the Zurich City Council over the Zurich church.[7] The key issue here was the break with the *corpus christianum* or Christendom. The church, Grebel and the Anabaptists thought, must be "free" of the state in order to stand properly apart from the "world" and be a faithful church. Adult baptism (or re-baptism, which is the meaning of ana-baptism) was the symbol of this break with the state church system. After Grebel baptized George Blaurock in January 1525, Zwingli saw that what was at stake was the nature of the church. He saw that a church gathered by believers' baptism and confession was incompatible with a state church and its parish system; yet he was unwilling to make such a radical break. The basic issue, as Littell noted, "was not the act of baptism, but rather a bitter and irreducible struggle between two mutually exclusive concepts of the Church."[8] The one can be termed the constantinian church or the church of Christendom; the other, the Believers' Church.

The Believers' Church tradition was also shaped significantly by the Puritan Separatists in the late sixteenth and early seventeenth centuries. These ardent restorationists were driven not so much by an eagerness to reject the state church as by a passion for the holiness of the church. They defined the church as "a company of people called and separated from the world by the word of God, and joyned together by voluntarie professions of the faith of Christ, in the fellowship of the Gospell."[9] They tended to reject Luther and Calvin's view that the Word and sacraments were the marks of the true church. The true church, they believed, was to be a gathered community of "saints," covenanted believers walking in the way of Jesus and adhering to the model of church they saw in scripture. They shared with the Anabaptists an equally ardent concern for restoring the simplicity and purity of primitive Christianity.[10]

From these two fountainheads—Anabaptism in Europe and Separatist Puritanism in England—arose the modern Believers' tradition. Over the centuries the historical expressions of this vision have been diverse and, some would say, chaotic. The following bodies are among those often listed as sharing, at least in significant ways, the Believers' vision of Christian discipleship: Waldensians, Anabaptists, Baptists (especially non-Reformed), Mennonites, Church of the Brethren, Society of Friends, Churches of Christ, Church of God (Anderson, Indiana), Russian Evangelicals, Plymouth Brethren, Assemblies of God, various other Pentecostals, some Methodists, South America's base ecclesial communities, and hundreds of other lesser known bodies and movements. Such a listing helps us know whom we are talking about. These groups all share notably in the Believers' distinct theological vision-a few may even share most of its distinctives; but all of them fall short of that vision, as any particular congregation or movement will do. Thus the mere listing of churches and movements that partook of the Believers' way of being Christian does not (or should not) define, but merely illumine, this vision. What we seek is not so much a historical definition as a theological one. We look for the "generative principles or ideas in terms of which...[this] Christian tradition can be grasped and from which its distinctive features can be seen to emerge."[11]

Numerous attempts have been made to set forth these distinctive features, ranging from Menno Simons in the sixteenth century to James McClendon in the twentieth. Menno Simons, leader of Dutch Anabaptism, set out six defining marks of the church. To the two defining Protestant marks (preaching the gospel and rightly observing the sacraments), he added holy living, brotherly and sisterly love, witness, and the cross (suffering).[12] In our time Stephen Neill, an Anglican bishop and spokesman for the modern ecumenical movement, moved away from the classical Protestant definition to a listing of the marks strikingly similar to that of Menno. Neill proposed that to the traditional Protestant marks of the church should be added missionary vitality ("fire on the earth"), suffering, and the mobility of the pilgrim.[13] More recently Donald Durnbaugh, in his major treatment of the Believers' Church, characterized it as marked by discipleship, missionary vitality, separation of church and state, mutual aid in community, and a distinctive kind of ecumenicity.[14]

Most recently, James McClendon, in a groundbreaking systematic theology seeking to articulate the "baptist" or Believers' vision for today, has listed the basic marks of this theological vision as biblicism, mission (or evangelism), liberty, discipleship, and community. Thus the Believers' Church can be defined theologically as "an eschatological community rooted in Scripture typologically understood, a community conceiving itself to have a martyr mission to the world, a community determined that it must obey God rather than men or women, a community living a transformed (that is, supernatural) life by the authority of the risen Christ, [and] a community disciplined for obedient service to Christ in a visible church."[15]

THREE THEOLOGICAL TRADITIONS

The place and significance of the Believers' vision as a distinct "third way" will become clearer by further contrasting it with the Catholic and Protestant ways of being Christian in the modern world. Here we will use these three ways as a model to help us simplify and contrast very complex traditions.[16]

A basic divide sets apart the Believers' tradition from the other two: its characteristic critique and rejection of the state church or the constantinian settlement. Understanding the Believers' vision requires that one understand this fundamental divide. Most in the Believers' tradition looked back to the constantinian shift—the rise of the state church—as marking the church's fall or at least its widespread corruption. This conviction marked a fundamental break with the Catholic and Protestant traditions, and shaped the Believer's vision from top to bottom (for fuller discussion of this shift see Chapter 8). Another important divide—the papacy—separates the Catholic and Protestant traditions. Protestants generally believed that the corruption of Christian faith occurred with the elevation of the Papacy, often dated to the sixth or early seventh centuries.

Lesslie Newbigin, in a now obscure but important work of 1954, suggested a key word and a central image of the church to define the basic focus of each of these three theological traditions.[17] For the Roman Catholic tradition the key word is "sacrament" and the central image of church is the "Body of Christ," particularly defined as the *corpus christianum* or Christendom. Membership in the church is established and maintained through sacramental incorporation, beginning with infant baptism. For the Protestant tradition the key word is "faith" and the central image of the church is the "congregation of the faithful"; that is, church happens where those who have been justified by faith gather. One becomes a member by being justified through faith (which makes problematic the practice of infant membership, as we will see below). For the Believers' churches the key word, as Littell, Bender and others also have pointed out, is "discipleship" or actually walking in the way of Jesus; the central image of the church is a "fellowship of the Spirit." That is, the Christian life is an actually experienced and received reality; thus membership takes place through the fresh reception of the Spirit by each one. In this view being a Christian means not simply partaking of the sacraments (where one might remain unformed as a disciple) or claiming to be justified by faith, a recipient of Christ's imputed righteousness (where one might also remain unformed as a disciple), but rather having one's very character transformed by the power of the Spirit to be like Jesus and thus to walk in his way.

The contrast between the Protestant vision of church and the Believers' vision becomes very distinct at this point. In classical Protestantism church was defined more as an event than as an institution. Calvin's famous definition of the marks of the true church, followed also by Luther, makes this clear: "Wherever we see the Word of God purely preached and heard, and the sacraments administered according to Christ's institution, there, it is not to be doubted, a church of God exists." In this view church is not so much an institution, as with the Catholic tradition, as an event; week by week preaching and sacramental ministry is what identifies the church. So for Luther, as long as one was justified by faith, his or her outward behavior might differ little from others in the culture. Christians, Luther taught, are at the same time righteous and sinner (*simul justus et peccator*), that is, as they look to Christ they possess Christ's imputed righteousness but as they look to themselves they are always sinners. Thus the true righteousness of faith could be hidden under an outwardly sinful life, and the faithfulness of the church might well be hidden under the formality, inertia, and sinfulness of an ecclesiastical body. Luther and Calvin, to be sure, sought a purer, more visible church. But their formal definitions of church left that dimension out. The church existed where the gospel was preached and the sacraments properly observed. No matter how poorly a church might do this, Calvin insisted, it was still a true church.

Early in his reform movement Luther toyed with the vision of a Believers' Church. In 1526 he proposed three kinds of assemblies for his reformed church: a Latin mass for the well-educated, a German mass for the uneducated, and a smaller household assembly for those who were serious about following Christ. "Those who want to be Christians in earnest and who profess the gospel with hand and mouth," Luther said, "should sign their names and meet alone in a house somewhere to pray, to read, to baptize, to receive the sacraments, and to do other Christian works." But he went on to confesses that "as yet I neither can nor desire to begin such a congregation or assembly, or to make rules for it, for I have not yet people and persons for it."[18] Luther never established this third kind of assembly in the Lutheran Reformation. Where it happened, of course, was among the Anabaptists, and when it did a great gulf opened between the two movements. The problem was that, despite their new insights, Luther and the other Protestant Reformers held prior allegiance to the medieval pattern of church and state. They did not break with the *corpus christianum*. All persons continued to be routinely baptized into the church as infants, which produced, as Luther himself commented, a steady stream of church "members" who did not yet believe, who had no faith, and to whom "the gospel must be publicly preached."

In the Believers' vision, being a Christian involves not just a formal possession of church membership but an actual possession of life in Christ (or in Pauline idiom, "Anyone who does not possess the Spirit of Christ does not belong to Christ"). The gift of God's Spirit is the starting point of Christian life and this gift is closely related to the practice of believers' baptism. A common phrase used to describe this emphasis has been "regenerate church membership." Newbigin points out that neither Protestant doctrinal orthodoxy nor Catholic apostolic succession could take the place of the church as a community of the Spirit or of regenerate members. This was a dimension significantly diminished in the Catholic and Protestant traditions.[19]

So if one asks these traditions, "Where is the church?" one gets three distinct answers. The Catholic tradition answers, "Where the magisterium exists as an unbroken institutional succession from the apostles." The classical Protestant tradition answers, "Where the gospel is preached purely and the sacraments faithfully observed." And the Believers' tradition answers, "Where the Holy Spirit is recognizably present with power to produce transformed lives."

Many of the Believers' Churches, especially the early Anabaptists, insisted that no authoritative structure makes a group an authentic body of Christ. No amount of biblical doctrine, no matter how theologically articulate or skillfully preached, makes a group an authentic body of Christ. Rather it must be living as Christ lived, or at least seriously striving to live as he lived. "Most basic in this vision," Harold Bender wrote, "was the conception of the essence of Christianity as discipleship. It meant the transformation of the entire way of life so that it should be fashioned after the teaching and example of Christ. The Anabaptists could not understand a Christianity which made regeneration, holiness and love primarily a matter of intellect, of doctrinal belief, or of subjective 'experience' rather than one of the transformation of life."

In this regard, some of the theologians among the sixteenth-century Believers' Church sound much like nineteenth and twentieth-century Churches of Christ in their understanding of conversion. For example,

Balthasar Hubmeier (d. 1528), one of the leaders of Swiss Anabaptism, wrote: "Mere faith alone is not sufficient for salvation. Yea, I confess that mere faith does not deserve to be called faith, for a true faith can never exist without deeds of love." And Dirk Phillips (d. 1568), leader of the Dutch Mennonites, said: "But this is the beginning and the end of the teaching of Christ, that we sincerely repent, believe the gospel, are baptized upon our faith in the name of the holy Trinity, and are diligent by the grace of God to observe all that Christ has commanded us (Mt. 28:20)."[20] Repentance, faith, baptism and obedience make up the true path of salvation.

Now I will briefly contrast these three traditions in their views of sacraments, eschatology, spirituality, ministry, ethics, and tradition.

Sacraments. For Roman Catholicism sacraments are channels of grace, somewhat like medicine for sick souls. The import of Augustine's view seems to be that being a Christian is somewhat like being hospitalized for life; although one convalesces and gets better, one must continue to take the medicine of the sacraments, for one never really gets well. For the Protestant the sacraments are constitutive of church, so church happens where this is done. For the Believers' tradition they are not so much sacraments (at least in the later connotation of that term) as signs and expressions of new community—they both express and create a new kind of concrete, social relationship that Christ, through the Spirit, brings into being.

For the first two traditions infant baptism was the norm. Believer's baptism became the defining norm of the Believers' tradition, and though it was done either by sprinkling, pouring, or immersion, it was always done upon a profession of faith by a believing person. The Lord's Supper for the Catholic tradition is a eucharistic mystery with a high altar. For the Protestant tradition, especially in America, the supper can be called a memorial ritual with a low altar, though there are many nuances here, and Luther would not fit that category. For the Believers' churches a communal meal is the appropriate image, and the dining table becomes the fitting symbol, not an altar.

Eschatology. A difference in eschatology also tends to mark the three traditions. The Catholic tradition can be called amillennial; the Protestant also seems basically amillennial, though with strong apocalyptic strains at times and an occasional postmillennial thrust (like many early nineteenth-century American Protestants, including Alexander Campbell). The

Believers' tradition by and large has been characterized by an apocalyptic eschatology (at times radical and revolutionary).[21] [For discussion of the eclipse of apocalyptic and its impact on discipleship, see Chapter 8.]

Spirituality. In both the Catholic and Protestant traditions, spirituality tended to have an inward or subjective focus. The problem for Augustine became disordered desires in one's heart, and so there's an intense introspection that begins to emerge with Augustine. The same is largely true in Protestantism. After the constantinian settlement, citizenship and church membership became almost synonymous, so there were many church members who had not experienced the new birth and who really were not committed to following Jesus. In the Believers' tradition spirituality was more outwardly focused. The problem is not just disordered inner desires but disordered lives, lives not conformed to the way of Jesus. Thus one must not only seek to feel kindly toward one's neighbor, one must also share with him, serve him, and forgive him (and of course refrain from killing him, even when Caesar demands it).

During the long process of the constantinian settlement, the Christian life more and more became a life of interiority. As Stanley Hauerwas put it, "When Caesar becomes a member of the church, the enemy becomes internalized. The problem is no longer that the Church is seen as a threat to the political order, but that now my desires are disordered. The name for such internalization in modernity is pietism, and the theological expression of it is called Protestant liberalism."[22] The Believers' vision has sought to resist this pietistic impulse that turns spirituality primarily into a private, subjectivized experience of God.

Ethics. In the Catholic tradition a two-level ethic emerged: one kind of ethic for the mass of nominal Christians who were willing to follow Christ in a partial way, and another for those, like the monastics, more willing to conform their lives to the way of Christ. Sacraments became the necessary means of grace for this nominal, unformed mass. To describe the Protestant tradition, Luther's phrase *simul justus et peccator* is useful: Christians are at the same time righteous and sinner. The two states are easily blended, thus accommodating the masses of Christendom and allowing a kind of "cheap grace." Justification by faith alone thus easily became, for Protestants, the necessary means of grace for Christendom's nominal, unformed mass.

The Believers' tradition has focused on the Sermon on the Mount as a guide for basic Christian discipleship, not as a higher ethic for the spiritually elite. If one asks, "How can one actually follow the Sermon on the Mount? It seems impossible!" the one holding up a Believers' vision would reply, "Yes, such a way is humanly impossible; the Holy Spirit, working through the community of faith, must supernaturally conform one's life to such a way." As John Yoder put it, "Christian ethics calls for behavior that is impossible except by the miracles of the Holy Spirit."[23]

In the Believers' vision, Christ's presence is experienced most fully, not mystically or privately, but when people serve each other, display the character of Christ, and carry out his mission in the world. Theologians of the Believers' Churches often critiqued the Protestant churches for preaching a "sweet Christ" who required only that one have faith. They believed that one must yield inwardly to God and be remade by the Spirit into a new person, that the believer's inner state of grace will be visible externally in lives conformed to Christ's way. Thus they expected the preaching of the gospel to produce visibly (morally) reformed congregations—congregations simply incompatible with those of Christendom.

Tradition. In the Catholic tradition the apostolic pattern, however one defines it, is only embryonic; it grows up in later ecclesiasticism. In Protestantism the attitude toward tradition can be expressed in Paul Tillich's phrase "the Protestant Principle." "What makes Protestantism Protestant," Tillich said, "is the fact that it transcends its own religious and confessional character, that it cannot be identified wholly with any of its particular historical forms."[24] Thus the shifting, event character of Protestant ecclesiology is here emphasized. It means in short that nothing should be god except God alone, which produces a perpetual suspicion and a tentativeness toward all church forms and traditions, including suspicion of Protestantism's own forms and traditions. The Believers' tradition, with its central restorationist impulse, has often scorned tradition as corrupt; however, it has often recognized the value, indeed the necessity of, healthy, properly apostolic tradition.[25]

Continuity. For the Catholic tradition there is no fall of the church, no break in continuity, only growth and development. Magisterial Reformers generally followed Augustine in praising Constantine and applauding the church's progress under the leadership of Christian rulers. The church did enter a period of decisive decline, and they usually marked the beginning of that decline at the point when the papacy assumed power over the temporal realm. For Luther the decline began in 606 when Boniface III accepted the title of universal bishop. For most magisterial Protestants the church's "sleep" began when Christian rulers failed to perform their God-given duty to keep the church pure. They wanted to restore the Christian ruler to his place of authority, overthrow the Papacy, and thus bring God's Kingdom to completion.

Proponents of the Believers' vision generally held, in contrast, that the church's decisive fall or corruption resulted, not from the failure of Christian rulers to keep the church pure, but from their very assumption of power over the church. The rise of the *corpus christianum*, symbolized by Constantine, had opened the church to the unregenerate and uncommitted, thus altering the fundamental character of its life and witness. The church sought worldly power and splendor, introduced "inventions" into God's ordained worship, and began forcing people to conform to its teaching and practices. Christian profession became a badge of good citizenship and a level of discipleship far below the call of Jesus became normal.

The Catholic, Protestant, and Believers' traditions represent three main ways of being Christian in the modern European context. In the new American nation a fourth way was to emerge.

CHURCHES OF CHRIST AND THE AMERICAN HYBRID

In the period of early American nationhood, as the principle of church-state separation was established by law, the established churches of European origin were forced (against their wishes) to embrace the principles of voluntarism and religious liberty. As Roland Bainton noted, the Believers' Churches had first exemplified these principles in sixteenth-century Europe (where they were anathema to all others), and that legacy was transmitted to America indirectly by way of the Puritan revolution.[26] The democratic ethos of the United States forced the magisterial church traditions into a new style of functioning where they were required to enter the marketplace and compete with other churches. The new institution that emerged was called the denomination.[27] We might call it a hybrid of Protestant and Believers' ecclesiologies.

Despite the strong new principle of American voluntarism, the deep habits of Constantinian Christianity, learned over centuries in Europe, were not readily unlearned and relinquished or even recognized. A powerful establishment mentality remained among American churches. As Paul Peachy put it, "Protestants [in America] built denominations after the breakup of Christendom in the same way that kings built ostensibly sovereign realms with the breakup of the Holy Roman Empire."[28] Beyond the aggressive building of denominational empires, the establishment mindset appeared particularly in the long Protestant crusade for a "Christian America" where the Protestant churches, though no longer allowed a legal establishment, nonetheless sought to dominate the culture through an unofficial establishment.[29] This ardent crusade continued, with considerable success, throughout the nineteenth century and into the twentieth. The result was the formation of a variegated but dominant Protestant "mainline."

The new American denomination was fundamentally market-driven. Nathan Hatch and others have shown that in the early American Republic populist democracy with its new marketing strategies brought a theological revolution to American Christianity. One result was the "commodification" of faith—the adaptation of the Christian message to the competitive, free marketplace. The very success of populist Christian movements like Alexander Campbell's was in part a function of this "democratization" and "commodification" of faith. Thus those groups that rapidly developed a simple "theology of the people" carried the day (Methodists, Baptists, and Disciples); those that equivocated about adapting to the populist demands receded (Congregationalists, Presbyterians, and Episcopalians).[30]

American Methodism provides a striking example of this dynamic. According to Hatch, Methodism in the first three generations of the Republic was "the prototype of a religious organization taking on market form." Between 1776 and 1850 it experienced a "miracle of growth," from fewer than three percent of all church members in 1776 to over 34 percent by 1850.[31] Barton Stone, Alexander Campbell, and the Churches of Christ were somewhat less successful than the Methodists in taking America by storm, but their rapid growth was also propelled by pronounced accommodation to the American "market."

Alexander Campbell proclaimed that his reform movement was unique, not just another Protestant attempt at reform. "We adopt no amendments of old systems, nor attempt putting new patches upon the tattered and filthy garment" of the Protestant sects. Our doctrine, he said, is identical with what the apostles taught and practiced. Therefore, "Let us not talk of the 'Old Baptists,' and the 'Reformed Baptists'—of Old Lights or New

Lights....Let us contend only for that sect of disciples called 'christians' first at Antioch." "We have nothing to do with human systems, and ought not to retard our chariot wheels by the friction of the calvinian or arminian five points. With Paul and Peter, and James and John in our hands, what have we to do with the speculations of these uninspired men!"[32]

Though distinguishing himself and his movement from Protestantism, Campbell did see his restoring work as the fulfillment of Protestantism. For the Protestant movement had begun with the proper ideals: reliance upon scripture alone, proclamation of the priesthood of all believers, and rejection of creeds and ecclesiasticism. But Protestantism remained too wedded to Rome and the "leaven of popery," and soon retreated from its great gains. It became enfeebled due to "errors long cherished" by its leaders, particularly the seeking of temporal power and the elevation of "little popes"—authoritative creeds and confessions. Campbell intended to pick up at the point Protestantism had gone wrong and complete the task, stripping away its creeds and speculative theological systems, putting in place a "new and improved system of hermeneutics," and thereby opening up a "brighter and better era." Indeed, within a few years he could claim that the "era of Restoration" far surpasses the "era of Reformation," and that these gains had elevated the nineteenth century as much above the eighteenth as the Protestant Reformation had elevated the sixteenth above the fifteenth.[33] He could thus defend Protestantism in principle (as in his famous 1837 debate with the Catholic Bishop Purcell), even while leading the campaign against the aspirations and methods of the Protestant "establishment" in America.

Campbell deeply imbibed many of the ideals of the Believers' vision, especially early in his career. But he finally proved himself fundamentally Protestant in his reflexes and sympathies—not the old magisterial Protestantism, of course, but the new American hybrid Protestantism that moved toward and occupied the cultural mainstream. By the 1840s Campbell was becoming more Jeffersonian (aristocratic and agrarian) in outlook than Jacksonian (egalitarian). As his movement faced the institutional challenges of maintaining unity and order, Campbell pulled back from the Jacksonian faith in the common man and the sovereignty of the masses. He decried the "mobocracy" (a favorite pejorative term) that Jacksonian policies seemed to be producing. One senses the sharp tension between the radical freedom and individualism of his early rhetoric and the more authoritarian, ordered emphasis of his later thought. He eventually came to share more of the perspectives associated with the Whig Party which was more aristocratic and elitist in outlook.[34]

In this shifting outlook, Campbell left behind much of the iconoclastic rhetoric of his early years. As his movement gained size and faced the challenges of institutionalization, he more and more took his stand with the Protestant mainline style. Expensive church buildings, for example, once the object of his ridicule and condemnation, became the cause for congratulation and pride.[35] He called for a more authoritarian kind of leadership. "There needs [to be] a censor of the Reformation Press," he wrote in 1841, "just as much as a church needs a bishop, [and] a family a head...."[36] He tried to assume such a role but noted the popular outcry. (Ironically, at a deeper level, he did in fact wield such authority and control in the movement.) He moved away from the strict patternism by which he had set forth the church's "ancient order" and denied extra-congregational authority. In 1849 he became president of the new American Christian Missionary Society, and by 1850 was calling for a national convention and sanctioning plans for ecclesiastical districts, though he had earlier denied that an area fellowship could ever be the church. "We now allude to the church," he could write in 1853, "not a church, but the aggregate of all the particular churches in a state, an empire, a world."[37]

In general, George Phillips argues that after 1840 Campbell's roots in structured Seceder Presbyterianism came more and more to the fore as his concern for the power and growth of the Disciples movement steadily increased. He claims that "nearly all the significant features of... [Campbell's early] period (extreme constitutionalism, primitivism, rejection of missionary and Bible societies) were abandoned by 1840."[38] Further, Campbell embraced a form of realized eschatology that tended to equate his restored church with the kingdom of God. And he tended, especially after 1840, to make American culture and institutions the "bearer of God's cause." (See Chapter 8 for more on this point.) Campbell's mature theology, in short, was the theology of a movement very much shaped by and at home in American democratic culture.

Churches of Christ were influenced deeply by Alexander Campbell but ambiguously so; they also partook deeply of the Believers' vision as mediated through Barton Stone and David Lipscomb, and aggressively opposed Campbell's shifts and about-faces in his later career. Campbell's legacy is thus complexly mixed. Protestant and Believers' church elements were creatively intertwined in Campbell's theology and practice, with the Protestant, mainstream elements becoming more pronounced as he and his movement aged. The Protestant elements in Campbell's theology endured most readily in the Disciples of Christ, who in their subsequent history moved steadily, though fitfully, toward the mainstream; the Believers' elements endured most readily in the Churches of Christ, who in their subsequent history retained more of a sectarian stance and strongly rejected (or, in subsequent generations, simply forgot) Campbell's later, more Protestant position.

David Lipscomb, perhaps the single most influential leader among southern Churches of Christ in the later nineteenth century, epitomizes this Believers' legacy as it impacted the movement. His radical congregationalism, separatist stance toward the world, rejection of ecclesiastical offices, apocalypticism, ardent pacifism and apolitical stance, and his stress on simple living and sacrificial discipleship are elements that impacted Churches of Christ and distinguished his vision from Campbell's (see Chapter 5).

THE BELIEVERS' VISION TODAY

The vision of the Believers' Church is experiencing resurgence in the late twentieth century. As we have seen, it powerfully influenced the formation of American denominationalism in the early nineteenth century, and now it is powerfully impacting American Christianity for a second time.

To understand this new influence we must understand the new cultural context. The unofficial Protestant "establishment" in America continued in force through the early twentieth century. But the post-World War I period began a "second disestablishment" whereby the Protestant cultural hegemony was gradually broken up by growing pluralism and secularization. The mainline began to recede. Some, like Paul Tillich, began to proclaim the end of the "Protestant era."[39] George H. Williams, one of the foremost historians of the Believers' Churches, noted in 1962 the early effects of this development. As "the mission of the churches everywhere is being reconceived in a basically hostile or alienated environment," he wrote, "Christians of many denominations are finding themselves constitutionally and in certain other ways closer to the descendants of the despised sectaries of the Reformation Era than to the classical defenders of a reformed *corpus christianum.*"[40]

If this was somewhat true when Williams wrote in 1962, it is much more true forty years later, when we are well on the other side of the "second disestablishment" and indeed what some are now calling a "third disestablishment" in the 1960s and 70s.[41] The Constantinian era is finally over, dislodged at last by the sheer force of pluralism. Over a decade ago George Lindbeck wrote that "Constantinian Christendom seems to be definitively ending, and reshapings of ecclesial thought and practice greater than those of the reformation and comparable, perhaps, to the fourth century may well be unavoidable."[42] Those who had enjoyed mainline or culturally dominant status now find many of their privileges revoked, their assumptions of power passé, their comfort levels assaulted, and their new status more like that of the historic Believers' Churches (who have always rejected establishment in principle-not simply when forced out of power-and accepted the role of dissenters or outsiders). Now these mainline denominations (or empires) are experiencing both numerical decline and ideological decay. Denominationalism is not about to disappear, but its traditional configuration is a far less significant indicator of Christian life today.[43] Indeed, we are entering a period some are referring to as a "new reformation," a period when traditional Protestant visions of church life, organization, and ministry are being fundamentally challenged and rethought, and where some of the historic emphases of the Believers' Churches are re-emerging in unexpected ways.[44] And to paraphrase Lindbeck, we probably "ain't seen nothing yet."

All around us today there are creative and restless stirrings among churches, with unsteady but persistent moves toward the recovery of community and discipleship. And these moves seem to have a good bit in common with earlier Believers' movements. Yet, as Paul Peachy argues, the old problem still runs deep:

> The ecclesiological idioms that shape the corporate experiences of Christians today still hail largely from establishment times. Church bodies, both Catholic and Protestant, with establishment pasts, largely maintain the traditional establishment-engendered institutional and liturgical modalities. Free church denominations, if and when their sectarian fervor cools, gravitate toward "mainline"

liturgical modes. Institutionally neither group, established or free, is responding directly enough to either the new situation or the biblical materials.[45]

The new situation is a culture of autonomous, increasingly rootless and fragmented individuals; a culture where social relationships tend to be shallow and arbitrary, and where social life is administered bureaucratically; a culture where, cut off from the solidarities of kinship and community, people increasingly carry the burden of "detached subjectivity," thrown back upon little more than their own preferences, tastes, and feelings to determine what is true and good. The biblical materials—especially the Gospels, 1 Corinthians, and 1 Peter—seem to present a picture of church life considerably removed from and challenging to much modern church life. As Lindbeck summarized, "The mainstream of early Christianity was sectarian in the [sociological] sense in which we use that term. It consisted of a small, strongly deviant minority, unsupported by cultural convention and prestige, within the larger society."[46] Today the challenges of our new cultural situation will be better addressed and the biblical vision of eschatological covenant community more faithfully embraced by forms of church life more akin to the Believers' vision.

It is ironic that Churches of Christ at this juncture in their history appear to find these creative stirrings and reorientations distasteful or perhaps simply uninteresting. Once deeply rooted in the Believers' vision of church (albeit ambiguously, as we have seen), Churches of Christ by the late twentieth century have largely left behind that vision's deeper impulses and ideals, so that now, just when the vision is gaining new plausibility and many have begun creatively reappropriating it, they seem to be sitting on the sidelines occupied by other interests.

This aloofness or disinterest, it seems to me, takes at least three different forms. (1) Many members, of course, remain confident that Churches of Christ alone have restored and preserved the True Church, and thus need pay no attention to the upheavals of the "apostate" denominational world. (2) Others seem relieved to have moved at last beyond the exclusivism that marked and still marks many Churches of Christ and to have joined the larger Christian world (at least in spirit, if not in deed). As a result, they now seek to play catch up with the mainline Protestant way (which has itself been sidelined) rather than embrace (again) the upheavals and perhaps the odium of the dissenters' way. Here too are some who, recently freed from a dry intellectualism, seek compensation and refuge in spiritual experientialism. (3) And there are many, whether old exclusivist or new ecumenist, who are simply unaware of the Believers' vision as a venerable and coherent "third way"—a vision that has significantly shaped the history of Churches of Christ and that today awaits fresh and creative appropriation.

I began this chapter with the question whether those zealous tract writers of days (only slightly) gone by were correct in claiming that Churches of Christ were "Neither Catholic, Protestant nor Jew." Certainly they showed little awareness of the long history of the Believers' tradition and little appreciation for some of its theological ideals; indeed, these writers wrongly assumed that it is possible to stand free of tradition's streams. But as this chapter shows, I believe they got one thing right—that there has indeed been a "third way" of being Christian, a way that is neither Catholic nor Protestant.

Should we seek to renew or reappropriate this "third way" today? Can it be renewed today? In our fragmented and rootless culture, it is in fact already happening among many Christians—by studied intentionality among some, by unstudied experimentation among many others. This vision renewed today will not and cannot simply reflect that of the sixteenth century or the nineteenth century, for the context which challenges us is very different from what challenged them. The sixteenth-century context was magisterial establishment; the nineteenth-century context was emerging denominationalism with its drive for unofficial cultural establishment. Our context is radically pluralistic, secular, and neo-pagan. Today all the Christian players have been disestablished and must function as cultural outsiders. Christians now find themselves in a missionary situation in their own culture (though many do not yet know it). The historic Believers' vision thus stands as a rich heritage and ready resource as Christians seek faithfulness in such a time.

Over the centuries the Believers' vision has offered pressing critique of mainstream Protestant practices and doctrines, and thereby often offended the defenders of Protestantism. But it must also be said that this vision continually presents a strong prophetic call to the Believers' Churches themselves, who in their historic forms remain broken embodiments of that vision. For the Believers' vision always provokes, challenges, and calls to greater faithfulness. As John Yoder put it years ago, this vision "gives more authority to the church than does Rome, trusts more to the Holy Spirit than does Pentecostalism, has more respect for the individual than does humanism, makes moral standards more binding than puritanism, is more open to the given situation than the 'new morality.' If practiced it would change the life of churches more fundamentally than has yet been suggested by the perennially popular discussions of changing church structures."[47]

As in centuries past, the Believers' vision continues to challenge those who are "at ease in Zion" to embrace more fully the New Testament vision of faithful discipleship. Among Churches of Christ the recovery of such a vision may require more than ordinary measures of God's empowering Presence.

Notes

1. Batsell Baxter and Carroll Ellis, "Neither Catholic, Protestant, nor Jew" (Nashville, TN: Hillsboro Church of Christ, n.d.), 5, 6. These claims are ubiquitous in the literature of Churches of Christ. For example, Reuel Lemmons, prominent editor and thought leader, said, "The Reformation Movement gave the world Protestantism. The Restoration Movement gave the world the Church of Jesus Christ." *Abundant Living* (Rosemead, CA: Old Paths Book Club, 1950), 164-65.

2. James Leo Garrett, Jr., "Preface," *The Concept of the Believers' Church* (Scottdale, PA: Herald, 1968), 5. Max Weber first used the term in *The Protestant Ethic and the Spirit of Capitalism*, trans. T. Parsons (New York: Charles Scribner's Sons, 1958), 145-46.

3. Ernst Troeltsch, *The Social Teaching of the Christian Churches and Groups,* trans. Olive Wyon (1911; New York: Macmillan, 1931), 2:993.

4. Harold Bender, "The Anabaptist Vision," *Church History* 13 (1944), 3-24. See also Albert N. Keim, "History of the Anabaptist Vision," *Mennonite Historical Bulletin* 54 (October 1993), 1-5.

5. Franklin Littell, *The Anabaptist View of the Church*, 2nd rev. ed. (Boston: Starr King, 1958), xvii, 77. See also Littell, *The Free Church* (Boston, MA: Starr King, 1957); "The Historic Free Church Defined," *Brethren Life and Thought* 9 (Autumn 1964), 78-

90, and "The Anabaptist Doctrine of the Restitution of the True Church," *Mennonite Quarterly Review* 24 (1950), 66-86.

6. See for example Walter Klaassen, *Anabaptism: Neither Catholic Nor Protestant* (Waterloo, Ont.: Conrad Press, 1973); Donald F. Durnbaugh, *The Believers' Church: The History and Character of Radical Protestantism* (1968; reprint ed., Scottdale, PA: Herald, 1985); James Leo Garrett, ed., *The Concept of the Believers' Church* (Scottdale, PA: Herald, 1968); and Paul A. Basden, David S. Dockery, eds., *The People of God: Essays on the Believers' Church* (Nashville: Broadman & Holman, 1991), 368 pp.

7. Harold S. Bender, *Conrad Grebel* (Goshen, IN: Mennonite Historical Society, 1950), 99-100; John H. Yoder, "The Turning Point in the Zwinglian Reformation," *Mennonite Quarterly Review* 32 (1958), 128-40.

8. Littell, *Anabaptist View of the Church*, 14.

9. Williston Walker, *Creeds and Platforms of Congregationalism* (Boston: Pilgrim, 1960), 78. See also James F. Maclear, "The Birth of the Free Church Tradition," *Church History* 26 (1957), 99-131.

10. For the definitive work on Puritanism primitivism, see T. Dwight Bozeman, *Live Ancient Lives: The Primitivist Dimension of Puritanism* (Chapel Hill, NC: University of North Carolina, 1988).

11. James McClendon and John Yoder, "Christian Identity in Ecumenical Perspective," *Journal of Ecumenical Studies* 27 (Summer 1990), 568.

12. *Complete Writings of Menno Simons*, 1496-1561, trans. Leonard Verduin and ed. John Wenger (Scottdale, PA: Herald, 1956), 739-44.

13. Stephen Neill, *The Unfinished Task* (London: Edinburgh House, 1957), 19-20.

14. Durnbaugh, *Believers' Church*, 209-99.

15. McClendon, *Ethics: Systematic Theology, Volume I* (Nashville: Abingdon, 1986), 27-35, and McClendon and Yoder, "Christian Identity," 571.

16. I realize that typologies can easily distort through oversimplification and freeze conversation, but they can also clarify complex historical issues.

17. Lesslie Newbigin, *The Household of God: Lectures on the Nature of the Church* (New York: Friendship, 1954).

18. "The German Mass and Order of Service, 1526," in *Selected Writings of Martin Luther, 1523-1526*, ed. T. G. Tappert (Philadelphia: Fortress, 1967), 387-426. See also George H. Williams, "'Congregationalist' Luther and the Free Churches," *Lutheran Quarterly* 19 (1967).

19. The Puritans of early Massachusetts provide an example of Protestants who sought to combine a stress on regenerate church membership with the theocratic ideal of an established church. Though they invested extraordinary energy, the experiment quickly proved to be ironic and unworkable. See Edmund S. Morgan, *Visible Saints: The History of a Puritan Idea* (New York: New York University, 1963).

20. Balthasar Hubmaier, *Balthasar Hubmaier, Theologian of Anabaptism*, trans. and ed. H. Wayne Pipkin and John H. Yoder (Scottdale, PA: Herald, 1989), 526; Walter Klaassen, ed., *Anabaptism in Outline: Selected Primary Sources* (Kitchener, Ont.:

Herald, 1981), 2.10.

21. Walter Klaassen, *Living at the End of the Ages: Apocalyptic Expectation in the Radical Reformation* (Lanham, MD: University Press of America, 1992).

22. Stanley Hauerwas, "Preaching as Though We had Enemies," *First Things* (1995).

23. Yoder, "Let the Church be the Church," *The Royal Priesthood: Essays Ecclesiological and Ecumenical* (Grand Rapids, MI: Eerdmans, 1994), 174.

24. Paul Tillich, *The Protestant Era* (Chicago: University of Chicago, 1957).

25. See John H. Yoder, "Anabaptism and History," in *The Priestly Kingdom: Social Ethics as Gospel* (Notre Dame, IN: University of Notre Dame, 1984), 123-34.

26. Roland Bainton, "The Anabaptist Contribution to History," in *The Recovery of the Anabaptist Vision*, ed. Guy Hershberger (Scottdale, PA: Herald, 1957), 317.

27. See Sidney E. Mead, "Denominationalism: The Shape of Protestantism in America," in *The Lively Experiment* (New York: Harper & Row, 1963).

28. Paul Peachy, "The 'Free Church': An Idea Whose Time Has Not Come," in *Anabaptism Revisited*, ed. Walter Klaassen (Scottdale, PA: Herald, 1992).

29. See Robert T. Handy, *A Christian America: Protestant Hopes and Historical Realities*, rev. ed. (New York: Oxford University, 1984).

30. Nathan O. Hatch, *The Democratization of American Christianity* (New Haven: Yale University, 1989), and R. Lawrence Moore, *Selling God: American Religion in the Marketplace of Culture* (New York: Oxford University, 1993).

31. Nathan Hatch, "The Puzzle of American Methodism," *Church History* 63 (June 1994), 188; Roger Finke and Rodney Stark, "How the Upstart Sects Won America: 1776-1850," *Journal for the Scientific Study of Religion* 28 (1988), 27-44. In this same period Congregationalists declined from 20.4 percent of church members to 4 percent; Presbyterians from 19 percent to 11.6 percent; and Episcopalians from 15.7 to 3.5 percent.

32. Alexander Campbell, "Reply to Epaphras—No. 4," *Millennial Harbinger* 3 (November 1832), 532; "The Crisis," ibid. 6 (December 1835), 597, 598.

33. Alexander Campbell, "Extract of the Opening Speech...at the Commencement of the Late Debate," *Millennial Harbinger*, new series 7 (December 1843), 529-31.

34. See Harold Lunger, *The Political Ethics of Alexander Campbell* (St. Louis: Bethany, 1954), 129-47.

35. Campbell, *Millennial Harbinger* (1853), 138-39.

36. Campbell, "Prefatory Remarks," *Millennial Harbinger* (1841).

37. Campbell, ibid. (1853), 307. See Anthony Dunnavant, "Alexander Campbell on the Structure of the Church," *Disciples Theological Digest* 4 (1989), 21-39.

38. George Phillips, "Differences in the Theological and Philosophical Background of Alexander Campbell and Barton W. Stone" (Ph.D. diss., Vanderbilt University, 1968), 208.

39. Tillich, *Protestant Era*.

40. George H. Williams, *The Radical Reformation* (Philadelphia: Westminster, 1962), 31.

41. Phillip E. Hammond, *Religion and Personal Autonomy: The Third Disestablishment in America* (Columbia, SC: University of South Carolina, 1992), and Robert S. Ellwood, *The Sixties Spiritual Awakening: American Religion Moves from Modern to Postmodern* (New Brunswick, NJ: Rutgers University, 1994).

42. George Lindbeck, "Scripture, Consensus and Community," *This World* 23 (Fall 1988), 16-17. See also Stanley Hauerwas and William Willimon, *Resident Aliens: Life in the Christian Colony* (Nashville, TN: Abingdon, 1989), 15-18.

43. Analysis of the mainline decline has become something of a cottage industry. See for example Leonard I. Sweet, "From Catacomb to Basilica: The Dilemma of Oldline Protestantism," *Christian Century* (November 2, 1988), 981 and Robert Wuthnow, *The Restructuring of American Religion: Society and Faith Since World War II* (Princeton NJ: Princeton University, 1988), 71-99.

44. See Greg Ogden, *Unfinished Business: Returning the Ministry to the People of God* (Grand Rapids, MI: Zondervan, 2003); William Beckham, *The Second Reformation: Reshaping the Church for the Twenty-first Century* (Houston, TX: Touch Ministries, 1995); Donald E. Miller, "The New Face of American Protestantism: A Second Reformation?" *Reinventing American Protestantism: Christianity in the New Millennium* (Berkeley, CA: University of California, 1997), 11-26; Charles Scriven, "The Reformation Radicals Ride Again," *Christianity Today* ; Rodney Clapp, *A Peculiar People: The Church as Culture in a Post-Christian Society* (Downer's Grove, IL: InterVarsity, 1996); Eddie Gibbs, *ChurchNext: Quantum Changes in How We Do Ministry* (Downer's Grove, IL: InterVarsity, 1999); and Lee Camp, *Mere Discipleship: Radical Christianity in a Rebellious World* (Grand Rapids: Brazos, 2003).

45. Peachy, "The 'Free Church?'" 184.

46. George Lindbeck, "The Sectarian Future of the Church," in *The God Experience*, ed. Joseph P. Whalen (New York: Newman Press, 1971),

47. Yoder, "Binding and Loosing," in *The Royal Priesthood*, 325.

CHAPTER EIGHT

LIVING IN LIGHT
OF LAST(ING) THINGS:
THE RECOVERY OF ESCHATOLOGY
FOR DISCIPLESHIP

FROM RESIDENT ALIENS TO ESTABLISHED CHURCH

The church's stance toward the world involves a great paradox. Early Christians expressed this paradox by speaking of themselves as "alien citizens." This image has deep roots in the New Testament. God's great people of faith "acknowledged that they were strangers and exiles on the earth" (Heb. 11:13). Though Christians are "aliens and exiles," they must "be subject for the Lord's sake to every human institution" (1 Pet. 2:11-14). Though their "commonwealth is in heaven," they live and patiently serve in this world (Phil. 3:20).

In the second-century, pagans puzzled over such attitudes toward the world. They wondered how the Christian church enabled its members "to set little store by this world, and even to make light of death itself." In response, an early Christian writer spoke of this stance as a marvelous paradox: "...though they are residents at home in their own countries, their behavior there is more like that of transients; they take their full part as citizens, but they also submit to anything and everything as if they were aliens. For them, any foreign country is a homeland, and any homeland a foreign country."[1]

During the first three centuries, the Christian church largely maintained this sense of being "resident aliens," a pilgrim people, a caravan community. But the fourth century brought epochal changes: the joining of church and state (symbolized by Emperor Constantine's conversion to Christianity) and the creation of constantinian Christianity. In using the term "constantinian" we are not so much concerned with Constantine the ruler or his conversion to Christianity in the year 311, but with Constantine as the symbol of an epochal shift in the whole conception of church and discipleship—a shift that had begun well before Constantine and that took many generations to work itself out. The term "constantinianism" is thus a shorthand term for a new era in Christian history.[2]

In the constantinian situation the makeup of the church changed dramatically. Up to that time Christians were a minority in the empire. They faced regular opposition and sporadic persecution. Being a Christian required courage and commitment. But after the Christian faith became officially sanctioned, and its profession a badge of respectability, almost everyone became a church member. Being a Christian required little courage, commitment, or sacrifice. Floods of half-committed and uncommitted people flowed into the church. The standards and expectations for discipleship had to be relaxed. Infant baptism, which required no explicit faith, replaced believer's baptism as the mark of church membership.

Christianity took on majority status. Indeed, the emperor Theodosius made it a civil offense *not* to be a Christian. With this new status church and world were fused in significant ways. The church began to view itself as responsible for christianizing the social order, for bringing all the institutions of society under the Christian umbrella. The result however was not just the Christianization of society; the result was also the widespread dilution of Christ's high calling in the church.

The Christianization of the Roman Empire thus was accompanied by the acculturation of the church. According to Ben Witherington, a primary factor in this acculturation was "the gradual acceptance of one form or another of realized eschatology that either made its peace with the world or assumed that worldly matters and material things were *adiaphora* [indifferent things]. As a result, the church gradually allowed the dominant culture to set the agenda in economic, political, and social matters (including the role of women)."[3] This situation gave rise to a two-level ethic (one for the masses, and one for those who wished to take discipleship more seriously), to a doctrine of the invisible church (because the visible church was so obviously deficient and mixed), and to a new way of understanding New Testament eschatological texts.

This shift had enormous consequences for Christian ethics or discipleship. John Yoder has argued that whenever Christian faith becomes an official or established ideology the Lordship of Jesus gets compromised. "Some other value—power, mammon, fame, efficacy—tends to become the new functional equivalent of deity."[4] Power rather than servanthood is glorified. Violence rather than peaceableness becomes an accepted way. The concrete and often radical way of Jesus gets compromised by the way of Roman imperialism and might or in modern times by the way of capitalism or nationalism or liberal individualism. The mission of Jesus becomes identified with or pre-empted by humanitarian causes and liberal notions of human self-fulfillment. The proper biblical name for this tendency is idolatry.

What, we may ask, is the relevance of all this for Christians in modern times? Have we not left the constantinian joining of church and state far behind? And is not American democracy built squarely on the disestablishment of religion? The U.S. Constitution *did* legally separate church and state and the Bill of Rights *did* guarantee freedom of religion. In this way the legal establishment of Christianity ended. But, as we saw in the previous chapter, the cultural establishment of Christianity did not. Indeed, a generic version of Protestant Christianity continued to function as a national or civic religion well into the twentieth century. For many citizens, America remained not only a Christian nation but a Protestant one, and the language of this faith was deeply intertwined in the rhetoric of patriotism. As one scholar recently put it, "Establishment by law ended in the nineteenth century. Establishment by cultural domination ended [only] in the twentieth." This kind of unofficial Christian establishment Yoder calls "neo-constantinianism."[5]

If this analysis is at all correct, then American Christianity has continued to face the problem of the effects of establishment on Christian discipleship. Only now the problem is framed differently. It is no longer the problem of the legal establishment of Christianity in the context of Roman imperialism or medieval feudalism, but rather the problem of the cultural establishment of Christianity in the context of liberal democracy.

DISCIPLESHIP IN A LIBERAL CULTURE

To understand the new form of this problem, we must grasp the basic features of the liberalism that undergirds our culture. Modern liberalism began in the Enlightenment of the seventeenth and eighteenth centuries. It took shape around the basic claim that people could free themselves from the clutches of tradition and find a set of universal, rational truths to which all reasonable people could give assent. The liberal claim was that with these universal, rational truths one could fashion a political and social framework in which people holding very different conceptions of the good life could live together peaceably. The wars of religion that had racked Europe for generations could be quelled. Individual convictions could be honored or at least tolerated. Diverse and even competing conceptions of the good could all find their place in a common culture.

In the liberal vision, every person would be free to live by whatever conception of the good he or she pleased just so long as that particular conception was not imposed in any way upon the rest of the community. The only vision of the good to be imposed upon the entire community is the liberal vision itself. Outside this, all that would be permitted is the expression of preferences. Persuasion, not coercion, would rule and social life would proceed through a process of debate and bargaining.

Thus a basic feature of liberalism is that there is no one overriding good (except, of course, the guardian principles of liberalism itself).[6] Society consists of compartmentalized spheres—politics, art, athletics, science, family, and religion, for example. The individual moves from sphere to sphere, pursuing his or her own preferences in each one. Acceptable rules, of course, must be formulated to guide these pursuits. And a key measure of the acceptability of these rules is that they permit people the maximum freedom to express and implement their preferences.[7]

This summarizes in broad and over-simple strokes the liberal ideology that fundamentally shapes modern democratic states. Thus liberalism in the broader historic sense in which I am using it is not confined to the political left. For this liberalism is not primarily a theory of government but a theory of society. This theory continues to form, to varying degrees, the working assumptions of both political conservatives and liberals, of Republicans and Democrats, of a George Will as well as a Ted Kennedy, of the Moral Majority as well as the American Civil Liberties Union.

Liberalism has had some strong and obvious beneficial results, perhaps chief among them the championing of freedom of religion. But a fundamental weakness appears in the moral vision it sponsors. The architects of Enlightenment liberalism proposed to ground morality in a set of universal, rational principles. But as it turns out, the very ground rule of liberalism—that all competing conceptions of the good be allowed as preferences—makes it very difficult for any ultimate good to be established in the public realm. As a result, societies formed by liberal individualism tend to give rise to the notion—as we see presently in America—that the moral life is but another form of consumer choice.8

In such a context, the exercise of freedom, choice, and autonomy come to be viewed as the essence of the moral life. Authentic morality becomes the freedom to choose and the willingness to take responsibility for one's choices. The good society then becomes a society providing the greatest amount of freedom for the greatest number of people. In such a society it becomes hard to escape the conclusion that the good is little more than the sum of people's individual desires and choices.9

A graphic illustration of this consequence can be seen in the controversy that emerged some years ago over the Arthur DeMoss Foundation's television advertisements opposing abortion. They were engaging, well-produced spots, and each one ended with the slogan: "Life. The beautiful choice." The New York chapter of the National Abortion Rights Action League mounted a campaign to counter the ads. Their advertisement reversed the theme, proclaiming: "Choice. The beautiful life." The *New York Times* report explained: "The spot centers on personal preferences in areas like food, religion, and hairstyles, then segues into the issue of 'Whether you have a baby—or an abortion.'" The point clearly is that *what* one chooses does not particularly matter, only *that* one freely chooses. Whereas the Christian faith proclaims the fundamental conviction that the truth makes one free, the liberal spirit of the age tends to proclaim the exact opposite: that freedom makes one true.10

This emphasis on freedom and choice as the essence of morality has given rise to the language of "values" as the dominant moral language of our time, and the task of "values clarification" as the prime moral exercise. Each person has his or her own values, and the task of moral development is the discerning and clarifying of one's personal values. James Edwards has argued that this dominance of "values" has put us in a situation of "normal nihilism." That is, a kind of moral nihilism is now the normal condition of our lives in Western culture. "To be a normal nihilist," Edwards says, "is just to acknowledge that, however fervent and essential one's commitment to a particular set of values, that's all one ever has: a commitment to some particular set of values."[11]

Edwards claims that no better example of this moral stance can be found than the modern suburban shopping mall:

> In air-conditioned comfort one can stroll from life to life, from world to world, complete with appropriate sound effects (beeping computers; roaring lions). Laid out before one are whole lives that one can, if one has the necessary credit line, freely choose to inhabit: devout Christian; Williamsburg grandee; high-tech yuppie; Down East guide; great white hunter.
>
> This striking transformation of life into lifestyle, the way in which tools, garments, and attitudes specific to particular times and places become commodities to be marketed to anonymous and rootless consumers: these are the natural (if also banal) expressions of our normal nihilism....Is it surprising that the New Jerusalem appears as several hundred thousand square feet of air-conditioned merchandise to be bought and sold?[12]

The modern university mirrors this development in liberal society at large. The university has become a giant cafeteria, with a vast buffet of courses that are supposedly "value-neutral." That is, they seek merely to offer an array of alternative views so that students can "make up their own minds." In the process they train the students to consider their own commitments as nothing more than opinions or "interests." They refrain from attempting to shape the students' lives toward greater conformity to an ultimate Good, and thus produce students who believe that all moral stances are "relative" because they are based on choice.[13]

The basic point is that when Christian faith becomes (unofficially) established in a liberal society a similar kind of dissipation occurs. Jesus' vision of the good gets reshaped or pre-empted by the liberal vision of tolerating competing goods. Liberal notions of freedom, rather than faithfulness to the cruciform way of Jesus, begin to define Christians' dominant standards.[14] Good citizenship in the liberal state tends to define good citizenship in the Kingdom of God. Christians learn to pursue their own desires rather than to curtail their desires for the sake of life in community. They get shaped more by capitalism's desire for acquisition rather than by Christ's call for contentment with little. State use of power and violence readily sets the standard for Christian sanction of power and violence. The gospel, in short, is domesticated and Jesus' Lordship compromised.

BEARING THE CROSS IN AMERICA

Alexander Campbell (1792-1866), the most influential shaper of the nineteenth-century Stone-Campbell movement, provides an example. Campbell well represents, especially as he grew older, what Yoder calls the "neo-constantinian" mindset as it took shape in young America. Campbell rejoiced in the legal separation of church and state, and gloried in the freedoms of American democracy. But he retained the fundamental constantinian conviction that the fulfillment of God's kingdom was tied to human empire, that a civil authority was the bearer of God's cause. Campbell ardently embraced the belief—common among Protestants in his day—that the gospel and Anglo-Saxon civilization formed a happy marriage and that together, in the not-too-distant future, they would triumph over the world. In other words, he so identified the destiny of the American nation with the fulfillment of God's redemptive purposes for humankind that "the [American] nation emerged as the primary agent of God's meaningful activity in history."[15]

Lyman Beecher, the noted Christian preacher, exemplified this outlook in Campbell's time. According to Beecher, true freedom was being fully realized in the American nation for the first time in human history; as a result, "nation after nation, cheered by our example, will follow in our footsteps, till the whole earth is free."[16]

Campbell shared this outlook with only somewhat less ardor than Beecher. He went through a period of disillusionment with American politics, spanning roughly from 1829-30 (when he was deeply disappointed by the Virginia Constitutional Convention) to the early 1840s. The low point came in 1840, during the Harrison-Van Buren presidential campaign, when Campbell remarked that Christians should not take an active part in politics because it was so corrupt.[17] But despite the often disappointing reality of American politics, Campbell in the 1840s heightened the prospects for America's role in the divine millennial scheme. He frequently made remarks like this: "Europe, Asia, and Africa look to Protestant America as the wonder of the age, and as exerting a preponderating influence on the destinies of the world. We have then, a fearful and glorious responsibility."[18]

The heightening of Alexander Campbell's stress on civil religion as the agent of the Christian millennium seems to parallel the dramatic territorial expansion of the United States between 1845 and 1848. This was the age of "manifest destiny" (a term first used by John O'Sullivan in mid-1845). During these three years the United States acquired about 800 million acres: Texas (1845), Oregon Territory (1846), California and New Mexico (1848), and millions of acres in the Great Lakes region. In the brief span of about 1,000 days the boundaries of the United States dramatically expanded to the Rio Grande River in the south, the Pacific Ocean in the west, and the 49th parallel in the north.[19] In such a time it truly seemed to many like Campbell that America was God's nation of destiny.

This conviction deeply shaped Campbell's view of discipleship, of what it means to profess the Lordship of Christ.[20] For him and many of his Disciples the marks of the true church were primarily doctrinal and formal, not ethical and communal.[21] They held up a precise New Testament blueprint or model for structuring the church, not so much a vision of a radically transformed kingdom community. They proclaimed believers' baptism by immersion as a formal ordinance required for salvation and church membership—not as a sign of entry into a community formed by trust in and radical obedience to a Christ who walked the way of the cross yet triumphed mightily over all the powers of this world.

Campbell of course thought that baptism should be followed by the "Christian life" and growth in grace, but he did not see the life of discipleship as particularly odd. After all, he and his followers were living in an especially propitious time—a blessed time when a democratic, Protestant-dominated, providentially-prepared nation stood poised to usher in the great millennial age. So he eagerly hitched the church to the rising American star, and saw the prospects as glorious indeed.

Discipleship thus remained a somewhat tame and culturally acceptable proposition, not a path especially marked by oddness or dislocation—and certainly not a path of persecution. Campbell made this stance surprisingly clear in his attacks on Walter Scott Russell (whose provocations we noted in Chapter 2 and traced more fully in Chapter 4). As we have seen,

Russell in one of his writings had insisted that Christians must "take up their crosses and bear them" after Christ. Campbell, attempting to expose and refute all of Russell's "heresies," objected: "There is now no cross under our [American] government. In other words there is no persecution in our country....Hence no man in the United States has to carry a cross for Christ's sake."22

Such pronouncements strongly suggest that Alexander Campbell failed to see the extraordinary nature of Jesus' ethic or the fuller significance of the confession that Jesus, not Caesar—Jesus, not liberal democracy—is Lord.

THE RECOVERY OF ESCHATOLOGY FOR DISCIPLESHIP

What is missing in such "neo-constantinian" versions of the Christian ethic is the New Testament's bold eschatological claim. The Christian ethic is grounded in this bold claim. The claim is that the triumph of God has been uncovered or revealed. The claim is that in Jesus' death and resurrection all the hostile "powers" of this present age have been disarmed and defeated, that God's kingdom has broken into history and thus, for the believer, brought an end to all other kingdoms. In Jesus' victory and in this new kingdom the believer sees the end of history. The believer, by faith, knows how history will turn out. This triumph is not visible to the human eye or audible to the human ear and cannot be known through any scientific research or statistical projection. It is known only through faith. The worldly "powers" continue to rage and threaten, but the believer "sees" that they are doomed—finished, already writhing in their death throes. The believer thus knows something that unbelievers do not know: that Jesus Christ now reigns as Lord of all, and further, that one day every knee will bow and every tongue confess that Lordship. Furthermore, believers not only know by faith how history will end, they also presently participate in that end through the presence of God's Spirit. "We are those," Paul said, "upon whom the ends of the ages have come" (1 Cor. 10:11). Knowing this truth and experiencing this power, the disciple can follow Jesus in all things, even in those things that seem utterly impractical and unworkable to those who do not know what Christians know, "see" what they see, and experience what they experience by the Spirit. This basic New Testament outlook can properly be called "apocalyptic."23

This apocalyptic vision eventually faded as the church became more institutionalized and powerful. John Yoder has shown that the constantinian shift brought a new way of understanding New Testament eschatological texts: "Before Constantine, one knew as a fact of everyday experience that there was a believing community but one had to 'take it on faith' that God was governing history. After Constantine, one had to believe without seeing that there was a community of believers, within the larger nominally Christian mass, but one knew for a fact that God was in control of history."[24] In other words, when everyone became a church member in the Christian empire both the level of discipleship in the church and the level of expectation for the inbreaking of God's new order in their midst diminished in tandem. The visible church was obviously such a mixed company that the true church had to be designated an invisible community revealed only at the last judgment.

This shift in Western Christianity gave rise to two quite different eschatological views. As Colin Gunton puts it, one view is "increasingly dualistic: this life is a preparation for the next, a training ground for a future destiny. The other stresses more strongly the [believing] community as the place where the conditions of the life to come may be realized in the here and now." The first view has generally characterized the "orthodox" mainstream of Western Christianity. The second view has been embodied mainly by the renewal and breakaway groups often judged to be "heretics." At the heart of this divergence was the doctrine of the Spirit, and specifically two different views of how the Spirit constitutes the church. Gunton and others have argued that the mainstream Western tradition, when measured against the New Testament, was marked by a major deficiency in its pneumatology. The New Testament emphasizes the eschatological dimensions of the Spirit who makes real in the present life of the community the victory of Jesus over the powers and brings rich foretastes of God's goal for creation. But the Western church has tended to postpone the effects of Jesus' victory to a promised afterlife and "the Spirit has tended to be institutionalized, so that in place of the free, dynamic, personal and particular agency of the Spirit, he is made into a substance which becomes the possession of the church....[The result is] claiming too much of a realization of eschatology, while expecting too little of the community as a whole."[25]

Churches of Christ have undergone their own shift from one type of eschatology to the other. The second, more apocalyptic type described above can be seen in an important strand of the tradition running from Barton Stone down through David Lipscomb and James A. Harding at the turn of the twentieth century. These three important nineteenth-century shapers of the tradition of Churches of Christ, in contrast to Campbell, lived out of an apocalyptic vision. (Let me note here that though all three men held some version of classic premillennialism, an explicit premillennial stance is not a necessary feature of apocalypticism.[26]) We examined Stone's apocalypticism and its shaping of his ethics in Chapter 5 and noted Lipscomb's influence briefly in Chapter 2. Here we look briefly again at Lipscomb and add the witness of James Harding.

Catching the spirit of Lipscomb's life, one of his contemporaries noted that he "lives in utter disregard of the notions of the world." In a characteristic passage, Lipscomb wrote that the "religion of Christ was not only adapted to the common people, but despite all theories to the contrary, they are those best fitted to maintain and spread that religion. The rich corrupt it, the rich pervert it to suit their own fashionable ways." "The rich, and worse, those not rich who aspire to ape and court the rich, are the greatest corrupters of the church," he wrote in a common refrain. When the rich embrace the faith, he said, "ninety times out of every hundred their influence is to corrupt the church, lower the standard of morality, and relax all discipline in a church." God's people, Lipscomb believed, rejected worldly fashion and sought simplicity. For this reason he was appalled in 1892 when he heard that an Atlanta church had spent $30,000 on its new building. "When I hear of a church setting out to build a fine house," he wrote, "I give that church up. Its usefulness as a church of Christ is at an end."[27] These attitudes of Lipscomb were grounded explicitly in his understanding of God's inbreaking rule on the earth.

James Harding lived his life according to what he called God's law of "special providence." This meant, he said, that he tried to choose his work by the needs of the kingdom "without taking into consideration my financial interests at all, except to believe that God would supply my every need, if I worked faithfully for him." His only employment contract, he said, was a Matthew 6:33 contract: "Seek first his kingdom and his righteousness, and all these things shall be yours as well." Such a contract guarantees everything one needs, no matter the circumstances, he insisted. It does not depend on whether one pleases people or not, on sickness or on health, or on the size of one's family—but only upon pleasing the Lord.

Such a contract makes one free like nothing else, for God is a friend more loving and kind than any earthly father or mother, and his promises of care and blessing are more sure.[28]

God's promises of care and commands to trust, Harding stressed, are just as plain and certain as "He that believes and is baptized shall be saved" (which was a favorite and often repeated text among Churches of Christ); to reject one teaching is just as much unbelief as to reject the other. Harding accepted both. Late in his life, he could write: "For thirty-six years I have endeavored to follow the directions of Jesus literally. I have avoided the accumulation of property....I have no house, no land, no stock, no property except that which we daily use, no money laid up for the future."[29] He said that he rarely possessed as much as fifty dollars at one time and, when he did, most often used it for immediate needs. Harding too grounded these practices in his apocalyptic vision of God's kingdom. Not surprisingly, many of his fellows thought that he had gone dangerously overboard in his trust of God.

This apocalyptic strand was quite influential but by no means monolithic in the tradition. When Campbell's postmillennial eschatology faded,[30] as it quickly did after 1860, a significant segment of Churches of Christ were left with a biblical restorationism that equated the kingdom of God with Campbell's restored church. As this doctrine hardened into a more rigid orthodoxy, the apocalyptic strand represented by Lipscomb and Harding was denounced and cast off in the early twentieth century (see Chapter 2 and Chapter 5).

With this casting off, the Churches of Christ completed the shift to the other type of eschatology mentioned above—the more conventional and dominant eschatology which stands at some remove from the New Testament vision. Having confined the Spirit to the Bible (not so much to the institution) and virtually equated God's Kingdom with their fully restored True Church, Churches of Christ by the early to mid twentieth century largely fit Gunton's description cited above: an over-realized eschatology and an under-realized discipleship. The Spirit's present eschatological work in the church was minimized or denied, thus doctrinally undercutting the very conduit of kingdom life and empowered discipleship. Rather than an eschatological or end-time community where salvation is presently being realized, the church becomes an institution where people are (often moralistically) prepared for salvation.

The church becomes more of a holding tank, a place to wait for rescue and for heaven, rather than an end-time community, a colony of heaven, where through the Spirit's presence the community tastes rich appetizers from the heavenly banquet.

The difference between these two conceptions of eschatology and of the church lies fundamentally in the doctrine of the Spirit and how the Spirit constitutes the church. The New Testament emphasizes the present eschatological work of the Spirit, and the Spirit's freedom and dynamism in the community; later Christian tradition, particularly after the constantinian settlement, tended to institutionalize the Spirit and assume that Christians were mostly only preparing for the end, not already partaking partially of it.

For several decades biblical scholars and theologians have been rediscovering and recovering the fundamentally apocalyptic vision of the New Testament.[31] This vision had been eclipsed and mostly discarded in the late modern period, especially among the more liberal. Many modern theologians were embarrassed by eschatology, embarrassed by Jesus the apocalyptic prophet, and disturbed by the whiff of the radical it contained. Many who recognized an imminentist eschatology in the New Testament, including some Church of Christ scholars, simply assumed that Jesus and/or Paul were wrong about the timing of the *parousia*. But today most biblical scholars are coming to agree that the eschatological vision is an irreducible part of the vision of both Jesus and Paul, and some theologians are beginning to insist that such a vision remains a vital component of faithful discipleship.[32] But the recovery of these insights for the life of modern churches yet remains a largely incomplete task.

Several years ago, in a roundtable discussion with students training for ministry, Gordon Fee, a widely respected New Testament scholar, was asked, "If you were to return to the pastoral ministry, what would you emphasize?" Fee answered quickly, "No matter how long it might take, I would set about with a single passion to help a local body of believers recapture the New Testament church's understanding of itself as an eschatological community." In recounting this incident, Fee commented that the "one feature that probably more than any other distances the New Testament church from us is the thoroughgoing eschatological perspective from which believers viewed everything that God had wrought through Christ and the Spirit."[33]

This task of recovery is aided by the new cultural situation in America. As we saw in Chapter 7, "Christian America," with its neo-constantinian assumptions and practices, was largely displaced after the 1960s, so that believers now find themselves in a situation much more like that of the pre-constantinian church. Believers have thus been forced into a situation where they again must lean by faith on God's governance of history rather than America's governance of it, and where the Christian community must recover or reinvigorate the vision and practices that can maintain such faith in a hostile environment. That means, in short, recovery of the New Testament's apocalyptic vision—the vision with which the church was launched and which enabled it to flourish in faith in the midst of pagan religion and state persecution.

The New Testament's eschatological vision is critical for the discipleship of the Christian community. In Ernst Käsemann's terse conclusion, "apocalyptic [was] the mother of all Christian theology"[34]—and, we might add, of Christian ethics. But the apocalyptic horizon soon receded in the emergence of what scholars have called "early catholicism," and that recession had profound theological and ethical repercussions. As Beker puts it,

> once one's perspective on an imminent theophany—such as we find in Paul—is displaced by a different outlook, Christian faith is deeply affected. In other words, whenever the church becomes preoccupied with its own security and survival in the world and thus with the issues of ministerial order, apologetics, and the hostility or acceptance of outsiders, it surrenders its passion for God's imminent kingdom along with its longing for God's cosmic promise of salvation....The gospel instills in us a passion which no 'delay of the *parousia*' or ongoing chronology of history can truly affect.[35]

The result of this eschatological shift was—and is today—accommodation to the world and an "in-group" mentality in the church.

When the apocalyptic vision grows dim or is lost, as it has in the modern West, Christian life becomes conventional and tame. "Sin-habits dull our faith into stodgy moralism and respectable boredom," as Eugene Peterson put it. The church grows comfortable and sleepy, easily bored, forgetting that it is engaged in a great battle, an army against armies. Members become doctrinaire and dutiful, finding solemn comfort in the habits and forms of the old ways. Some readily retreat into a pietistic individualism, seeking the private sweetness of the Spirit's caresses but without the public buffetings that usually attend Christ's odd way. Mention "apocalyptic" and some believers may think you are talking about a new video game or the latest Star Trek movie.

But from time to time this state of affairs gets shaken up. Now and then, as Peterson says, "crisis rips the veneer of cliché off everyday routines and reveals the side-by-side splendors and terrors of heaven and hell." Apocalypse thus works as a kind of arson: "it secretly sets a fire in the imagination that boils the fat out of an obese culture-religion and renders a clear gospel love, a pure gospel hope, a purged gospel faith."[36]

Recovering a Lost Language

For some time I have found myself caught in the dilemma that has become the dilemma of much traditional Christianity, whether more conservative or more liberal. I find myself in a faith tradition that, though once quickened by a robust apocalypticism, now not only has lost that vision but, by and large, no longer finds it intelligible. I find myself in a community of faith that no longer speaks, as it were, the New Testament "language" of apocalyptic.

I grew up speaking a broken version of this language; it was still "spoken" some around my early household of faith (primarily as the legacy of David Lipscomb), but it had become by then only a kind of second language—second to the language of the One True Church fully restored. And second languages usually do not fare very well in the long run. Over the last decade or so I have tried hard to relearn this language and to "speak" it before my students and before those with whom I worship each week. But I have done so with limited intelligibility.

I remember vividly the day in class several years ago when one student got it. It was an upper division Christian Ethics course in a Christian university, and the class was full of bright, ambitious, and affluent students, most of them the children of Christian homes. We had spent a couple of weeks on the New Testament apocalyptic vision, contrasting it with the more familiar conventional Christian eschatology and showing how that vision shaped and undergirded Christian discipleship. Then for several more weeks I had come back to that vision time and again as we dealt with various other matters. Susan was an intense, serious, and rather out-spoken student aiming for a career in public service. One day in class about mid-semester she gave a big "Aha!" She appeared stunned. She said she had grown up in church but had never heard this before (which could, perhaps, be more a statement about her attentiveness and under-standing in church than of what was said and done there). She said that, if this was the New Testament vision, Christians—like her—would have to seriously rethink what it means to follow Christ today. Most others in the class, as I recall, got the information (for the exam) but I am not sure how many of them actually got it.

It may well be, of course, that I do not speak the language very well or that I speak it in a degenerate dialect. But my own fluency, I think, is not the central problem; neither is my skill as a teacher. It is rather that this language no longer remains a living language in my community of faith. Some people, to be sure, remember a good bit of the vocabulary. They still use some of the old words. But the old words have taken on different, more bland meanings. The grammar and syntax of apocalyptic have become foreign. And as a result some of the ways of discipleship that are defined and supported by that New Testament "language" no longer make much sense.

What we require is a recovery of the "idiom of apostolic apocalyptic."[37] But such recovery is deeply challenging. The trouble, it appears to me, is that apocalyptic cannot be translated faithfully into another language or idiom. It is a distinct idiom, and disciples must learn to "speak" it. Or rather we should say that disciples must be taught it, and be taught it by those in the Christian colony who "speak" it fluently. But when the colony has forgotten its native language through its eagerness to do business with its neighbors, how can that language—along with the social practices it enables—be recovered? That question remains one of the most fundamental and difficult questions with which I continue to wrestle.

Revelation 5 gives us a dramatic vision of the apocalyptic reality that transforms Christian language and practice.[38] The scene opens with a figure sitting on heaven's throne holding a scroll that is "sealed with seven seals." John the seer realizes that no one in heaven or on earth can open the scroll and declare its message, and so he begins to weep. But an elder's voice consoles him: stop weeping, he says; the Lion of the tribe of Judah has conquered and can open the scroll. And then the lion appears, but in the form of a Lamb "looking as if it had been slain." The Lamb takes the scroll, and immediately heaven's worshippers, joined by all of creation, lift up a great hymn of praise: "Worthy is the Lamb, who was slain" (5:8-14).

The sealed scroll, we may readily assume, symbolizes the secret of human destiny. The tears of the seer we may take as the tears of us all as we experience and contemplate earth's sorrows and evils-the persecutions, the endless wars, the ravages of disease, suffering, death. Why does human history go on? Why does not God end it all? And the Revelation gives us an answer near the close of the scene: "You are worthy to take the scroll and open its seals, because you were slain, and with your blood you purchased men for God from every tribe and language and people and nation. You have made them to be a kingdom and priests to serve our God, and they will reign on the earth" (5:9-10).

Why does this earthly drama continue? Because God is forming, here and now in the course of earth's history, a new race of human beings, a race called out from every race. Human history's basic and last task is the forming of a new community on the earth. It is a community formed by the Lamb that was slain and governed by the "politics of the Lamb." The sacrificial death of Jesus, through the power of the Spirit, has already formed this people. They are already a new people, a "kingdom of priests." And this new people is meant to rule the world under its risen Lord. But not as Caesar ruled, not as dictators and presidents now rule—not by swords and spears or tanks and bombs; not by might and power; not by the "politics of the lion." The Lamb's new nation will conquer, indeed, but by the very way of the Lamb, the very way that Jesus lived and died— triumph through a cross.

In the eyes of the world, which measures everything by the politics of power, compromise, and personal preference, the "politics of the Lamb" will appear strange and unworkable. It will appear much the same way to Christians whose fundamental convictions remain indebted to the modern tradition of liberal individualism. And indeed, in the short run this "politics" or way of living as a distinct people will often seem to fail. Yet the final outcome is certain, for in the heavenly hymn of Revelation 5 the Lamb has already passed his triumphal power to his kingdom of priests.

THE GREAT CULTURAL BAZAAR

This conviction about the triumph of the Lamb stands at the center of the New Testament's eschatological vision. Without such a vision, I am convinced, the church cannot occupy its proper minority stance in a liberal culture or in any other culture; without it, Christian communities will find it hard to resist setting up a flashy bargain table to hawk their wares in the great cultural bazaar.

In New Testament perspective, two realms (or aeons) exist side by side in human history. One is the world of sin and death, the other is the new humanity which makes up the body of Christ. Each of these two realms manifests itself socially or culturally. The old realm or "world" shows itself in the structures of human society in general (with its materialism, sensuality, racial barriers, economic conflicts, and declarations of human autonomy). The new realm (or aeon) shows itself in the church with its new social order or politics which is taking shape under Christ's Lordship and is modeled after the way of the cross.

This new order (now becoming visible in the church) must be kept uncontaminated by the old (the "world"). It must maintain a distinctive quality of existence. It must uphold radically different values, treat people in radically different ways, and nurture within its community a different view of reality. It must maintain an ethos where following the way of the cross becomes intelligible rather than appearing as blatant "foolishness"—which will always be how it appears to the world.

This means that the church must remain a distinct and, in a significant sense, a withdrawn community. It must live in opposition to the "world." When we say that, however, we must speak carefully. Paul does not instruct the church to close itself off from the secular world (which would, in any case, be impossible) or to cease all association with the immoral people of the world (1 Cor. 5:9-10). There must be separation, to be sure, "but not of the usual kind. The church is not prohibited from entering the world; the world is excluded from entering the church."[39]

The church thus does not simply withdraw from the "world" or adopt a passive stance toward social evil. Some kinds of apocalypticism promote such passivity and withdrawal but that is exactly what makes them unbiblical and unchristian.[40] But the church does stand apart from the "world" as a distinct entity. Rejecting the constantinian assumption of Christianity's majority status, we must assume that the faithful Christian community will always occupy a minority status in its culture—even in a so-called "Christian" culture. This separate, minority status does not mean isolating oneself from society or failing to participate in it. It certainly does not mean self-righteously elevating oneself above other sinful human beings. To the contrary, this sharp disavowal of the "world" and its values is done for the sake of the "world," for the love of the "world." The church remains a distinctive, minority community, not to isolate and protect itself, but because it believes that it can best serve the "world" by being faithfully and fully the church.

By seeing its minority status and becoming a distinctive and set-apart community, the church serves the world by enabling the world to see its true plight or lostness. As the realm of estrangement from God, the world lives by a clouded and distorted vision of reality. For this reason the world does not know that it is the world. It cannot recognize itself. It cannot name its most basic problem—rebellion against God and declaration of its own autonomy. In the language of John, it lives in darkness. Thus, as Stanley Hauerwas has written, "the church serves the world by giving the world the means to see itself truthfully."[41]

The church's first and highest calling, therefore, is to be the church. Richard Neuhaus put it clearly: "Because Christ is Lord, Caesar is not Lord. By humbling all secular claims to sovereignty, the church makes its most important political contribution by being, fully and unapologetically, the church."[42] It shuns violence and retaliation, and thus helps the world see the way of peace. It eschews control and manipulation of people, and thus shows the world the way of respect and equality. It breaks down racial and social distinctions in its midst, and thus shows the world the sinfulness and injustice of its divisions between people. It lets go of its possessions with joy and gladness, and thus exposes the world's idolatrous attachment to its money and possessions. In short, it proceeds by way of the "politics of the Lamb."

The church thus serves as the "light of the world." In this way at least part of the world may be able to recognize itself as "world." Part of the world may be able to see its lostness and deception, its chaos and sin. At the same time, however, much of the world will scorn the church for attempting to show the world its true nature.

The Christian eschatological vision is not only about *what comes last* but just as importantly it is about *what lasts*. To practice the "politics of the Lamb" means to testify faithfully to the way the world will be when God is through with it. But more, it means to embody that testimony, to live in the already inbreaking end-time reality even as we await its fullness. Walking in such a way means living in the dynamic fellowship of the Spirit and in the bright light of last(ing) things.[43]

Notes

1. *Epistle to Diognetus* 5.5.

2. On this momentous shift see John Yoder's seminal essays, "The Otherness of the Church" (1961), in *The Royal Priesthood: Essays Ecclesiological and Ecumenical*, ed. Michael G. Cartwright (Grand Rapids, MI: Eerdmans, 1994), 53-64, and "The Constantinian Sources of Western Social Ethics," in *The Priestly Kingdom: Social Ethics as Gospel* (Notre Dame, IN: University of Notre Dame, 1984), 135-47. See also Robert Lee Williams, "Persecution," in *Encyclopedia of Early Christianity*, ed. Everett Ferguson, et. al. (New York: Garland, 1990), 713-17, and Timothy D. Barnes, *Constantine and Eusebius* (Cambridge, MA: Harvard University, 1981), 48-53. For a very readable overview of this shift and its implications for contemporary Christians, see Rodney Clapp, *A Peculiar People: The Church as Culture in a Post-Christian Society* (Downers Grove, IL: InterVarsity, 1996), 22-31.

3. Ben Witherington, *Women in the Earliest Churches* (Cambridge: Cambridge University, 1988), 219.

4. Yoder, "The Constantinian Sources of Western Social Ethics," in *The Priestly Kingdom*, 137.

5. William Lee Miller, *The First Liberty: Religion and the American Republic* (New York: Alfred Knopf, 1986), 350; Yoder, *Priestly Kingdom*, 142. For extensive documentation of America's unofficial Protestant establishment, see Robert T. Handy, *A Christian America: Protestant Hopes and Historical Realities*, rev. ed. (Oxford, 1984); for the early period see Richard J. Carwardine, *Evangelicals and Politics in Antebellum America* (New Haven, CT: Yale University, 1993).

6. The moral neutrality of the liberal state is, of course, an illusion. As J. Budziszewski put it: "The scandal of Neutrality is that its worshipers cannot answer the question 'Why be neutral?' without committing themselves to particular goods—social peace, self-expression, self-esteem, ethnic pride, or what have you—thereby violating their own desideratum of Neutrality." *True Tolerance: Liberalism and the*

Necessity of Judgment (Transaction, 1993). Richard Neuhaus underscores the same basic point: "one problem with the naked public square is that it never remains, it cannot remain, naked. Exclude explicit moral judgment from the public square, and moral judgments that dare not speak their name will come in to take their place." "The Couture of the Public Square," *First Things* (December 1993), 68.

7. In this characterization of liberalism, I have drawn on Alasdair McIntyre, *Whose Justice? Which Rationality?* (South Bend, IN: University of Notre Dame, 1988), 335-48. For a critique of McIntyre and a more positive assessment of liberalism, see Jeffrey Stout, *Ethics After Babel* (Boston: Beacon, 1988).

8. The liberal political tradition contains considerable diversity in moral outlook, so I am speaking here of broad tendencies. See Nancy L. Rosenblum, *Liberalism and the Moral Life* (Cambridge, MA: Harvard University, 1989).

9. Stanley Hauerwas, *The Peaceable Kingdom: A Primer in Christian Ethics* (South Bend, IN: University of Notre Dame, 1983), 7-9.

10. See Roger Lundin, "The Ultimately Liberal Condition," *First Things* (April 1995), 22-27.

11. James Edwards, *The Plain Sense of Things: The Fate of Religion in an Age of Normal Nihilism* (University Park, PA: Pennsylvania State University, 1996), 47.

12. Ibid., 50, 55.

13. Stanley Hauerwas, "How Christian Universities Contribute to the Corruption of Youth," in *Christian Existence Today* (Durham, NC: Labyrinth, 1988), 24-43. See also McIntyre, *Three Rival Versions of Moral Enquiry: Encyclopedia, Genealogy, and Tradition* (Notre Dame: University of Notre Dame, 1990), p. 219.

14. On this point see Max Stackhouse, "Piety, Polity, and Policy," in *Religious Beliefs, Human Rights, and the Moral Foundation of Western Democracy*, ed. Carl Esbeck (Columbia, MO: University of Missouri, 1986), 23.

15. James H. Smylie, "National Ethos and the Church," *Theology Today* (1964).

16. On the widespread blending of civic liberty and Christian faith in this period see Nathan Hatch, *The Sacred Cause of Liberty: Republican Thought and the Millennium in Revolutionary New England* (New Haven, CT: Yale University, 1977), 170-75, and Sidney Mead, "The Nation with the Soul of a Church," *Church History* 36 (1967), 262-83.

17. See George Phillips, "Differences in the Theological and Philosophical Background of Alexander Campbell and Barton W. Stone" (Ph.D. diss., Vanderbilt University, 1968), 87-92.

18. Campbell, *Popular Lectures and Addresses,* p. 179. See Richard T. Hughes and C. Leonard Allen, "From Primitive Church to Civil Religion," in *Illusions of Innocence: Protestant Primitivism in America, 1630-1875* (Chicago: University of Chicago, 1988).

19. Thomas Hietala, *Manifest Design: Anxious Aggrandizement in Late Jacksonian America* (New York: Cornell University, 1985), 2.

20. This paragraph and the next three are adapted from Leonard Allen, "Testing the Metal of Pacifism," in *Proclaim Peace: Voices of Christian Pacifism in America Outside the Historic Peace Churches,* ed. Theron F. Schlabach (Urbana, IL: University

of Illinois, 1996).

21. Campbell could write that the "distinguishing characteristic [of the current reformation] is, A RESTORATION OF THE ORDINANCES OF THE NEW INSTITUTION TO THEIR PLACE AND POWER." "The Ordinances," *Millennial Harbinger*, new series, 7 (January 1843), 9.

22. Alexander Campbell, "Opinionisms—No. 1," *Millennial Harbinger*, 5th series, 2 (August 1859), 436-37.

23. To call Paul's framework of thought "apocalyptic" is not to say that Paul writes in the genre of apocalyptic. As J. C. Beker puts its, "Paul is a writer of letters and not of apocalypses; he uses apocalyptic motifs but not the genre of apocalypse. Whereas the apocalyptic composition often concentrates on a timetable of events or on a program for the sake of calculating apocalyptic events, Paul stresses to the contrary the incalculability of the end....Paul emphasizes the unexpected, the suddenness and surprising character of the final theophany (1 Thess. 5:2-10). Moreover the incalculable nature of the end motivates Paul to restrain severely his use of apocalyptic language and imagery....Thus the delay of the *parousia* is not a theological concern for Paul. It is not an embarrassment for him; it does not compel him to shift the center of his attention from apocalyptic imminence to a form of 'realized eschatology,' that is to a conviction of the full presence of the kingdom of God in our present history. *Paul's Apocalyptic Gospel: The Coming Triumph of God* (Philadelphia: Fortress, 1982), 48-9. See also Ben Witherington, *Jesus, Paul and the End of the World: A Comparative Study in New Testament Eschatology* (Downers Grove, IL: InterVarsity, 1992), 23-35.

24. Yoder, *Priestly Kingdom*, 85-6.

25. Colin Gunton, "The Community: The Trinity and the Being of the Church," *The Promise of Trinitarian Theology* (Edinburgh, Scotland: T & T Clark, 1991), 65.

26. In Christ's first coming, Barton Stone said, "he abode but a few years on earth; in his second coming he will abide 1000, and not leave the world, till he [has]... assigned to each one his eternal portion." In 1833 Stone wrote that when Christ returns the saints who are alive will be changed from mortal to immortal "and reign with the Lord on the earth 1000 years—this is the first resurrection. The second resurrection is of the wicked, which shall take place after the 1000 years are finished." Barton Stone, "The Millennium," *Christian Messenger* 7 (October 1833), 314. James Harding wrote: "During this thousand years, Christ and his saints reign; but the rest of the dead live not again till the thousand years have expired....This millennial reign will be on the earth," and it will be a time when Christians will enjoy a "perfect rest from sin." James Harding, "The Kingdom of Christ vs. the Kingdom of Satan," *The Way* 5 (October 15, 1903), 929-31. For David Lipscomb's views, see *Civil Government: Its Origin, Mission, and Destiny and the Christian's Relation to It* (Nashville, TN: McQuiddy, 1889).

27. David Lipscomb, "A Visit to Chattanooga," *Gospel Advocate* 36 (April 3, 1889), 214; Lipscomb, "Fine Houses for Worship," ibid. 39 (January 28, 1892), 52. See Anthony Dunnavant, "David Lipscomb on the Church and the Poor," *Restoration Quarterly* 33 (1991), 75-85.

28. See for example, James Harding, "The Greatest Hindrance to the Spread of the Gospel," *The Way* 3 (March 6, 1902), 377-79, and "In Whom Shall We Trust?" ibid. 3 (April 18, 1901), 18-20.

29. James Harding and L. S. White, *The Harding-White Discussion* (Cincinnati, OH, 1910).

30. See James H. Moorhead, "The Erosion of Postmillennialism in American Religious Thought, 1865-1925," *Church History* 53 (March 1984), 61-77.

31. See N. T. Wright, *Jesus and the Victory of God* (Minneapolis, MN: Fortress, 1996), and Klaus Koch, *The Rediscovery of Apocalyptic: A Polemical Work on a Neglected Area of Biblical Studies and Its Damaging Effects on Theology and Philosophy* (London: SCM, 1972).

32. On Jesus, see N. T. Wright's recent, major contribution to this recovery, *Jesus and the Victory of God;* on Paul, see the work of J. Christian Beker, *Paul's Apocalyptic Gospel;* for Christian theology, see Jürgen Moltman, *The Way of Jesus Christ: Christology in Messianic Dimension* (Minneapolis, MN: Fortress, 1993). Wright says, for example: "To postpone the effectiveness of his [Jesus'] victory to an after-life, as has been done so often in the Christian tradition, or to transform it into the victory of true ideas over false ones…is to de-Judaize Jesus' programme completely. It is to fail to take seriously his stark prayer for the kingdom to come, and God's will to be done, on earth as it is in heaven." The first Christians followed neither of these two options: "they announced and celebrated the victory of Jesus over evil as something that had already happened, something that related pretty directly to the real world, their world. There was still a mopping-up battle to be fought, but the real victory had been accomplished. That was the basis of their announcement to the principalities and powers that their time was up. That was the basis of their remarkable joy…." (659).

33. Gordon Fee, *Paul, the Spirit, and the People of God* (Peabody, MA: Hendrickson, 1996), 49.

34. Ernst Käsemann, "On the Subject of Primitive Christian Apocalyptic," in *New Testament Questions of Today* (Philadelphia, PA: Fortress, 1969), 137.

35. J. Christiaan Beker, "The Promise of Paul's Apocalyptic for Our Time," in *The Future of Christology*, ed. Abraham J. Malherbe and Wayne A. Meeks (Minneapolis: Fortress, 1993), 157-58, 159. Moltmann points to a specific example: how modern Christians view the healing miracles of Jesus. "Once this eschatological horizon disappears," he argues, "the [healing] miracles cease to point to the beginning of the new creation of all things; and they then stand on their own as marvels in an untransformed world." The healing stories will regain their relevance to us, he concludes, to the extent that we restore the eschatological horizon of New Testament faith. *The Way of Jesus Christ*, 189.

36. Eugene Peterson, *The Contemplative Pastor: Returning to the Art of Spiritual Direction* (reprint ed, Eerdmans, 1993), 41.

37. Yoder, "Armaments and Eschatology," *Studies in Christian Ethics* 1.1 (1988), 47.

38. I am dependent here on John H. Yoder in "The Politics of the Lamb," *Seek Peace and Pursue It: Proceedings from the 1988 International Baptist Peace*

Conference, Sjovik, Sweden, ed. H. Wayne Pipkin (Memphis, TN: Baptist Peace Fellowship, 1988), 69-76, and James McClendon, *Doctrine*, 98-100.

39. Robin Scroggs, *Paul for a New Day* (Philadelphia: Fortress, 1977), 52.

40. Yoder argues that "Schweitzer's thesis, generally accepted by liberal theologians, that the eschatological expectancy of the early church led to ethical irresponsibility, is simply wrong, exegetically and historically." "Peace without Eschatology?" in *The Royal Priesthood*, 157-58. Indeed, apocalyptic expectancy formed the very foundation of Jesus' and Paul's ethical teaching.

41. Hauerwas, *Peaceable Kingdom*, 101-102.

42. Richard J. Neuhaus, "Christianity and Democracy," *Center Journal* (Summer 1982), 9-25.

43. I am indebted to James McClendon for this last phrase, which also serves as the title of this essay. His systematic work exemplifies what it means to bring eschatology from its place at the rear—and sometimes only as an afterthought—to its properly central place in Christian doctrine. *Systematic Theology, 2: Doctrine*, 69-102.

CHAPTER NINE

THINGS UNSEEN:
A MODERN CHURCH AFTER MODERNITY

Today Churches of Christ are a modern church entering a world in which modernity is losing its dominance. This reality, probably more than any other factor, accounts for the swift and disorienting changes besetting Churches of Christ at the close of the twentieth century. Indeed, the changes underway are more profound and sweeping than those most worried about change seem yet to realize.

Various voices within the tradition are examining the symptoms and attempting to diagnose the illness. One voice is F. LaGard Smith, former professor of law at Pepperdine University and accomplished Christian author. In his book, *Who Is My Brother?* (1997), Smith asserts that Churches of Christ are undergoing a "quiet revolution," and that few seem properly concerned. A growing number of members are quietly but quickly coming to acknowledge as fellow Christians all those who have faith in Jesus regardless of how they understand and practice baptism. Caught up in a "frenzy of ecumenical fervor," Smith argues, Churches of Christ are presently experiencing a "radical abandonment of settled doctrine" regarding matters like baptism and fellowship. The Protestant "faith only" doctrine is replacing the historic insistence on the essentiality of baptism, with the result that their "exclusive circle of fellowship" is breaking down. Churches of Christ therefore are facing a sharp and troubling crisis of identity.[1]

Smith is a skilled polemicist who speaks the language of traditional members, articulating their unease in this topsy-turvy time and shoring up the doctrinal system they have long embraced. His book belongs to a venerable genre: defense of Churches of Christ as the One True Church over against the "doctrinally rebellious denominations." Written with more skill and charity than most works in the genre, it nonetheless sharply restates the exclusive view of fellowship traditionally held by Churches of Christ. With urgency and deep concern, the author lays out what he sees as the underlying causes of this "quiet revolution": biblical illiteracy, the frenzy for church growth, the impact of the Promise Keepers movement, and the retooling of the traditional theology to justify what people have already decided to do.

Smith is correct that Churches of Christ are indeed undergoing a crisis of identity, a crisis bringing disarray, deep unrest, and dissipation. For the doctrinal system that Smith and numerous others are now trying to shore up against extensive erosion has comprised the core tradition of Churches of Christ for well over a century. Without this system it is unclear who or what they will be. Without it, to the minds of many members, they would have little reason to be a separate body at all. Without it they would have to forge a new identity—an arduous, uncertain, and psychologically stressful undertaking.

But the factors Smith holds up as causes of this "quiet revolution" are themselves mostly symptoms of a much larger, more momentous shift.

A MODERN CHURCH AFTER MODERNITY

One of the central themes of this book has been that the theology of Churches of Christ—their way of reading the Bible, their philosophical assumptions, and their basic worldview—was formed in the context of the moderate Enlightenment in eighteenth-century England and early nineteenth-century America. This meant not only embracing Baconian natural science as a grid for reading the Bible, but also accommodating the new individualism and populism of American democratic culture.

The vigorous embrace of these powerful cultural forces was essentially hidden by the illusion that Churches of Christ had escaped tradition.

They had become first-century Christians, nothing more or less. No creed but the Bible. No timeworn, human ideologies to pervert their vision. No faded or contrived imitations. Just Bible facts. Just the thing itself.[2]

For good or for ill—probably for both—the world that upheld such assumptions is collapsing, and a new era is emerging. We are now in a time of worldview change. The modern worldview, with its built-in secular biases and boundless confidence that humans could manage, unite, and control the world, is being dislodged. Some would say it is crumbling.

According to Diogenes Allen, the modern worldview was built upon four key foundational pillars: (1) the assumption that the idea of God was superfluous to the modern project; (2) the confidence that morality could be based on reason apart from revelation; (3) the inevitability of cultural and scientific progress; and (4) the conviction that all knowledge is good. Each of these pillars is crumbling, with the result that the structure of modernity is toppling. Though the postmodern era presents new and dangerous challenges to Christians, it means a new freedom for Christians to profess their faith more fully and less apologetically. And it means that Christian theologians "no longer need to labor within the tight, asphyxiating little world of the Enlightenment or to become premodern."[3]

The reasons for this shift are complex. To put it simply, the human spirit cannot remain vigorous and strong while breathing the steadily dissipating air of modernity. As people have climbed up the mountain of modernity the air has gotten thinner and thinner, and they have found themselves gasping for breath. Furthermore, the modern age simply has not made good on some of its boldest promises, especially the promise of steady progress toward social utopia. The "technological bluff"—the long-unquestioned conviction that technology will one day solve our problems—has been called. As Thomas Oden put it, the "leaky condom" provides an apt symbol of the failure of modernity. The prestige of scientific definitions of reality is diminishing; the invisible spiritual realm is now becoming more real and palpable to Western people.

Most scholars and cultural analysts agree that the long-dominant, modern worldview is receding, if not collapsing, but it is difficult to say what is emerging. Many are calling it "postmodern," a term that has somewhat different meanings across different disciplines. According to one influential theorist, "the word postmodern...designates the state of our culture following the transformations which, since the end of the nineteenth century, have altered the game rules for science, literature, and the arts." In its simplest form, he says, it means "incredulity toward meta-narratives." In the modern West the meta-narrative or overarching, controlling story was the Enlightenment story of scientific and cultural progress that emerged and became dominant over the last three centuries.[4]

But in the postmodern period this grand narrative has been overturned, indeed the very possibility of such narratives is rejected. Instead there is only a proliferation of "belief systems," all of them local and personal. As Walter Anderson put it,

> This postmodern world looks and feels in many ways like the modern world that preceded it; we still have the belief systems that gave form to the modern world, and indeed we also have remnants of many of the belief systems of premodern societies. If there is anything we have plenty of it is belief systems. But we also have something else: a growing suspicion that all belief systems—all ideas about human reality—are social constructions.[5]

Other theorists of the postmodern have pointed to a basic shift in the socio-economic structure of Western society, a shift from management by rational bureaucracies to a more open, fluid, and dynamic culture resulting from new developments in technology and education.[6]

I advance no particular theory of the postmodern; I use the term reluctantly, and then primarily to mean that the worldview or ethos called modernity has been, for some time, receding and being replaced by something else; that something else is whatever comes after the modern. And what comes after modernity is not one thing but an array of things, all of which can be characterized in certain broad strokes but which probably defy, for now, a general theory of the "postmodern."[7]

The following are some of the generally recognized broad features of this new era:

> (1) A sharp increase in the rate and amount of cultural change; a culture where high technology and mass media create change more rapidly than any previous culture.
> (2) The social construction of reality.
> (3) The loss of supposed universals and common goods. As

people become more and more aware that we live not in a single Culture but among many cultures, this awareness creates the sense that truth is relative and that "the good" is determined by one's own tastes and preferences.

(4) A loss of confidence in and profound uneasiness about science.

(5) A strong sense of the ironic, the growing sense that the best laid plans and best intentions often turn out to have contrary, even opposite, results.

(6) An awareness of the inescapability of tradition and community.

(7) The resacralization of a world that has become secular.[8]

In a world after modernity, there is more openness to the transcendent and spiritual realm. For more than two centuries Christian faith has been on the defensive against the steady encroachment of the secular and scientific worldview. Christian intellectuals and apologists have, to varying degrees, sought to accommodate that worldview. But now, with the decline of the modern worldview, believers can embrace more easily the full wealth of historic Christian convictions, some of which—miracles, the Trinity, and the Holy Spirit, for example—were readily sacrificed or compromised to accommodate modernity. Churches of Christ, like other conservative Christian traditions, ardently opposed theological modernism with its anti-supernatural bias and ready embrace of the spirit of the age; but ironically the theological tradition running from Campbell down to present-day churches has been notably shaped and compromised by the spirit of its founding age: the moderate Enlightenment and American democracy.

Nowhere is this seen more clearly than in matters of the Spirit and Spirituality. As we saw in Chapter 3, the main trajectory of the tradition has held a "Word only" view of the Spirit's present work and has held that, since the first century, God has worked only through "natural," not "supernatural," agency. As Z. T. Sweeney put it with memorable simplicity, "God does no unnecessary work, and the work of the Paraclete is not necessary now." This stance has meant not only a staunch cessationist view of all miracles and *charismata* but the consignment of many other New Testament texts to a first-century ghetto. The exhortation to call the elders for healing prayer in James 5:13-15, for example, no longer applies, for the elders obviously had miraculous power to heal, and since miracles have ceased, no one can possess that power anymore. Prayer brings forth no miracles; Christians are to pray for God's providence to aid the sick, and "God works his providence through natural laws—the doctors, nurses, medicines, technologies, as well as the prayers of the saints."[9]

In 1865 J. B. Grubbs stated that "No one of prominence in the brotherhood has ever advocated that miracles have been used by God since the first century."[10] Though not technically correct—Barton Stone and others in his early circle believed God continued to work miracles—this statement does generally describe the tradition both before and after 1865. In general, the tradition has read the Bible through a grid which sharply separated the "natural" and the "supernatural," limited Divine agency in the present age to the "natural," and assigned the experience of Divine Presence only to Bible times. This grid was forged only in modern times and is largely foreign to the world of the Bible itself.[11]

The impact of such a modern grid on the interpretation of scripture was focused deftly by Karl Barth when he wrote that the question, "What is within the Bible? has a mortifying way of converting itself into the opposing question, Well, what are you looking for?" He added: "We shall always find in the Bible as much as we seek and no more."[12]

After modernity, such a modern interpretive grid will appear more and more problematic. Not only will it become more of a problem exegetically and theologically in light of Biblical reality, but also more of a problem in its relevance and appeal to people open to and hungry for Spiritual reality and experience. The idea of a limited, first-century age of miracles—that miracles were necessary for completing and verifying Scripture and establishing the church but after that was done ceased to occur—has been in decline for several generations. By 1930, this view had lost its dominant role in English-speaking Protestantism.[13] From the 1960s to the 1990s interest in and openness to the miraculous dramatically increased. In 1995, for example, a *Time* magazine poll found that 69% of all Americans believed in the possibility of miracles in the world today. This development, Robert Mullin recently noted, has been one of the most remarkable occurrences in American Christianity during the last thirty years.[14] It is one sign of what has been called the collapse of modernity's "brass heaven" and the emergence of a worldview more open to the power and presence of God.

Churches of Christ, no doubt, will continue to react against the trendy and fashionable spiritualities of the time, the running after spiritual experiences, the charismatic hype and excesses portrayed in the media—and there will be considerable substance to their critique of these trends. But their own theological tradition, which has tended to be reactionary rather than constructive, ill-equips them for the recovery of a robust and balanced Spirituality based in the triune life of God. In recent years a good number of Church of Christ members have been drawn to the wave of small groups studying material like Henry Blackaby's *Experiencing God* (1992) that comes out of the Baptist "deeper life" tradition,[15] and to books like Richard Foster's *Prayer: The Heart's True Home* (1994) with roots in Quaker spirituality. These materials clash sharply with some of the basic theological tenets of Churches of Christ; but the embrace of these materials can be seen as a kind of grassroots critique of a tradition devoid both of language to talk about experiencing God and a theological framework able to account for and discipline such experience.

After modernity, the more "charismatic" or "third wave" expressions of Christian faith will continue to form a major part of the vanguard of the Christian movement around the world. These churches take many forms and cannot be viewed as a monolithic movement; nor should they necessarily be lumped together with the crass and sensationalized variety visible in the American media. They are a major force in worldwide Christianity and prominent theologians are taking them seriously.[16] But Churches of Christ have been, and likely will remain, unable to enter into any significant, constructive dialogue with this huge, mission-oriented part of God's Kingdom today. For traditionalists the matter is clearcut and simple: these movements are all bogus since miracles and the *charismata* have ceased to occur.[17] For progressives the matter is more complex: charismatics are embarrassing as well as politically incorrect within the tradition, and the charismatic style is beyond their experience and comfort zones. Further, some progressives, like the traditionalists, still have worldview barriers to charismatic reality, though, unlike the traditionalists, they would not use the old cessationist arguments and proof texts to nullify it.[18] In general Churches of Christ maintain a strong distaste for all things "charismatic," and the fear of excess outweighs any positive features they might be able to acknowledge.

After modernity, it is not that Churches of Christ need to "get in step" with the (post)modern culture and adopt its vocabulary so they can be more relevant and attractive to the denizens of this strange new age; rather, it is that the challenges of this new era can reopen doors to Christian truth that were closed or seldom used in modernity and lead to the reintroduction of Christian practices that have atrophied in its thin air. The jarring and shaking of these times can awaken Christians to a more faithful and robust practice of their faith and to a fuller confession of its historic truth.

TRINITARIAN THEOLOGY AND SPIRITUAL LIFE

By far the most important recovery of neglected Christian practice and truth that the change of eras is making possible, particularly for Churches of Christ, is a practical or functional doctrine of the Trinity. This claim may sound odd to many Christians, and perhaps even unintelligible at first—which may in itself be a sign of the problem we face.

The doctrine of the Trinity has been in steady recession in the modern period, and this eclipse stands behind the rise of modern unitarian, rationalistic, Christological, and other heresies. The reasons for the decline are at least two. First, the traditional Western Trinitarian doctrine was increasingly judged to be an inherited dogma that was dense, arcane, and of little relevance to Christians and to the modern world. It was viewed as remote from the actual needs and concerns of believers. Some Christian leaders thus became hostile to the doctrine and many became indifferent. Second, the traditional doctrine did not fare well against the criterion of "reasonableness" that became ever more dominant in the Enlightenment. The Deists and other proponents of "natural religion" found the doctrine an offense to reason and simply lopped it off. Most others did not reject the doctrine outright, but it became functionally peripheral to a Christian faith increasingly measured and limited by the canons of human reason. This more subtle form of eclipse can be seen in the line of "supernatural rationalism" that runs from the Christian philosopher John Locke down through Alexander Campbell and other progressive Christian thinkers of the eighteenth and early nineteenth centuries.[19] In Robert W. Jenson's judgment, "the inherited doctrine of the Trinity was by the opening of the nineteenth century nearly defunct in all those parts of the church open to modernity."[20] To put the matter over simply, God's relationality was overshadowed by mechanism. Mystery was eclipsed by method.

Others forms of eclipse have been added to these older ones in more recent years. Some biblical scholars, for example, have in effect become binitarian by insisting that the New Testament does not compel us to make a person out of the Spirit as in traditional Trinitarian doctrine.[21]

All this is not to say that the traditional Trinitarian doctrine in the West was free of problems. These older Enlightenment, as well as the more recent, rejections of Trinitarian doctrine are based, in part, on the assumption that the classic Western doctrine *is* the doctrine of the Trinity. But the received Western doctrine (strongly indebted to Augustine for its formulation) was marked by abstract, heavily philosophical analysis and alien, Hellenistic assumptions about deity. God was assumed, for example, to be "impassable" (or passionless), an attribute that directly counters the biblical story of God's anguished interaction with Israel. As a result, the classic form of the doctrine, with its distortions, helped precipitate its modern eclipse.

The new environment that many like to call "postmodern" is aiding the recovery of a robust and more sound Trinitarian faith and practice. The recovery of the doctrine was launched in the early twentieth century by Karl Barth, though his own doctrine was not sufficiently freed from the Western distortions. Over the last twenty-five years other theologians from a variety of traditions have advanced this recovery in fresh and faithful ways.[22]

What has emerged from these efforts is a recovery of God's relationality—or what is sometimes called the social Trinity (see John 17:20-26). In this view God is understood as a community of persons rather than as three modes of being. God is not a solitary, domineering individual who rules through arbitrary exercise of power but rather the perfect model of loving community—becoming vulnerable, entering into partnership, sharing the divine life, loving like a parent. As a contemporary spiritual writer has put it:

God is not a solitary.
That is why He is not alone.
He is a Trinity.
If He were only unity, He would be a solitary.
But, being love, He is a Trinity, Father, Son, and Spirit.
The Father is life, and He is the source of all things;
the Son is the image of the Father, and He is light;
the Holy Spirit is the love which unites them,

and He is a divine person.

God, being love, is communication....

The love of the Trinity is the new kind of love proposed to man.

But it is impossible to live it without the Trinity within us.

That is why the Christian is 'inhabited.'

He is 'inhabited' by the Trinity.

"Anyone who loves me will be true to my word, and my Father will love him; we will come to him and make our dwelling place with him" (John 14:23).[23]

In this view God is essentially dynamic, relational, and ecstatic (going outside oneself). God is the very paragon of love in relationship, of living in intimate community and submissive freedom—the God who loved Israel like Hosea loved Gomer and who so loved the world that he sent his only Son. And God invites human beings, his creatures, to share the rich life and fellowship of the divine community, and through partaking of that life to become like his Son.[24]

The basic problem faced by Churches of Christ at this juncture lies here, and it is fundamentally doctrinal or theological. Defenders of the tradition, like LaGard Smith, deplore "doctrinal dithering" and issue strong calls for doctrinal purity. I agree. And that, ironically, is the deepest problem with Smith's book and its genre—doctrinal deficiency. The long lineage of polemical writings in this genre, as a whole, has slipped away from the central, anchoring, orienting doctrine of the faith: the Trinity. Indeed, the doctrinal tradition as a whole has been off-center. Though most leaders have affirmed the Father, Son, and Spirit, Churches of Christ have had a very weak doctrine of the Trinity.

This may at first appear to be an odd, even outlandish, claim. "Of course we believe in the Father, the Son, and the Holy Spirit. Three in one, one in three. What's the problem?" The problem is not believing in the Father, Son, and Spirit, of course; any serious biblicist does that. The problem is a Trinitarian theology and practice, a functional doctrine of the Trinity that centers and deeply shapes not only one's theology but especially one's worship. There is a large difference between affirming a doctrine of the Trinity and being Trinitarian.

As I have stressed over and over to theology students over the years, the doctrine of the Trinity is not about some strange heavenly arithmetic that theologians like to play with. It is rather a kind of shorthand for referring to what we know of God now that Jesus has come and the Spirit has been poured out. Though a deep mystery, the Trinity is a crucially practical doctrine—practical in the sense that it fundamentally shapes our practices. For the way we understand God's way of loving and relating to people sets the pattern for how his followers conduct their life together and carry out their ministry to the world.

The Trinity provides our pattern or exemplar for unity and fellowship. God leads a relational life as Father, Son, and Spirit. That life is characterized by submissive love, as each member of the Trinity pours his life into the other. In God's own self there is an abundant outpouring of life, so abundant that it overflows and creates community with God's creatures—those outside the relationship within God. Through the sending of the Son and the outpouring of the Spirit, God pours this rich life into his creatures. As Diogenes Allen puts it: "The life of the Trinity is a perfect community and it is the kind of community for which we long; it satisfies our craving to be loved perfectly and to be attached to others properly."[25]

We partake of the Trinitarian life in several ways: sacramentally (to use a word that is awkward for Churches of Christ) through observing Christ's ordinances, doxologically as we draw near to God and God to us, charismatically (another awkward word) through divine gifts of grace, and pneumatologically through the mystery of the indwelling Spirit. The Trinity is the doctrinal center and fulcrum of the Christian faith. To change the metaphor, it is the prism through which all other doctrinal features of the faith are lighted and put in perspective. Indeed, the Trinitarian doctrine encapsulates and preserves the uniquely Christian view of God's relational character.

When this doctrine functionally recedes, as it has done in the modern period, there are many, often subtle, consequences. One easily falls prey to sectarianism or overly narrow views of God's Kingdom; to various forms of legalism, all of which misconstrue the nature of God's relationality; to authoritarianism, which misconstrues the character of Christ's exercise of authority; to spiritual triumphalism, which downplays the cruciform nature of discipleship; to spiritual elitism, which distorts the purpose of the Spirit's power and gifts; to constricted or mechanical understandings of the ordinances or sacraments in Christian life; and other assorted ills, heresies, and disruptions in the life of the church.

One example can be seen in what one observer has called "a morbid fondness for controversy" in the movement.[26] The rancor and division that has so marked the tradition of Churches of Christ is not simply an unfortunate consequence of garrulous or prideful personalities (one will always have those in good supply); rather it is a theological problem. "Having decimated our own brothers through years of infighting," LaGard Smith laments, "we have rendered ourselves unable to fight the real enemy."[27] True. But the traditional theological agenda he defends is virtually guaranteed to continue it. This is why I say that the basic problem is a fundamental doctrinal weakness in the tradition that has the effect of skewing basic Christian practices like unity, peaceableness, and forgiveness.

Another result of the eclipse of Trinitarian faith and practice among Churches of Christ is their exclusive view of fellowship in Christ. Though Alexander Campbell and certainly Barton Stone did not take an exclusivist stance, a staunch exclusivism began to emerge in Campbell's reform movement by the early 1830s. This exclusivism remained a strong and swelling stream among the conservatives who eventually became the Churches of Christ. Moses E. Lard, Tolbert Fanning, David Lipscomb, E. G. Sewell, James A. Harding, and Austin McGary—all mid to late nineteenth-century leaders who played a major role in the formation of the Churches of Christ as a distinct and separate tradition—held staunchly to an exclusivist position. "I mean to say distinctly and emphatically," Moses Lard wrote in 1863, "that Martin Luther, if not immersed, was not a Christian...I recognize no human being as a Christian who is not immersed." In 1887 James Harding affirmed that the unimmersed "are not in the kingdom, not in the church, not in Christ; but they are out of Christ, in the world, in their sins." For many in the movement, immersion itself was not sufficient—one must be immersed for the right reason. A strict exclusivist in Texas said, "We do not recognize Baptists as Christians, because they have not been baptized for the remission of sins."[28] This latter view became dominant among Churches of Christ by the early twentieth century; and throughout the century most congregations have not accepted Baptist baptism (and certainly not infant baptism) but insisted that a person must understand the proper purpose of baptism for it to be valid.

The exclusivism that marked the early Churches of Christ continued down through the mid to late twentieth century. In 1963 Reuel Lemmons, a prominent editor and preacher among mainstream churches, said that the hope of salvation is not extended to the unimmersed; rather, believer's immersion for the remission of sins is "essential to salvation, essential to citizenship in the kingdom of God, and essential to the fellowship of the saints." Furthermore, no one can serve and worship God acceptably in a "denomination"; the "Lord's church" is an entirely different institution, and today the Churches of Christ are identical with that church founded on the day of Pentecost.[29] Thomas B. Warren, long-time editor of an influential periodical, *The Spiritual Sword,* and vehement champion of an even stricter exclusivism, often stated flatly that everyone who has not submitted to proper baptism (as Churches of Christ have traditionally interpreted it) will be eternally lost, no matter how sincere their faith or how pious their lives.[30] And most recently LaGard Smith has put a slightly softer spin on the traditional exclusivism by making a distinction between "faith fellowship" and "'in Christ' fellowship": the first is what Christians share with all those who love God and profess faith in Jesus but who, because they have not experienced the new birth according to the biblical pattern, are "still outside the boundaries of the kingdom"; the second is what Christians share with Christ and with all those who have been baptized as adults for the remission of sins.[31]

With such a view Churches of Christ in effect denied the Christian status of most believers outside their own ranks—though many were reluctant to put it so bluntly.[32] As a logical result, they have been almost completely uninvolved throughout their history in any cooperative or unitive efforts with the "denominations," for they have approached them typically as non-Christians in need of conversion rather than as fellow Christians in need of reformation.

In a 1983 study of Churches of Christ's attitude toward other denominations, Myer Phillips concluded that, despite the significant growth of a softened, more inclusive attitude beginning after 1960, the "attitude of sectarian exclusivism is probably still the attitude reflected by most Church of Christ leaders and spokesmen."[33] By the end of the twentieth century the traditional exclusivism had given up more ground, but the momentum of the tradition still remained strong enough that the politics controlling most congregations, colleges, and other institutions did not allow open, "official" fellowship even with Baptists, much less non-immersionist believers. Even many of today's progressive leaders who, in private conviction, have broken with the tradition of exclusivism still remain constrained by it in public practice. The old dogma is breaking down considerably across both pulpit and pew—Smith calls it the "quiet revolution"; but the claim to be the One True Church over against all the denominations—a claim virtually unquestioned until the early 1960s—yet remains the elephant in the living room of Churches of Christ.

The pivotal issue in the exclusive view of fellowship has been the role of baptism as initiation into life in the Spirit. The "rediscovery" of baptism "for remission of sins" was a key turning point in Campbell's new reformation movement in the 1820s. When preached in the context of "mourner's bench" conversions, it drew thousands of believers seeking more explicit assurance of forgiveness into the Disciples movement. But Churches of Christ, for whom this doctrine has been so central, missed a key point in Campbell's view of baptism as initiation. Early in his career then again in 1837 and after, Campbell made a subtle but crucial distinction: though Christ's blood actually cleanses from sin, baptism "formally" cleanses. Baptism thus serves as a formal sign of forgiveness and gives the believer an assurance of salvation that the unimmersed cannot experience. "The present salvation," he concluded, "never can be so fully enjoyed (all things else being equal) by the unimmersed as by the immersed." Similarly, he also distinguished between "inward and outward Christians," asserting that it was possible for one who sincerely mistook the outward baptism to possess the inward."[34] Among the branch of his heirs that became Churches of Christ this point was entirely lost.

In practice over the years Churches of Christ have taken a high view of baptism, insisting that baptism does not just stand for something but that it does something. And that is good. Baptism and other Christian ordinances are channels of divine life and grace. They are empowering. They are dynamic and life-giving. They shape and train Christians to be disciples. When one neglects them one is deprived of measures of divine life. As James McClendon puts it, they are performative signs that bring believers more and more into the divine life and draw them more and more into the way of Jesus.[35]

Such a high view of the ordinances or sacraments, however, requires a firm rootage in a proper Trinitarian theology, that is, in a proper understanding of God's relational nature. Otherwise one too easily makes them magical or mechanical. Or one pronounces that the divine life can flow only in this way and in no other way. Certainly baptism is the normal sign of Christian conversion and initiation. But as Campbell put it, he that "infers that none are Christians but the immersed, as greatly errs as he that affirms that none are alive but those of clear and full vision."

The revivalistic milieu of early America, which focused so heavily on the private conversion experience, decimated the role of the ordinances or sacraments in many Christian traditions. But today some of those traditions are beginning to rediscover believers' baptism and some are calling for weekly communion. It is not surprising or accidental that this renewed emphasis and recovery comes at the same time that churches in America have been culturally disestablished and forced to function more and more as outsiders. Methodist theologian Stanley Hauerwas says (with tongue only partially in cheek) that one of the goals in his ethics class at Duke Divinity School is to make Methodist ministers feel guilty for not celebrating the Eucharist every week in their churches.[36] This is not a time for preachers, teachers, and pastors in Churches of Christ to be surrendering or downplaying a high view of baptism and weekly communion. Indeed, their challenge is to deepen and enrich the meaning of these practices by centering them more deeply and explicitly in the Trinitarian life of God.

In becoming more fully Trinitarian in practice, Churches of Christ especially face the challenge of developing a Trinitarian doctrine of the Holy Spirit.[37] Here the barriers of their tradition are high and forbidding. Here the long reach of the "dirt philosophy" remains most firmly felt (see Chapter 4). Yet after modernity, as we have seen, the atmosphere is more hospitable precisely at this point. After several centuries of being desacralized, the world is being resacralized. The world of things unseen is becoming less and less foreign to more and more people. After modernity, in fact, the challenge becomes, not so much creating openness to spiritual reality and experience, but rather constraining and disciplining it so that believers' lives are conformed to the way of Jesus and the practices of God's Kingdom. Trinitarian doctrine is our chief tool for constraining and focusing the spiritual effulgence of a resacralized world that will always be prone to spiritual narcissism and illusion. It is also our chief tool for opening up believers to the power and presence of the living God when they have constricted that reality through accommodation to modernity.[38]

So the challenge becomes, both for Churches of Christ (who have overly minimized that reality) and for other churches (who have, at times, overly magnified it), to recover a discipleship rooted in a Trinitarian pneumatology. Christian discipleship involves following the risen Lord, in the power of the Spirit, to the glory of God the Father. In the Trinitarian economy the present work of the Spirit is primarily eschatological. That is, the Spirit, using means that are finite and contingent, anticipates and makes real the life to come in the present life of the Christian community. Full and faithful discipleship, then, is supernatural or Spirit empowered; the believer walks in a way and engages in practices that are humanly impossible but that in the power of the Spirit become possible. When discipleship is not rooted in the Spirit's power it gets tamed or toned down to what seems humanly possible, simply reasonable, and culturally appropriate.

Certainly in their churches members of Churches of Christ have experienced the Spirit's empowerment to various degrees—they have sought to practice Christ's ordinances faithfully, have learned to pray, and have sought to love and serve one another and the weak; but their doctrine has not adequately accounted for or supported this experience and their language has not adequately named it. Further, their worship has lacked Trinitarian language and shape. This doctrinal deficiency has inhibited and often distorted practice. At this juncture, Churches of Christ need to recover a fuller Trinitarian faith to correct and refocus their doctrinal and liturgical tradition. Gordon Fee, gathering up the fruit of his extensive exegesis of all the Spirit texts in Paul, has put this recovery in terms that can resonate with Churches of Christ: "a genuine recapturing of the Pauline perspective will cause the church to be more vitally Trinitarian, not only in its theology, but in its life and Spirituality as well. This will mean not the exaltation of the Spirit, but the exaltation of God; and it will mean not focus on the Spirit as such, but on the Son, crucified and risen, Savior and Lord of all."[39] After modernity, such recovery has become more possible.

DILEMMAS OLD AND NEW

Nicholas Wolterstorff, a noted philosopher and deeply committed Christian, recently observed: "The thinkers of the Enlightenment hoped to bring about a rational consensus in place of fractured tradition. That hope has failed. In my judgment it was bound to fail. It could not succeed."[40] This judgment about the Enlightenment as an intellectual movement can also be applied to Christian movements like Alexander Campbell's that partook of the same spirit and envisioned a similar goal. Campbell and other early nineteenth-century restorationists hoped to bring about a rational consensus in place of a badly fractured Christian tradition. But that hope has failed. Indeed, its failure has been apparent for several generations. Campbell's movement itself, after all, spawned several new traditions, themselves reflecting the steadily growing pluralism and fragmentation of democratized Christianity; and Churches of Christ themselves have evolved into numerous subdivisions, some of them deeply estranged from one another.

But though the failure has long been apparent, Churches of Christ did not recognize it, indeed could not recognize it. For the theological tradition that shaped them (which was all the more powerful for being unacknowledged) required a rational consensus; and it carried the deep assumption that every honest, rational individual could—and would— read the Bible alike. That after all was a basic assumption of Baconian science and theology as Campbell had articulated it; and, as we have seen, that assumption had soon become a hidden, ideological fixture in the movement. Only now is that ideology beginning to be recognized and critiqued. For the most part Churches of Christ have continued to expect (and demand) a rational doctrinal consensus—if not a consensus that triumphantly sweeps the Christian world in a dawning millennium as Campbell envisioned, at least one achieved in a small but faithful enclave of truth and rationality.

Not only has the Enlightenment hope for rational doctrinal consensus failed, but as Wolterstorff noted, it was bound to fail. It could not succeed. For the Enlightenment epistemology was based on the erroneous assumptions that context and community do not matter, that one can stand free of tradition, and that the only path to truth is the unencumbered individual weighing the factual evidence and exercising his or her rational powers. These assumptions were enormously powerful and attractive—and remain so for many people in Churches of Christ—but they no longer stand. If nothing else, the sheer force of pluralism and fragmentation has overturned them. We are being forced to recognize the boundedness and embeddedness that marks human life and human knowing. Such recognition tempers the presumption (and indeed the arrogance) that has marked the modern spirit, and allows us to face more fully the way we actually come to our deepest convictions.

Facing up to the failure of the Baconian hope for Christian unity based on doctrinal consensus and to the weakness in the epistemology that undergirded it presents an enormous—and perhaps insurmountable—challenge for Churches of Christ at the present juncture. Put most simply, this failure strikes at the heart of the tradition; to face up to it will require a fundamental reorientation of the tradition. There are resources for such reorientation within the tradition itself, as we have seen somewhat in this book.[41] The Disciples of Christ, another main branch of the Stone-Campbell heritage, have tapped into some of those resources and used them on their fitful and ill-timed twentieth-century journey toward mainline Protestantism. But Churches of Christ, now over a hundred years separated from the Disciples, have their own weighty tradition with their own selective interpretation of the founding story. Those other resources and strands of the story are deeply buried and long forgotten, and even when unearthed seem to many like strange, unworkable, and probably dangerous relics.

To work at theological reorientation within a tradition, it seems fair to say, one must first be conscious of having or being a tradition. But in my experience of teaching in a seminary and in dozens of congregations over many years, it has required a momentous and difficult step for people in Churches of Christ to acknowledge that they are deeply part of a human tradition. For their powerful and ever-present tradition had taught them that they were only New Testament Christians, not part of any human, and hence "denominational," tradition.[42] Thus the very step of entering into historical consciousness and attempting to own up to the tradition was itself a kind of departure from the tradition. Most of those who have made this journey, I have observed, have found the new vista wonderfully freeing and spiritually uplifting, but at the same time it has left them with the dilemma of what to do with their anti-tradition tradition.

For a generation or so a cadre of Church of Christ biblical scholars, along with a few theologians, have been attempting, to varying extents, to reorient the tradition in significant ways. These leaders have broken with the traditional Baconian hermeneutic, the old exclusivism, and the doctrinal system that undergirded it; and, in more recent years, some have broken with the old Enlightenment assumptions about tradition. If one contrasts the assumptions and theological method of these progressive leaders with, for example, the assumptions and method of *Sound Doctrine—Volume I* (1920) by Nichol and Whiteside, a work that served for two generations and more as a basic "catechism" for Churches of Christ, one finds them worlds apart.[43] As a whole, however, these scholars and theologians remain reluctant, for political and personal reasons, to acknowledge the extent to which they have broken with their doctrinal tradition and taken up new methods of biblical interpretation and theological reflection.

The agenda of the progressives has been heavily shaped by an outside tradition—the late modern tradition of historical-critical biblical studies located mainly in the secular academy. They tend to work with the confidence that, through such historical-critical methods, they have acquired, finally, the key to opening up the text and discovering "what the first hearers would have heard." They are attempting more or less self-consciously to embrace their own church tradition while acknowledging—and sometimes even embracing (privately at least)—the larger Christian community with its many traditions. They are historically conscious and critical, to varying degrees, and seek theological correction and enrichment of their tradition.[44] Their influence has steadily grown as they have trained a sizable group of ministers and younger professors who are now exerting a spreading influence.

Some of this new generation of progressive leaders, in fact, are sounding more and more like traditionalists in their rhetoric: the tradition may be flawed in notable ways, they seem to be saying, but at least it provides a bulwark against the powerful onslaught of trendy and vacuous attempts at cultural relevance. They hold up the Church of Christ tradition as a bulwark and refuge against change, though ironically in their own theologies they have broken with key aspects of the tradition and adopted ways of interpreting the Bible drawn from a foreign tradition—the modern academy. And having made these breaks with some defining features of the tradition, they are having trouble defining theologically the nature of the tradition they hold up as a bulwark.

This situation points to the dilemma faced by the new progressive church leaders as they grapple with their modern church in a (post)modern context. At one level it is a personal dilemma—an acute discomfort with, or at least a deep ambivalence about, the tradition and yet a strong loyalty and familial attachment to it. At another level the dilemma is theological. Can this particular tradition, so deeply grounded in the early modern thought world and so long isolated from the larger Christian world, be theologically overhauled without losing itself or at least losing what made it dynamic over the last century? Can one leave behind or change its time-honored method of biblical interpretation, its relentless polemic against the church as denomination, its century-and-a-half-old insistence that instrumental music in worship is not only inappropriate but in fact sinful, its unique dispensational arrangement of scripture (see Chapter 3)—can these things, and others, be altered and yet the tradition dynamically maintained? Can one leave behind these deep convictions and practices and remain who Churches of Christ have claimed to be?

Churches of Christ became a sizable and dynamic Christian movement in twentieth-century America. Their appeal was the claim to have restored the True Church that had been corrupted and lost by human denominational traditions. Many thousands of Baptists, Methodists, Presbyterians, Lutherans, Catholics, Pentecostals, and believers from sundry other Christian churches were taught that they were not True Christians and converted to the True Church. Indeed, most of the evangelistic literature of twentieth-century Churches of Christ, until recently, focused on such "conversions." It was standard practice—and remains so among traditionalists—to speak of a Baptist, a Pentecostal, or a Catholic becoming a "New Testament Christian" and a member of the "Lord's Church." These claims and practices were integral to the tradition; a whole doctrinal system undergirded them.[45] This system and its practices remain intact for many members, and, as we saw earlier, popular polemicists like LaGard Smith and numerous others continue to defend and promote it aggressively.[46] And understandably so, for this exclusivist system—whether articulated in strident and blunt tones or in more gentle, tactful ones—has been at the heart of the tradition, especially in the twentieth century.

To adopt a non-exclusive, more denominational view of the church, which most all of these younger, progressive, academy-trained leaders have done, is to have made a most fundamental departure from the core of the Church of Christ tradition over the last century and more—though some of these leaders, concerned for institutional continuity and growth, usually downplay the extent and significance of this move. Whether one judges such a departure as good and necessary or as troubling and dangerous, the problem remains. Can the tradition, which admittedly is faltering, be stabilized and even renewed when many of its traditionally deep convictions are only accommodated or played to and no longer held as deep convictions? I doubt it. The new theologians are attempting to build their new doctrinal edifice upon the old or to supplant the old with what they judge to be more healthy doctrine, but the result will be something quite different. And that something different will, especially in this time when fracture and diversity is the order of the day, most likely bring new division and subdivision. But then that is not a new story for Churches of Christ or indeed for American Christianity.

The dilemmas do not all lie with the young progressives, however. The traditionalists have their own dilemmas at this juncture. The older people among them remember some of the glory days—the post-World War II years when the ranks of Churches of Christ were swelling, when vigorous debates with denominationalists were still the order of the day, and when the message of the One True Church was unambiguous and powerful. Those days have passed, and many people feel troubled and fearful, perhaps guilty, and certainly disoriented. Their congregations, for the most part, are stuck, either settled into a defensive holding pattern or wracked by the tensions of young families pressing for change and renewal. Some traditional leaders mount vigorous polemical campaigns to sound the alarm; others of a gentler, less combative nature quietly grieve what they interpret as the spiritual blindness and apostasy of those who break with the doctrinal system that upholds Church of Christ exclusivism. The language of "going off" to the denominations, long part of Church of Christ vocabulary, still sounds frequently in the ranks, though it is becoming more and more a whisper instead of a shout.

In some larger suburban congregations, particularly west of the Mississippi River, those who still use the traditional vocabulary and embrace the traditional doctrinal system have become a distinct minority. As the pressure mounts for them, they either speak up for the tradition in face of persistent attempts at change or quietly seek a more traditional congregation. The leaders of these progressive congregations, for the most part, still know the traditional language and doctrine but do not believe parts of it; they try, however, to accommodate the tradition enough to remain a Church of Christ. That means, at the present juncture, worshipping without instrumental music, practicing weekly communion and believers' baptism by immersion for the remission of sins, maintaining a congregational polity with a plurality of elders, continuing to use the basic rhetoric of restoration, and upholding a non-charismatic or cessationist interpretation of the gifts passages. For the present it also involves maintaining the traditional role and place of women in the church, though some congregations are engaging in discussion of the issue and a very few are beginning to change their practices somewhat.

Nothing has been more central and distinctive to the identity of Churches of Christ in the last century than the practice of worshipping without instrumental music. Far from a mere preference or a guiding principle, it was a strict prohibition based on an interpretive method that viewed everything not commanded or exampled in the New Testament as forbidden. Instrumental music was, in short, a sin, an act of rebellion against God's design for true worship. A cappella worship became one of the most distinctive features of Churches of Christ and thus a central element in its ethos and identity.[47] Striking examples of the proportions that this issue has assumed are the following two statements, both published recently in a leading, mainstream church magazine: "the introduction and use of mechanical instruments of music into Christian worship," wrote an influential Bible commentator and preacher, "is sinful and is perhaps the most sinful thing that any true church of our Lord could do in this generation." Another well-known preacher said that "instrumental music only lets the cat out of the bag....After they bring in the instrument, baptism is no longer essential, and the church is just another denomination among denominations."[48]

Traditionalists believe that instrumental music in worship is sinful and puts one out of fellowship with God, though sometimes they hold this view less polemically and more quietly. Almost no progressive leaders believe instrumental worship to be sinful, though many believe it would be divisive (and thus sinful) to embrace or impose it at present. Beyond this shift, the progressives continue the practice of *a cappella* worship for various reasons: some believe it best because it reflects the practice of the primitive churches; a good many prefer it because they grew up with it; some think it a good safeguard against the transformation of worship into entertainment; some put a new spin on the tradition by saying that there should be a place for *a cappella* churches within the larger Christian world; and some simply accommodate the practice as a political necessity. All of these reasons may be good rationales for continuing the traditional practice; but all of them are departures from the rationale of the core tradition, and will not satisfy many traditionalists—indeed, such reasons will probably not be strong enough to maintain the tradition widely among progressive churches in the long run. In most Christian colleges operated by Churches of Christ, whether run by traditionalists or progressives, full-time faculty members can still be dismissed for worshiping regularly with a group using instrumental music.

For *a cappella* worship to continue to be a defining feature of Churches of Christ it must be held as a deep conviction. For in this music-saturated culture and with a generation of Christian young people—not to mention the unchurched—who can embrace the traditional practice only with a great and arduous leap, the force of mere preference and accommodation will not carry the tradition forward for long. Most of the traditionalists and some of the progressives know this. So the one group seeks to shore up the doctrine supporting the practice and thus protect Christians against apostasy; the other hardly ever mentions the traditional doctrine except in preferential or political terms, with some envisioning a time when this practice too becomes part of a tolerable diversity within the tradition.

The universities and graduate schools of religion supported by Churches of Christ tend, of course, to be the centers of progressive thought. The theological dilemmas and political tensions they face are ever shifting and often intense. Speaking at a conference on the restoration ideal in America hosted by Abilene Christian University, David Edwin Harrell, social historian of the Stone-Campbell movement and lifelong member of Churches of Christ, said: "Places such as Abilene Christian University, where there is an honest effort to encounter both past and present, find themselves living in delicate tension. Although some individuals thrive in that tension, for the most part such institutions form bridges that transport people back and forth from one cosmos to another."[49]

Both progressives and traditionalists today share one of the tradition's oldest dilemmas: the place of creeds or confessions of faith. Though vociferously claiming to be non-creedal and to have the Bible as their only doctrinal standard, Churches of Christ, of course, have long possessed a creed. Traditions cannot cohere and continue without them. Functional creeds or statements of faith are the product of theological reflection in the face of pressing needs and challenges facing a tradition. But the creed of Churches of Christ is informal and mostly unacknowledged, a fact which makes critiquing it both hazardous and haphazard. Open and orderly theological reflection is difficult, especially when many of the participants do not think they are doing theological reflection. The word "theology" has finally become acceptable in some quarters in recent years but is still viewed by many as something either superfluous or dangerously "denominational." Modernity could sustain the Churches of Christ claim to "pure" objectivity and creedlessness, but in a (post)modern age when we are increasingly recognizing the tradition-determined nature of our convictions and communities, and when the Enlightenment claim to "pure" objectivity has been exposed as illusory, the claim to creedlessness will be increasingly untenable and unworkable.

The dilemmas touched on here, along with others, will continue to press and swell as Churches of Christ move further into this new era. As the pressures and tensions mount, many traditionalists will retrench further into the comforting confines of their traditional doctrinal system with its stark exclusivism. Progressive leaders with a high tolerance for tension will continue to work creatively with the tradition, attempting by fits and starts to shape it into something new. Between these two groups will be a steadily shifting, increasingly diverse, generally affluent middle group, loyal to the tradition but uncomfortable with its harder features and key parts of its traditional theology. A sizeable and motley group of others, weary of the growing tensions, will simply let go and find themselves free falling in the grace of God and, willy nilly, into the church catholic.

After modernity, it will be particularly difficult for a modern church tradition that does not know it is a modern church to deal self-consciously with the new challenges and opportunities of this inchoate new era. It will be difficult even to name properly the deeper causes of the unrest and sense of vertigo they are experiencing. But Churches of Christ have sought sincerely for almost two centuries to be a people faithful to God and to live under the authority of God's Word as they understood it. The pressures and disarray of this time can serve to renew a fresh and ardent seeking after God. And God has promised sustenance, wisdom, and direction for those who seek him in the humility that crisis can bring.

Notes

1. LaGard Smith, *Who Is My Brother? Facing a Crisis of Identity and Fellowship* (Malibu, CA: Cotswold, 1997). Smith is the author of *Out on a Broken Limb* (Eugene, OR: Harvest House, 1986), a popular expose of Shirley McLaine's New Age views.

2. Examples of this language are not hard to find: "The church of Christ is not a denomination in the current sense of that word; it is the thing itself....The church of Christ has no part or lot in denominationalism...." John T. Hinds, "Is the Church Denominational?" *Gospel Advocate* 73 (August 6, 1931), 972. See also Wayne Jackson, "Denominationalism," *Gospel Advocate* 145 (November 2003), 22-4.

3. Diogenes Allen, *Christian Belief in a Postmodern World* (Louisville: Westminster/John Knox,1989), 1-6, 7. On the failure of the Enlightenment's moral project, see the seminal work of Alasdair McIntyre, *After Virtue* (Notre Dame, IN: University of Notre Dame, 1984), 51-61. Allen writes: "Although the intellectual situation today is vastly more favorable than it has been in recent centuries, the dust from the collapse of the modern mentality has not yet settled so that everyone can see clearly that we are in a new situation" (6).

4. Jean-Francois Lyotard, *The Postmodern Condition: A Report on Knowledge*, trans. Geoff Bennington and Brian Massumi (Minneapolis, MN: University of Minnesota, 1984), xxiii, xxiv.

5. Walter Truett Anderson, *Reality Isn't What It Used to Be* (San Francisco: Harper & Row, 1990),

6. For example, Peter Drucker, *The Landmarks of Tomorrow: A Report on the New Post-Modern World* (New York: Harper & Row, 1957).

7. The "postmodern," viewed as a reaction against the "modern," remains in significant ways tied closely to the modern, just as protests against grammar must still be written using grammar. Indeed, some of what is called "postmodern"—like deconstructionist theories—might better be termed "ultra-modern" or "radically modern." For wise and insightful general treatment, see Albert Borgmann, *Crossing the Postmodern Divide* (Chicago: University of Chicago, 1992); David Harvey, *The Condition of Postmodernity: An Inquiry into the Origins of Culture Change* (Cambridge, MA: Basil Blackwell, 1984); and Leszek Kolakowski, *Modernity on Endless Trial* (Chicago: University of Chicago, 1991).

8. In addition to the works cited above, see J. Richard Middleton and Brian J. Walsh, *Truth Is Stranger Than It Used to Be: Biblical Faith in a Postmodern Age* (Downers Grove, IL: InterVarsity, 1995), and Thomas C. Oden, *After Modernity, What?* (Grand Rapids, MI: Zondervan, 1992). For a brief survey of the transition from modern to postmodern and its implications for Christian mission, see Craig Van Gelder, "Mission in the Emerging Postmodern Condition," in *Between Gospel and Culture: The Emerging Mission in North America,* ed. George R. Hunsberger and Craig Van Gelder

(Grand Rapids, MI: Eerdmans, 1996), 113-38.

9. Stephen D. Fishel, "Shall We Pray for the Sick?" *Spiritual Sword* 25 (July 1994), 34-7.

10. J. B. Grubbs, "The Miraculous and the Providential," *Lard's Quarterly* 2 (July 1865), 349.

11. If the tradition generally has constrained the New Testament's spiritual world view by its embrace of early modern assumptions, some academy-trained scholars in the tradition now maintain many of those same constraints—and more—through use of late modern critical methods. As avowed conservatives, they reject Bultmann's demythologizing program but actually employ a more subtle and acceptable version of the same method. Gordon Fee's description seems apt: "Whether one believes such things [as the Pauline *charismata*] happened or not, of course, depends almost altogether on one's worldview. The so-called Enlightenment has had its innings, and moderns, helped along by the phenomenal advances of modern scientific discovery, are prone to unbridled arrogance, leaving Paul and his churches to their own world-view—in which they believed in such things—but rather casually dismissing them in terms of reality. Bultmann, for example, speaking for many, caricatured the 'three-storied universe' of Paul and his contemporaries. So prevalent is this worldview that many evangelicals, conservative in their theology and therefore incensed at Bultmann's 'rationalism' which so casually dismissed the Pauline affirmations, adopted their own brand of rationalism, as a way of explaining the absence of such phenomena in their own circles: by limiting such Spirit activity to the apostolic age." *God's Empowering Presence: The Holy Spirit in the Letters of Paul* (Peabody, MA: Hendrickson), 887-88.

12. Karl Barth, *The Word of God and the Word of Man* (New York: Harper, 1957), 32.

13. The concept first emerged in the Protestant Reformation where it served as a polemical tool of Protestants against Catholic claims to miracles; it remained strong among Protestants until the mid-nineteenth century, but from 1850 to 1930 came under strong attack. Since 1930 it has been in steady decline. See Robert Bruce Mullin, *Miracles and the Modern Religious Imagination* (New Haven, CT: Yale University, 1996), 1-30.

14. Ibid., 262.

15. On Blackaby and the "deeper life" tradition, see Gary Furr, "'The Road of Ashes': Spirituality and the Prospects for Disillusioned Baptists," in *Ties That Bind: Life Together in the Baptist Vision*, ed. Gary A. Furr and Curtis W. Freeman (Macon, GA: Smyth and Helwys, 1994), 127-49.

16. For recent examples of critical yet appreciative assessments of the diverse "charismatic" movements by widely-respected theologians, see N. T. Wright, *Bringing the Church to the World: Renewing the Church to Confront the Paganism Entrenched in Western Culture* (Minneapolis, MN: Bethany, 1992), 137-47; James Wm. McClendon, *Systematic Theology, 2: Doctrine* (Nashville, TN: Abingdon, 1994), 434-39; and Clark Pinnock, *Flame of Love: A Theology of the Holy Spirit* (Downers Grove, IL: InterVarsity, 1996).

McClendon, a "baptist," writes: "the wider significance of Pentecostals for today's theology cannot merely be the rather patronizing insight that these, too, are God's children. Of course they are, but a theology that sees only that would be as backward as those apostles who reluctantly concluded that Gentiles could after all be disciples of Christ! Rather I believe that what the Spirit is saying by means of the Pentecostal revival is that all God's children must be pentecostal—since all share the same Spirit, since all are called to be missionaries, since all require fellowship in the Spirit. The highly visible ecstasy-and-fellowship of Pentecostals is the Spirit's fresh signal that ecstasy and fellowship are the distinguishing marks of the Spirit of God—the gifts of God who is Spirit and who in coming to us brings us into intimate relation with the Spirit and with one another. This does not mean that all of us must adopt each element of Pentecostal doctrinal teaching. By logic, we cannot, for…the concrete details vary crucially among Pentecostals themselves….The necessary message of Pentecostals…is that the reality of present enjoyment in the Christian life, of Spirit-given full salvation now (albeit only a rich foretaste of eternal salvation) is fully claimed and rightly shared by all who bow the knee to Jesus Christ as Lord" (437-38).

17. For representative treatments by traditionalists, see James D. Bales, *Miracles or Mirages?*; Jimmy Jividen, *Miracles: From God or from Man?* (Abilene, TX: Abilene Christian University, 1985).

18. For my limited purposes in this chapter I use the simple categories of "progressive" and "traditionalist" to describe basic forces presently at work in Churches of Christ. For an attempt at a more complex taxonomy of the present "camps" and tensions, see Douglas Foster, *Will the Cycle Be Unbroken?: Churches of Christ Face the Twenty-First Century* (Abilene, TX: Abilene Christian University, 1994), 89-98.

19. John Locke's *The Reasonableness of Christianity as Delivered in the Scriptures* (1695), towers over this lineage. On "supernatural rationalism" see Chapter 2.

20. Robert W. Jenson, *Christian Dogmatics* (Philadelphia: Fortress, 1984), 1:150.

21. See for example C. F. D. Moule, *The Holy Spirit* (Oxford: Mowbray, 1978), 43-51. This form of eclipse has a few proponents among Church of Christ scholars.

22. Particularly noteworthy are Jürgen Moltmann, *The Trinity and the Kingdom: The Doctrine of God* (San Francisco: Harper & Row, 1981); Karl Rahner, *The Trinity*, trans. Joseph Donceel (London: Burns and Oats, 1970); Eberhard Jüngel, *The Doctrine of the Trinity*, trans. Horton Harris (Edinburgh: Scottish Academic Press, 1976); John D. Zizioulas, *Being as Communion: Studies in Personhood and the Church* (London: Dartman, Longman, and Todd, 1985); and Robert W. Jenson, *The Triune Identity* (Philadelphia: Fortress, 1982). Noteworthy works focusing particularly on the practicality of the Trinitarian doctrine include Catherine M. LaCugna, *God for Us: The Trinity and the Christian Life* (San Francisco: Harper & Row, 1991), and L. Gregory Jones, *Transformed Judgment: Toward a Trinitarian Account of the Moral Life* (Notre Dame, IN: University of Notre Dame, 1993).

23. Carlo Carretto, *The God Who Comes* (Maryknoll, NY: Orbis, 1974), 79, 83.

24. Recent advocates of the social Trinity include Colin Gunton, *The Promise of*

Trinitarian Theology (Edinburgh: T & T Clark, 1991); Wolfhart Pannenberg, *Systematic Theology*, trans. Geoffrey Bromiley (Grand Rapids, MI: Eerdmans, 1991), 1:259-336; LaCugna, *God for Us*; Ted Peters, *God as Trinity: Relationality and Temporality in Divine Life* (Louisville, KY: Westminster/John Knox, 1993); Moltmann, *The Trinity and the Kingdom,* esp. 171-76; and Pinnock, *Flame of Love*, 21-48.

25. Diogenes Allen, *The Path of Perfect Love* (Cambridge, MA: Cowley, 1992), 52. This is one of the best discussions of God's relational life and how that life creates community with human beings. See pp. 39-59.

26. Lester G. McAllister and William E. Tucker, *Journey in Faith: A History of the Christian Church (Disciples of Christ)* (St. Louis, MO: Bethany, 1975), 235.

27. Smith, *Who Is My Brother?*, 154.

28. Moses Lard, "Do the Unimmersed Commune?" *Lard's Quarterly* 1 (September 1863), 44, 49; James Harding, "Bro. McGarvey's Reply Reviewed," *Gospel Advocate* 29 (May 25, 1887), 321; W. K. Homan, *The Church on Trial or The Old Faith Vindicated* (Dallas: Aldridge & Co., 1900), 50. See also David Lipscomb, "Oppose the Beginnings of Error," *Gospel Advocate* 37 (November 28, 1895), 757, and Austin McGary, "Re-Baptism," ibid., (May 28, 1884), 338.

29. Reuel Lemmons, "The Boundary of Brotherhood," *Firm Foundation* 80 (August 13, 1963), 514; "Denominationalism Versus Sectarianism," ibid., 79 (July 31, 1962), 482; and "The Church of Christ," ibid., 95 (May 16, 1978), 306.

30. An entire issue of *The Spiritual Sword* 10 (January 1979) was devoted to this point. Warren wrote: "One cannot be saved without being baptized in the name of (by the authority of) Jesus Christ, and one cannot be baptized in the name of Jesus Christ unless he is baptized in order to be saved—not because he thought he was already saved before he was baptized" (p. 3) This view, of course, excludes from salvation most members of the Baptist Church. See "It is Sinful to Enter the Baptist Church" and "It is Sinful to Remain in the Baptist Church," ibid., 11 (January 1980).

31. Smith, *Who Is My Brother?* Lines like this appear from time to time: "In all of England there are fewer than fifty congregations of the church" (p. 99), by which he means Churches of Christ. In a final chapter, however, the author does allow that God in the end will exercise divine mercy and clemency in ways that will most likely surprise everyone.

32. On the history of Church of Christ exclusivism, see Myer Phillips, "A Historical Study of the Attitude of the Churches of Christ toward Other Denominations" (Ph.D. diss., Baylor University, 1983), and Arthur Murrell, "The Effects of Exclusivism in the Separation of the Churches of Christ from the Christian Church" (Ph.D. diss., Vanderbilt University, 1972). Perhaps the earliest book to reject the pervasive exclusivism was M. F. Cottrell, *Refocusing God—the Bible and the Church* (Denver: By the author, 1962), but its impact seems to have been negligible. A 1966 book, *Voices of Concern*, did attract considerable attention. In it Logan Fox, longtime preacher and missionary, wrote: "As I seek now to understand how I was taught that the Church of Christ is the 'one and only true church' I find no particular name coming to mind.

Rather does this central dogma of our brotherhood so permeate the area that its source cannot be discovered...it is taken for granted and never questioned. One may play at being open-minded; in fact, such play is encouraged....But one never really questions whether we are in truth the true church. To do so is taboo, unthinkable." "Destiny or Disease?" in *Voices of Concern*, ed. Robert Myers (St. Louis: Mission Messenger, 1966), 14.

33. Phillips, "Attitude of the Churches of Christ toward Other Denominations," 329.

34. For a fuller treatment of this issue, see my book, *Distant Voices: Discovering a Forgotten Past for a Changing Church* (Abilene, TX: Abilene Christian University, 1993), 32-38, 55-62. Campbell's linking of baptism with assurance of forgiveness was a feature of his Calvinist heritage: "Nor [is]...water an instrument of our forgiveness, regeneration and renewal... ," Calvin wrote in 1536, " it is only the knowledge and certitude of such gifts that are found in the sacrament." *Institutes of the Christian Religion* (1536), 110.

35. James Wm. McClendon, "Baptism as a Performative Sign," *Theology Today* 23 (October 1966), 403-16, and his *Doctrine*, 386-96.

36. Stanley Hauerwas, *In Good Company: The Church as Polis* (Notre Dame, IN: University of Notre Dame, 1995), 5.

37. Over a decade ago Albert Outler spoke of the urgent need for "an updated pneumatology that includes historical perspective along with the opening horizons of a postmodern and global age." Significant works attempting to do this include: Killian McDonnell, "A Trinitarian Doctrine of the Holy Spirit," *Theological Studies* 46 (1985), 191-227; Moltmann, *The Spirit of Life: A Universal Affirmation* (Philadelphia: Fortress, 1992); and Pinnock, *Flame of Love*.

38. For fuller development of this paragraph in relation to Churches of Christ, see my book, *Participating in God's Life: Two Theological Crossroads for Churches of Christ*, with Danny Swick (Siloam Springs, AR: Leafwood Publishers, 2002).

39. Fee, *God's Empowering Presence*, 902. See also his more popular treatment of Trinitarian pneumatology in *Paul, the Spirit, and the People of God* (Peabody, MA: Hendrickson, 1996), 36-48.

40. Nicholas Wolterstorff, *John Locke and the Ethics of Belief* (Cambridge: Cambridge University, 1996), 246.

41. See Allen, *Distant Voices* (1993).

42. F. D. Kershner, a conservative Disciple writing in the early twentieth century, noted this perpetual dilemma. The movement found itself in the strange position, he observed, of being "a party whose basis consisted in opposition to the whole party idea—an unsectarian sect, a non-denominational denomination—a very particular and distinct people, pleading for an idea in its essence catholic and universal. This anomalous position has always embarrassed our work." "Progress of Restoration Principles," *Christian Standard* 53 (August 17, 1918), 1403.

43. C. R. Nichol and R. L. Whiteside, *Sound Doctrine—Volume I* (1920; reprint ed., Abilene: Abilene Christian University Bookstore, 1954). C. R. Nichol's *Pocket Bible*

Encyclopedia, an alphabetically arranged, ready-reference version of the same doctrinal system, sells over 10,000 copies a year for ACU Press.

44. See Thomas H. Olbricht, "Religious Scholarship and the Restoration Movement," *Restoration Quarterly* 25 (1982), 193ff.; James Thompson, "New Testament Studies and the Restoration Movement," ibid. 223ff.; and Don Haymes, "The Silence of the Scholars," *Mission* 8 (September 1974), 70-85.

45. This doctrinal system was spelled out most clearly and simply in the twentieth century by Nichol and Whiteside's *Sound Doctrine-Volume I* (Clifton, TX: Nichol, 1920). A more recent statement of this system is Leroy Brownlow, *Why I Am a Member of the Church of Christ* (Ft. Forth, TX: Brownlow Publishing), a work widely used around mid-century and still in circulation.

46. Smith, *Who Is My Brother?*; Smith, *The Cultural Church: Winds of Change and the Call for a New Hermeneutic* (Nashville, TN: 20th Century Christian, 1992); Howard W. Norton, "The New Hermeneutic—A Sign of Apostasy?" *Gospel Advocate* 134 (February 1992), 12-14; William Woodson, "A Scriptural Critique of the New Hermeneutic," *Spiritual Sword* 21 (April 1990), 35-38. Woodson says that rejecting the time-honored interpretive method and adopting a "new hermeneutic" "virtually negate(s) the restoration principles which have brought unity to the churches of Christ for almost two hundred years" (35-36).

47. Among the vast polemical literature on this subject, see for example these recent and representative articles: Guy N. Woods, "Why Churches of Christ Do Not Use Instrumental Music in Worship," *Spiritual Sword* 24 (April 1993), 17-24; Hugo McCord, "Is Instrumental Music a Matter of Indifference?" *Spiritual Sword* 26 (April 1995), 33-34; J. W. Roberts, "Instrumental Music Is Unauthorized and Unprecedented," *Gospel Advocate* 134 (May 1992), 38-43; Bruce Harris, "Instrumental Music in Worship Is Sinful," *Firm Foundation* 102 (August 27, 1985), 511; Earl I. West, "The Instrumental Music Controversy in American Church History," *Missions in Crisis, Abilene Christian University Annual Bible Lectures, 1988* (Abilene, TX: ACU, 1988), 177-91; Jimmy Jividen, "Instrumental Music: A Point of Controversy," *Gospel Advocate* 138 (January 1996), 22-24; and Dan Chambers, "Pleasing God: A Case for Vocal-Only Praise," *Gospel Advocate* 145 (November 2003), 38f.

48. Burton Coffman, "The Sinful Use of Instrumental Music," *Gospel Advocate* 137 (October 1995), 22; Charles Hodge, "Facing the Instrumental Music Question Again," ibid. 140 (February 1998), 24. Hodge concluded: "How important is the instrumental music issue? The entire future of our movement is at stake. May God have mercy upon us" (25).

49. David Edwin Harrell, Jr., "Epilogue," in *The American Quest for the Primitive Church*, ed. Richard T. Hughes (Urbana, IL: University of Illinois, 1988), 241.

EPILOGUE
RENEWAL AND THE POLITICS OF CHANGE

This is a momentous time in Western culture and in the Christian movement around the world. Awakening is occurring. Bold mission thrusts are
underway. The church faces both new promise and new peril. Some are
seeing that in North America Christians are now faced with the challenge
of adopting a missionary stance toward American culture, of seeking to
form "missionary congregations" rather than being content with churches
that support missions.

Yet Churches of Christ remain, to a large extent, insular and inert,
fixed in maintenance or preservation mode, intramurally preoccupied,
impaired both by defective theology and traditionalism. We are living in
one of the great periods of evangelism in Christian history; but Churches
of Christ have drifted into a backwater in the swirling, churning river of
Kingdom advancement. The diverse, burgeoning, worldwide "charismatic" movements at the forefront of this spreading flame they have viewed,
for the most part, as little more than a vast scourge upon the earth. Behind
this attitude is both the eccentric doctrine of the Spirit we have explored
earlier in this book and a deep-rooted spirit of ecclesial separatism, a spirit that, though now in sharp retreat, continues to keep Churches of Christ
isolated from and condescending toward other Christians.

Some cultural observers have claimed that we are entering a post-denominational age. Certainly denominational loyalties are markedly receding and the old denominational map is becoming less useful to navigate the American Christian terrain.[1] As George Marsden put it, when people have discovered that all brands of gasoline are basically the same, what they look for is octane. So with denominationalism. For more and more people, spiritual power and vitality is what they seek, not so much a particular brand of church. Further, new, "back-to-the-Bible" churches claiming to be non-denominational are springing up like mushrooms, making claims that sound a lot like the early Churches of Christ. Yet Churches of Christ are hardly involved; indeed, open sympathy and involvement would be cause for suspicion and perhaps disenfranchisement.

The problem faced by Churches of Christ is not how to convince denominationalists to embrace the True Church—that could be viewed as a preoccupation only so long as one thinks one is living in a basically "Christian" culture—but rather how to be faithful disciples in (post)modernity. The challenge is to maintain the cruciform practices of the Kingdom in the context of liberal tolerance, radical individualism, and the emerging neo-paganism.

God appears to be working in powerful and fresh ways at this juncture in history. Some of the old polarizations are breaking up and old alienating labels are becoming less functional. There is an opening, a ripeness, that seems to arise in the shake-up and disorientation that comes with the passing of one era and the emergence of another.

The face of the church in America will continue to change, perhaps dramatically, in the next generation. For Christians of all stripes are now being forced to disengage from the old (neo-)constantinian habits that have enabled them to feel so comfortable and at home in American culture. And as these old habits are being broken, Christians' true identity as strangers and pilgrims is being renewed, and ways of being the church more suited to the pilgrim life are fitfully emerging.

Churches of Christ, along with the other Christian traditions, will be forced more and more to face up to the realities of becoming missionaries in their own culture and of forming missionary congregations. And missionary congregations in our chaotic (post)modern culture will look and function differently from the churches of "Christian America" that we have grown accustomed to. Indeed, the new cultural status of Christians calls for "a new, post-Christendom definition of the church."2

A prominent example of the new missional thrust toward (post)modern culture is the "Emergent Church" movement—a loose, relational network of church leaders who have entered into conversation about the nature of the emerging culture and how to become missionaries to/in it. The point, says one of its leading spokesmen, "is not having a gospel that postmodern people like, nor is it starting postmodern churches....Rather, the point is having churches that bring the gospel of the kingdom of God to postmodern people with a style of incarnation that resonates with (and in fact continues) the original Incarnation."3

An important part of this shift is the correction—and indeed transformation—of the secular worldview that has pervaded the modern period and underwritten the bureaucratic, scientific culture, which in turn has molded modern churches. Sociologist Donald Miller, in his sympathetic study of the "new paradigm churches" that are revolutionizing American Protestantism, says that these churches are breaking sharply with modern assumptions about reality. His chief examples are the large networks of churches associated with Calvary Chapel, Vineyard Christian Fellowship, and Hope Chapel. He calls these Christians "postmodern primitivists": postmodern in that they "refuse to absolutize the last 200 years of science-dominated thinking," and primitivists because they look to primitive or first-century Christianity for "a radical spirituality that undermines the cynicism and fragmentation of many postmodern theorists." "New paradigm Christians are quite comfortable," says Miller, "with an epistemology that breaks with critical thought and interjects God into everyday experience, denying the sacred-profane split" that became normative in the Enlightenment.4

Another closely related aspect of the ecclesial shift underway is the renewal of the church as a community of the Spirit. This has been one of the strengths of the Believers' tradition over the centuries as it lived in perilous and persecuted disestablishment. And now with the newly disestablished status of American Christianity, the renewal of Spiritual community has again become a pressing concern. But in our present environment, for all its talk of "community," it becomes difficult to speak clearly or properly of Christian community. Liberal culture with its intense individualism isolates people thereby producing a great "need for community," but with its fundamental commitment to autonomy, self-determination, and voluntarism the community it produces only superficially resembles Spirit-formed community. As Robert Wuthnow noted in his study of the current small group movement in America, today's small groups are typically based only on "the weakest of obligations: come if you have time; talk if you feel like it; respect everyone's opinion; never criticize; leave if you become dissatisfied."[5] Such individualistic community easily and regularly masquerades as Christian community, making Christians rightly wary of community for the sake of community. But despite these obstacles, the renewal of Spiritual community will continue as Christians take up afresh their status as strangers and aliens, and as they reach out to people broken and estranged by the ravages of (post)modern secular culture.

For Churches of Christ, the politics of the ecclesial shift now underway will be difficult, often excruciating. Old centers are not holding. New, delicate alliances will attempt to replace them. Among the progressives there will be ever-shifting accommodation to the new and finessing of the old, beginning with the traditional Church of Christ "creed." To traditionalists it will look like duplicity and breach of principle. And maybe, to some extent, it will be, for that is the nature of most politics. Bold Kingdom witness may not fare well amid the keen tracking of ever-shifting political sensitivities and the aggressive catering to the tastes and wishes of old and new customers.

At one level, these changes can be viewed as the old "sect to denomination" process proceeding like clockwork (as H. R. Niebuhr described in general and as David Harrell has documented extensively in the Stone-Campbell tradition).[6] This transformation is both a sociological process (moving from less affluent and respectable to more affluent and respectable) and a theological process (moving from harder, narrower claims to softer, wider ones). Among Churches of Christ, this shift has been underway since at least the 1960s but is only now becoming widely visible. Only now are younger people who have already made this shift widely coming into positions of power in the congregations and schools. The progressive schools serving Churches of Christ are not only promoting this shift, they are, perhaps more fundamentally, simply responding and adapting to it.

Some progressive leaders among Churches of Christ seem bent on achieving mainline status. Embarrassed by their tradition's isolationist and somewhat anti-intellectual past, its garrulous polemical style and rough-hewn ways, they have set out to imitate the more respectable ways—the institutional methods, liturgical style, and theological sophistication—of the middle-brow mainline Protestant churches. But with the collapse of America's "Christian" culture in the 1960s, these mainline churches have themselves been sidelined. They have experienced sharp membership declines, identity crises, and loss of their dominant voice in the culture. The Disciples of Christ began that journey long before Churches of Christ, and Ronald Osburn has noted the irony of the outcome: he says they finally made it to the mainline but just at the time of the mainline's disestablishment.[7] That was thirty-five years ago. Churches of Christ may seek to play catch-up, but when or if they do they will find themselves not in the mainline but still on the sideline.

Churches of Christ constitute a rivulet in the great stream of God's Kingdom on the earth. Some of the very language and terms of the intramural arguments and discussions they are absorbed in would sound quite odd to the ears of many Christians today. Every tradition, of course, has its in-house discussions, its distinctive emphases, and (to the eyes of outsiders) odd practices. That's okay. Such issues are worth arguing about—up to a point. But it is long past time for Churches of Christ to acknowledge and openly participate in the great stream of historic, trinitarian Christian faith, a stream variously muddied and polluted, to be sure, but a stream that nonetheless has proclaimed the love of the Father, known the grace of the Lord Jesus, and experienced the fellowship of the Holy Spirit.

As for the "quiet revolution" that so troubles traditionalists, not all the change stirring and troubling Churches of Christ today is due to secularism, biblical illiteracy, or cultural sellout, as the polemicists seem to think. Some of it is, of course. But some of it is a fitful critique of and move away from earlier (nineteenth century) cultural accommodation by the tradition itself. Alexander Campbell's theological system was a critical response to early nineteenth-century revivalism and an effective accommodation of the new spirit of individualism and liberty set loose in America. But his theology was deeply shaped by the culture of that time, including the bold conviction that one could stand free of culture and tradition and "just read the Bible." David Lipcomb's theological stance was deeply formative for Churches of Christ, as it combined Campbell's hermeneutical principles with a countercultural apocalypticism. But his theology was deeply shaped, to cite just one example, by the culture of "true womanhood" dominant in mid-nineteenth-century America (as we saw in Chapter 6).

We do not have the option of choosing between a cultural church and a non-cultural church; culture is the unavoidable medium of the church's life. It has always been a "cultural church," and some of the present ferment has come as people have realized that nineteenth-century enculturation and accommodation was not eternal and in some respects no longer healthy or appropriate.

Restorationists like Churches of Christ are usually tempted to think of renewal as the return to or recovery of some past golden age that has slipped away. But Ray Anderson got it nearly right, I think, when he wrote that

> the [renewed] church does not emerge out of its past. When it attempts to do this it resorts to strategies of resuscitation rather than experiencing the power of resurrection. In its attempts to be contemporary the church usually arrives a decade, if not a generation, too late. The renewed church emerges in the present out of its future. As in the case of everything related to the creative life and power of God, the future of the church exists first and then its present.

He adds that when the church's theme song becomes "'Blest Be the Tie That Binds,' it will get all tangled up in its own apron strings. The Spirit of Christ cannot be tethered to institutional programs nor contained in the straitjacket of ecclesial politics."[8]

There was no golden age of the church. We want there to have been. We like nostalgia. But the church has always been in trouble of one sort or another as it sought to live out the good news of the Kingdom of God. Whether being blind-sided by its culture, idolizing its successes, buckling under worldly pressure, or simply nodding off, the church has always been less than golden. And so it is today. It is not some golden era we look back to; rather, it is the challenge of the present as we take up—in the power of the Spirit and the hope of the coming Kingdom—the opportunity to correct and leave behind past forms of unfaithfulness.

The extent to which Churches of Christ will be able to do this at this time of changing eras will depend on their openness to the renewal of their theology, particularly a functional Trinitarian theology, and their openness to God's Spirit. But the Spirit of God is a power they will not be able to manage in good modernist fashion, and that just may be the catch. For a tradition that does not believe in miracles today, it just may take one for Churches of Christ to break out of modernity's hold and to step briskly up to the front line of the gospel's engagement with the powers of the present age.

Churches of Christ may well find a measure of fresh success in this new era, but it will not be under the banner of their traditional theology. Already, most of the pockets of vitality and growth have quietly broken with or significantly revised that theology. What the younger generation of members will do with the tradition as the passion of the new continues to press against the inertia of the old is hard to say. But since many of this new generation now believe in miracles, they may well get fresh glimpses of things unseen after all.

Notes

1. See Robert Wuthnow, *The Restructuring of American Religion: Society and Faith Since World War II* (Princeton, NJ: Princeton University, 1988), 71-99, and Wade Clark Roof, "The Church in the Centrifuge," *Christian Century* (November 8, 1989), 1012-14.

2. Craig Van Gelder, "A Great New Fact of Our Day: America as Mission Field," in *Between Gospel and Culture*, 57-68. Regarding this challenge, Lesslie Newbigin wrote: "We have lived for so many centuries in the 'Christendom' situation that ministerial training is almost entirely conceived in terms of the pastoral care of existing congregations. In a situation of declining numbers, the policy has been to abandon areas (such as inner cities) where active Christians are few and to concentrate ministerial resources by merging congregations and deploying ministers in the places where there are enough Christians to support them. Needless to say, this simply accelerates the decline. It is the opposite of a missionary strategy, which would proceed in the opposite direction—deploying ministers in the areas where the Christian presence is weakest." *The Gospel in a Pluralist Society* (Grand Rapids, MI: Eerdmans, 1989), 235-36.

3. Brian McLaren, "A Letter to Friends of Emergent," www.anewkindofchristian.com. See also McLaren, *The Story We Find Ourselves In: Further Adventures of a New Kind of Christian* (Jossey-Bass, 2003); Dan Kimball and others, *The Emerging Church* (Grand Rapids: Zondervan, 2003); and Chuck Smith, Jr., *The End of the*

World...As We Know It: Clear Direction for Bold and Innovative Ministry in a Postmodern World (Colorado Springs: Waterbrook, 2001).

4. Donald E. Miller, *Reinventing American Protestantism: Christianity in the New Millennium* (Berkeley, CA: University of California, 1997), 25, 125.

5. Robert Wuthnow, *Sharing the Journey: Support Groups and America's New Quest for Community* (New York: Free Press, 1996).

6. H. Richard Niebuhr, *The Social Sources of Denominationalism*; David Edwin Harrell, "The Emergence of the Church of Christ Denomination" (booklet, 1971).

7. Ronald Osburn, "The Irony of the Twentieth-Century Christian Church (Disciples of Christ): Making it to the Mainline Just at the Time of the Mainline's Disestablishment," *Mid-Stream* (1989), 293-312.

8. Ray Anderson, *Ministry on the Fireline: A Practical Theology for an Empowered Church* (Downers Grove, IL: InterVarsity, 1993),

ALSO AVAILABLE

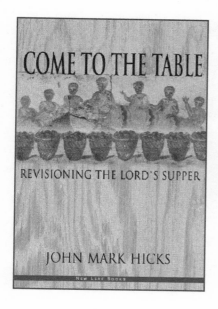

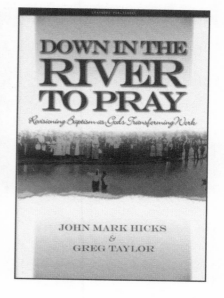

"a wonderful, comprehensive and
engaging invitation to deeper
understanding of and participation
in the Lord's Supper."
—William Willimon

"a must-read for all who believe that
the work of reform is not done"
—Philip Kenneson

$12.99 205 pages

"a compelling picture of our
baptismal identity"
—Robert Webber

"Every congregation should
thoroughly study this biblical,
historical, theological, and
practical portrait of baptism."
—Gary Holloway

$14.99 280 pages

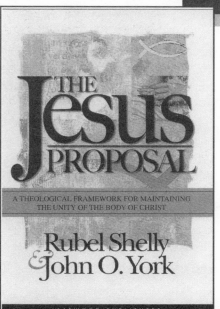

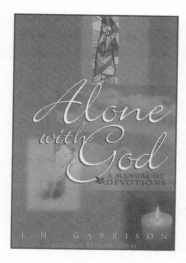